INSIDE SPORT
2 E
PSYCHOLOGY

Costas I. Karageorghis, PhD, CPsychol, FBASES

Peter C. Terry, PhD, FBASES, FAPS

Human Kinetics

243 792

Library of Congress Cataloging-in-Publication Data

Karageorghis, Costas I., 1969--
  Inside sport psychology / Costas I. Karageorghis, Peter C. Terry,
    p. cm.
  Includes bibliographical references and index.
  ISBN-13: 978-0-7360-3329-9 (soft cover)
  ISBN-10: 0-7360-3329-7 (soft cover)
  1. Sports--Psychological aspects. 2. Sports sciences. I. Terry, Peter C., 1952-- II. Title.
  GV706.4.K373 2011
  796.01--dc22
                              2010033594

ISBN-10: 0-7360-3329-7 (print)
ISBN-13: 978-0-7360-3329-9 (print)

The Web addresses cited in this text were current as of October 2010, unless otherwise noted.

Acquisitions Editor: Peter Murphy; **Managing Editors:** Cory Weber, Julie Marx Goodreau; **Assistant Editors:** Rachel Brito, Derek Campbell; **Copyeditor:** Patsy Fortney; **Indexer:** Bobbi Swanson; **Permission Manager:** Martha Gullo; **Graphic Designer:** Joe Buck; **Graphic Artist:** Tara Welsch; **Cover Designer:** Keith Blomberg; **Photographer (cover):** Torsten Blackwood/AFP/Getty Images; **Photo Asset Manager:** Laura Fitch; **Photo Production Manager:** Jason Allen; **Art Manager and Illustrator:** Kelly Hendren; **Associate Art Manager:** Alan L. Wilborn; **Printer:** McNaughton & Gunn

Human Kinetics books are available at special discounts for bulk purchase. Special editions or book excerpts can also be created to specification. For details, contact the Special Sales Manager at Human Kinetics.

Printed in the United States of America   10 9 8 7 6 5 4 3 2

The paper in this book is certified under a sustainable forestry program.

Human Kinetics
Web site: www.HumanKinetics.com

United States: Human Kinetics
P.O. Box 5076
Champaign, IL 61825-5076
800-747-4457
e-mail: humank@hkusa.com

Canada: Human Kinetics
475 Devonshire Road Unit 100
Windsor, ON N8Y 2L5
800-465-7301 (in Canada only)
e-mail: info@hkcanada.com

Europe: Human Kinetics
107 Bradford Road
Stanningley
Leeds LS28 6AT, United Kingdom
+44 (0)113 255 5665
e-mail: hk@hkeurope.com

Australia: Human Kinetics
57A Price Avenue
Lower Mitcham, South Australia 5062
08 8372 0999
e-mail: info@hkaustralia.com

New Zealand: Human Kinetics
P.O. Box 80
Torrens Park, South Australia 5062
0800 222 062
e-mail: info@hknewzealand.com

E2305

To my children, Anastasia and Lucia; my wife, Tina; and my parents, John and Anastasia.

—Costas Karageorghis

To my children, Dominic and Lucas; my loving partner, Victoria; and her son, Finn.

—Peter Terry

The book is also dedicated to our many wonderful students, past and present, from whom we have drawn inspiration and learned so much.

CONTENTS

FOREWORD

One of the greatest competitive athletes in history, U.S. discus thrower Al Oerter, was considered to be a man who competed at his best when it mattered most. Being a four-time Olympic champion testifies to that, especially when you consider that he was not ranked number one in the world in any of the Games that he won! But for me, there were two very good reasons why he prevailed as the Olympic champion from 1956 to 1968. First, he considered the Olympic Games to be the greatest contest of athletic prowess on planet Earth, and to him it really mattered as a test of himself not just as an athlete but also as a man.

The second characteristic that really set him apart from his rivals was that he had such a positive, strong mental attitude. To paraphrase the great man, "I never set out to beat the world. I just set out to do my absolute best." He was able to maximize his sport performance from a simple psychological perspective that he had rationalized himself, and it worked.

I remember all too well my first international athletics meeting in the old GDR (East Germany). I was number one in Britain so had no problem consolidating my status on a domestic front, but when I came face to face with three Eastern Bloc giants in the changing rooms, my heart sank. I thought that their immense size and perceived strength were to be the beating of me before we had even entered the arena. I was beaten before I started. Al Oerter's psychology now rings loud in my ears.

Dr. Karageorghis and Professor Terry have written a book that not only explores theoretical principles, research findings, and anecdotal evidence; but it also assists in maximizing sport performance from a psychological perspective. It offers competitors, coaches, students, and teachers the techniques that enable athletes to engage in an optimal mental state, and it presents strategies for dealing with the stressful situations that sport can conjure up.

In my capacity as a television commentator I am lucky to travel all over the world observing and contributing to great sporting events. An Olympic 100-meter final on the track is a superb example of "people watching" as well as a demonstration of who is the fastest man or woman on Earth. When the cameras close in on the athletes before the start, it is an opportunity for the world to catch a glimpse of the competitors in their final preparation for what could be the most important moment of their lives. Often you get a few clues about how they are handling the experience of severe pressure.

I have often thought that sport is an art form as well as a science. The scientific approach to training and competition is a well-trodden path, and the artistic nature of a superb sport performance is by definition a truly wonderful spectacle to behold. If you can experience this firsthand as I do, you are very lucky indeed.

The authors of *Inside Sport Psychology* have come to realize that their area of expertise is as much an art as a science. I celebrate this as a real breakthrough in understanding, simplifying, and truly getting inside sport psychology.

Paul Dickenson
BBC TV sports commentator and former
international hammer thrower for Great Britain

PREFACE

This book is primarily for athletes, coaches, team managers, and students of sport psychology. It also carries many important messages for the parents and guardians of aspiring athletes. The principles that are promoted transcend the sporting arena and are applicable to those who wish to excel in other fields of human endeavor: It is not unusual nowadays for sport psychology techniques to be applied in business and the performing arts, or indeed any other performance-oriented environment.

Virtually all athletes and performers recognize the importance of psychology; nonetheless, many consider their state of mind to be a random performance factor over which they have little control. They may be unsure of how to develop their psychological skills, motivation, and mental toughness. The aim of this book is to provide a structured and theoretically grounded approach to developing the psychological aspects of training and competition. In addition to the topics that one might expect in such a text (e.g., motivation, self-confidence, competition anxiety), there is a great deal of unique and original material that stems from our applied experiences and research publications.

Athletes often wonder how it would feel to lock into their optimal mental state at will. The likelihood is that their performances would be far more consistent. It might also be easier for them to achieve their goals and they would never need to bemoan the fact that they "weren't in the mood" or "didn't feel up for it." Such a positive mental approach to sporting competition can be achieved through training the mind using principles that are quite similar to those applied when training the body. In fact, the mind offers myriad resources that can be harnessed for the purpose of maximizing athletic performance. A consequence of learning mental skills is that their gradual development can lead to even greater enjoyment of sport.

Inside Sport Psychology uses examples predominantly from sports that are popular in Europe and the Commonwealth of Nations, such as soccer, rugby, tennis, and track and field, to illustrate the psychological principles. We have also considered the North American readership by using examples from sports that are popular in that region. Nonetheless, the style and outlook of this book differ from those of scores of sport psychology texts targeted at the North American market. This book integrates theoretical principles, research findings, anecdotal evidence, psychological measures, and applied interventions that are supported by our wide-ranging experiences.

All chapters share a similar format to help readers absorb the material and use it readily. Each topic is first defined and contextualized by using clear definitions of psychological terms. Second, the main theory or theories underlying the topic are explained using plain English to orient readers to the conceptual foundations of the interventions that follow. Along with the theory, key findings from recent research are provided to illustrate the potential effectiveness of interventions, developmental issues (i.e., changes across the lifespan), and gender differences.

Third, problem areas and roadblocks that are sometimes encountered when applying sport psychology techniques are discussed. Where appropriate, this discussion takes place immediately following the presentation of specific interventions. Fourth, the mainstay of each chapter is a detailed presentation of the most effective intervention techniques related to the topic. Because some of these interventions are applicable across topics (e.g., self-confidence and motivation), links throughout the text enable readers to quickly locate all of the material that may be relevant to them.

Finally, each topic is summarized using a synthesis of the main themes covered in the chapter. This synthesis includes a recap of the most important practical implications for athletes, coaches, team managers, students, and parents or guardians. The summaries can be revisited as *aide-mémoires* for the material covered in the chapters.

Chapters also address how well certain techniques are likely to work and when they might best be used. For example, we do not recommend positive self-statements as a singular intervention strategy for athletes experiencing low self-esteem; this can cause them to adopt negative counterstatements. This is because our minds can begin to question and challenge repeated positive self-statements.

Competitors often wish to know how they can overcome a motivational slump or how to focus better in critical situations. One of the primary aims of this book is to provide techniques that enable athletes to reproduce their optimal mental states and develop sound coping strategies for the stressful situations that sport can conjure. The interventions are based on theoretical principles stemming from the cutting edge of sport psychology research. We are both award-winning researchers and have acted as consultants to thousands of sportspeople. This gives us a unique insight into the application of theory in real-world situations. Over the years, we have come to realize that sport psychology is as much an art as a science.

Many of the exercises are as applicable to coaches and team managers as they are to athletes. Sport leaders play a vital role in delivering the fundamental principles of sport psychology and satisfying the needs of athletes. Indeed, fulfillment of athletes' psychological needs is a philosophy that lies at the very heart of this text. To this end, approaches such as getting athletes involved in the decision-making process, developing their sense of competence through the attainment of bite-sized goals, and promoting strong interpersonal relationships are explored. These approaches are underscored by a wealth of anecdotal evidence from some of the world's best-known athletes.

We have each produced a chapter on the application to sport of our specialist area of research. Karageorghis presents his groundbreaking work on the application of music within the sport domain and provides several music-related interventions that can be used to boost performance (chapter 8). In a chapter on mood and emotion, Terry explains how mood profiling can increase the likelihood that athletes will experience an optimal mindset for performance. He also demonstrates the application of mood profiles in a range of sporting contexts including the monitoring of training load (chapter 5).

Following an introduction that outlines the main facets of sport performance and provides guidance on maximizing skill learning (chapter 1), the remaining chapters cover important topics in contemporary sport psychology. Chapter 2 addresses motivation and includes some interesting self-assessment tests as well as a range of approaches on goal setting and overcoming slumps in motivation. Chapter 3 examines self-confidence, the guardian angel of performance, providing a range of novel approaches on how to bolster athletes' self-belief.

Chapter 4 focuses on competition anxiety with a detailed explanation of the anxiety–performance relationship followed by an array of anxiety control techniques. Chapter 6 spotlights concentration with applied examples to help the reader understand various types of concentration. Chapter 7 explores visualization and self-hypnosis using a range of innovative techniques that can enhance the consistency of performance. With judicious use, the contents of this book will help bridge the gap between sporting potential and sporting performance.

ACKNOWLEDGMENTS

We gratefully acknowledge Dr. David-Lee Priest (Brunel University) for his research assistance during the preparation of this book. We also thank Ted Miller (Vice President of Special Acquisitions at Human Kinetics) for his helpful comments on an earlier draft of the book.

1

Sport Psychology Applications

In training everyone focuses on 90 percent physical and 10 percent mental, but in the races it's 90 percent mental because there's very little that separates us physically at the elite level.

—Elka Graham, Australian swimming legend

We have written this book principally for athletes, but it is equally useful for coaches and team managers, students of sport psychology, as well as the parents and guardians of aspiring athletes. It may also interest those who are striving to excel in other fields of human endeavor such as business or the performing arts. This is because many of the psychological principles associated with excellence in sport can be applied universally.

Ask any champion athlete whether psychology is vital to success, and the answer every time will be a resounding *yes*. What many athletes and coaches are unsure about is how precisely to develop psychological skills and the mental approach to training and competition. Our aim is to provide a structured, easy-to-use guide to help athletes and coaches develop the psychological aspects of performance. The contents of this book should serve as an ideal complement to athletes' existing skills and physical aptitudes for their chosen sports.

Clearly, the mental aspect of performance can vary from day to day. If this were not the case, Tiger Woods would always win the US Open, Usain Bolt would always win the Olympic 100-meter title, and Brazil would always win the FIFA World Cup. The huge appeal of sport stems from its unpredictability: We never know for sure who's going to win. It is precisely this uncertainty that can be a source of great frustration for athletes and often accounts for thoughts, feelings, and behaviors that are not conducive to good performance.

One of the main challenges for athletes and their coaches is to be able to produce strong performances consistently, week in and week out. A lack of consistency is often what prevents people with considerable skill and ability from reaching the pinnacle of success for which they seem destined. The funny thing is that athletes have much more control over the consistency of their performance than they might imagine.

This book is certainly not a magic wand, and it won't transform someone without the right physical makeup into a Serena Williams, Jenson Button, or Cristiano Ronaldo. What it will do is enable athletes to concentrate far better, guide them toward improving their self-confidence, reduce the number of times they choke in pressure situations, and perhaps help them to conquer that opponent who has hitherto gotten the better of them.

No one can really afford to be an analogue athlete in a digital age. There is now huge interest in how to enhance sport performance using state-of-the-art methods. Athletes and coaches should take advantage of the wealth of sport science knowledge and research to give themselves the best possible chance of success. With margins of victory and defeat so slight, such knowledge can be the difference between triumph and disaster.

Applied sport psychology is closely related to its parent disciplines of psychology, physical education, and sport science. It has become extremely popular over the last three decades because coaches and athletes have begun to realize just how much of sporting performance depends on the mental approach. We would argue that applied sport psychology is both a science and an art. It is a science insofar as key principles from psychology are applied to sport often with the goal of enhancing performance, but it can also be considered an art because finding the right mix of applied interventions takes great skill, imagination, guile, and creativity.

Hence, you cannot expect to apply sport psychology out of a textbook in the same way that you can cook a gourmet meal or build a kit car. A detailed knowledge of a wide range of scientific principles is required because these underpin the area. Yet these principles need to be applied artfully. That is why you should be selective in what you decide to use from this book. Many techniques are presented, and although some will be entirely relevant to many people, they will not work for all.

In addition to enhancing performance, applied sport psychology is concerned with improving the experience of sport as a whole. A good sport psychologist equips athletes with skills that help them in many other aspects of their lives. They also educate athletes and coaches so that they eventually become self-sufficient. Competitors are taught a repertoire of mental skills and interventions to be used as and when required. Applied sport psychology is therefore about empowering athletes to improve their performances in the sporting arena while also enriching their lives.

This introductory chapter continues with a warm-up exercise (see exercise 1.1) and a brief history detailing the evolution of applied sport psychology. We then consider the constituent parts of sporting performance and focus in great detail on the development of key skills. This includes coverage of how to organize practice sessions to maximize skill learning; our advice draws upon the very latest research on skill development. We will go on to explore the intriguing nature-versus-nurture debate in sport and complete the chapter with a brief recap of the main points.

Exercise 1.1
What's Within Your Control?

Take a moment to reflect on all the excuses you have made in the past when you lost to an opponent or team you knew deep down that you could have beaten. Write down the list of excuses on a piece of paper before you go any further.

We are confident that your excuses may have included some of these: *I lost my focus at a critical moment, I wasn't feeling 100 percent, I was worried about what my teammates might say if I missed, I just talked myself out of it, I got too wrapped up in the referee's poor decisions,* or *I kept thinking about the consequences of not winning.*

Now go through the list and mark each excuse with either WMC for *within my control* or OMC for *outside of my control.* Add up the number of WMCs and OMCs. What you will most probably find is that the number of WMCs (factors within your control that caused you to underperform) far exceeds the number of OMCs. If this is indeed the case, it means that you lost as a result of poor psychological skills. This is something you might seek to rectify.

HISTORICAL USE OF SPORT PSYCHOLOGY

The interdependence of mind and body has fascinated people since ancient times. The celebrated Greek philosopher Plato popularized the maxim "healthy mind in a healthy body," which captures the essence of sport psychology. This is because many professional practitioners adopt a holistic approach wherein the general wellbeing of athletes is considered equally as important as their performance levels. In addition, many of the principles described in this book (skill formation, competitive tactics, emotional control) have their roots in traditional Chinese culture.

The exact birthplace of sport psychology is shrouded by historical uncertainty, although the efforts of early pioneers can be traced to central Europe. As early as 1830, the German scientist Carl Friedrich Koch published an article on "the psychology of calisthenics." This was followed, a few decades later, by Wilhelm Wundt's skill-related experimental work conducted at the University of Leipzig in 1879.

In the USA, just before the turn of the twentieth century, Norman Triplett of Indiana University produced one of the first journal publications on sport psychology, which addressed psychological factors in cycle racing. He found that the presence of another contestant "served to liberate latent energy not ordinarily available." Nowadays, we call this influence of the presence of others *social facilitation,* and Triplett's contribution is widely acknowledged as a landmark in social psychology.

The first use of the term *sport psychology* is credited to the founder of the modern Olympic movement, French nobleman Pierre de Coubertin. In 1900 he published an article titled "La Psychologie du Sport" and went on to write extensively on psychological aspects of sport until his death in 1937. Notwithstanding de Coubertin's contribution to the field, few of the early writings or experiments were systematic, progressive, or clearly defined within the context of sport.

The first person to make a career out of sport psychology was American psychologist Coleman Griffith, who is often referred to as the grandfather of sport psychology. In 1925 the University of Illinois asked Griffith to work with coaches in the hope that there would be some positive consequences for their athletes. Griffith's interventions contributed to the University of Illinois winning two national championships and three Big Ten championships in American football.

Griffith opened the first sport psychology laboratory in the USA and taught the first course in the subject. He also published the first two textbooks, which have long since been considered classics, *Psychology of Coaching* (1926) and *Psychology of Athletics* (1928). Many of Griffith's experiments were more concerned with the learning and retention of motor skills than with what we would today consider sport psychology. He was fascinated by topics such as reaction time and anticipation skills. Griffith's laboratory was forced to close in 1930 when the university withdrew its funding as a result of the Great Depression.

In 1938 Griffith became the first sport psychologist to work with a professional team: the Chicago Cubs baseball team. His appointment was made at the behest of the club's owner, William Wrigley Jr. (the chewing gum magnate), but it was ardently resisted by the team manager, Charlie Grimm. Griffith produced a fascinating study on the personality of the players, although he did not enjoy a great deal of competitive success with the Cubs. This may well have been due to the team manager's resistance to Griffith's services, but his efforts left the door ajar for the thousands of sport psychologists who followed.

Sport psychology gathered considerable momentum in the 1960s particularly through the work of two psychologists at San Jose State University, Bruce Ogilvie and Thomas Tutko. Like Griffith before them, they were very interested in how personality influenced sport performance. Ogilvie and Tutko courted controversy through the extensive use of a paper-and-pencil test known as the Athletic Motivation Inventory (AMI), which they claimed could accurately measure the motivation of athletes.

These pioneers of sport psychology advised coaches on the selection of athletes based on the results of the AMI. Other prominent psychologists of the time argued that selections could not be made on the basis of questionnaire results and that such tests were hardly worth the paper they were written on. This debate raged on for many years. For his many contributions, Bruce Ogilvie became known as one of the fathers of applied sport psychology in North America. He shares this title with Rainer Martens, a former professor of sport psychology at the University of Illinois, who founded the publishing company Human Kinetics.

Another American, Charles A. Garfield, visited the former USSR in the late 1970s and noted the considerable investment in athletic-related research since the 1950s as part of the Soviet space program. The race to be the first into space led the USA and USSR governments to explore highly innovative methods that might increase the endurance, resilience, and adaptability of astronauts.

Thinking outside the box in this way drove Russian scientists toward successfully employing ancient yogic techniques to control mental processes in space. The techniques they adopted were called *self-regulation training* or *psychic self-regulation*. These were used to control emotions such as the anxiety associated with living in zero gravity, as well as bodily functions such as muscular tension and heart rate.

The self-regulation techniques were not systematically applied to Russian athletes until a generation later, at which point the outstanding success of Soviet Bloc countries across a wide range of sports in the 1970s and 1980s enthralled the world. The state-sponsored selective schooling of young athletes, intensive training delivered by highly educated coaches, optimal nutrition, and sport psychology techniques created a conveyor belt of champions who were at the forefront of world sport right up until the fall of the Iron Curtain in 1991. Western sport authorities learned a great deal from this highly structured approach, and following disappointing performances at major events such as the 1976 Olympic Games in Montreal (where Eastern European countries enjoyed a medal bonanza), Australia, the UK, and the USA began to take sport psychology very seriously.

Following the successful application of sport science by Soviet Bloc countries, Western athletes became very interested in sport psychology. In the 1980s, governing bodies of sport throughout the West were encouraged to employ consultant psychologists to work with athletes, coaches, and team managers.

Initially, those interested in sport psychology based their interactions and interventions on theories and research from general psychology. As time went on, however, a number of sport-specific theories were developed and tested. For example, Rainer Martens and colleagues' book *Competitive Anxiety in Sport,* which described multidimensional anxiety theory, or how anxiety influences sport performance, was hugely influential.

By the 1990s, the number of sport psychology journals had increased, and scholarly bodies such as the International Society of Sport Psychology and the Association for Applied Sport Psychology organized frequent scientific meetings. The discipline had well and truly arrived and was duly recognized as a bona fide branch of psychology by organizations such as the American Psychological Association, the Australian Psychological Society, and the British Psychological Society.

Despite the strong scientific underpinnings of modern-day sport psychology, there are many reported instances of so-called charlatans working with managers and players, even at the elite level. Names such as Uri Geller, Mystic Meg, and Eileen Drewery are familiar to those who regularly read British tabloid newspapers. Many others who are not known publicly routinely tout their services to professional clubs. Although such individuals may appear to do some good initially, perhaps by lending a sympathetic ear or providing a prematch pep talk, their practices are generally not based on a sound methodology, and they are not licensed or accredited to provide such services. Accordingly, we urge you to exercise caution and to seek out qualified and recognized practitioners.

A high-profile case illustrates this point. The former England soccer manager, Glenn Hoddle, enlisted the services of faith healer Eileen Drewery to work with the national squad in preparation for the 1998 World Cup in France. Hoddle had a 20-year association with Drewery that began when he dated her daughter as a teenage player. At the age of 17, Hoddle was taken aback by an offer from Drewery of psychic help to fix a torn muscle, but he found that the injury miraculously disappeared following some "remote healing." During the 1990s, a string of professional footballers visited Drewery's home, including England internationals Paul Merson, Ian Wright, and Paul Gascoigne. Most of the 1998 World Cup squad had been directed to have sessions with Drewery, but

Major Sport Psychology Organizations Around the World

American Psychological Association (APA)—Division 47: www.apa.org/about/division/div47.aspx

Asian South Pacific Association of Sport Psychology (ASPASP): www.aspasp.org

Association for Applied Sport Psychology (AASP): http://appliedsportpsych.org

Arbeitsgemeinschaft für Sportpsychologie (ASP; German Sport Psychology Society): www.ispw.unibe.ch/asp

Australian Psychological Society (APS) —College of Sport Psychologists: www.groups.psychology.org.au/csp

British Association of Sport and Exercise Sciences (BASES) —Sport and Exercise Psychology Interest Group: www.bases.org.uk/Sport-Psychology-Interest-Groups

British Psychological Society (BPS) —Division of Sport & Exercise Psychology: www.bps.org.uk/spex/spex_home.cfm

Canadian Society for Psychomotor Learning and Sport Psychology (SCAPPS): www.scapps.org

De Vereniging voor SportPsychologie in Nederland (VSP; Dutch Society for Sport Psychology): www.vspn.nl

Εταιρεία Αθλητικής Ψυχολογίας (ΕΑΨ; Hellenic Society of Sport Psychology): www.sportpsychology.gr

Federación Española de Psicología del Deporte (FEPD; Spanish Sport Psychology) Federation: www.psicologiadeporte.org

Fédération Européenne de Psychologie des Sports et des Activités Corporelles (FEPSAC; European Federation of Sport Psychology): www.fepsac.com

International Society of Sport Psychology (ISSP): www.issponline.org

North American Society for the Psychology of Sport and Physical Activity (NASPSPA): www.naspspa.org

Schweizerische Arbeitsgemeinschaft für Sportpsychologie (SASP; Swiss Society for Sport Psychology): http://sportpsychologie.ch

Sociedade Portuguesa Psicologia do Desporto (SPPD; Portuguese Society of Sport Psychology): www.sppd.com.pt

Società Italiana di Psicologia dello Sport (SIPSIS; Italian Society of Sport Psychology): www.psicologiadellosport.it

Société Française de Psychologie du Sport (SFPS; French Society of Sport Psychology): www.psychodusport.com

Svensk Idrottspsykologisk Förening (SIPF; Swedish Sport Psychology Association): www.svenskidrottspsykologi.nu

many claimed to feel very uncomfortable about this. When the press caught wind of the story, it ran and ran. Eventually, Hoddle was dismissed as the England manager.

As a consequence of such cases, governing bodies of sport are now very mindful about whom they hire and their scientific credentials. The new millennium has witnessed a considerable expansion of the training available for aspiring sport psychologists. It's actually so extensive that, in some countries, it takes longer to qualify as a sport psychologist than it does as a general medical practitioner! Athletes and coaches looking to engage the services of a sport psychologist should be certain that the person is accredited, licensed, or chartered by a recognized national body (see Major Sport Psychology Organizations Around the World on the previous page).

Before hiring a sport psychologist, keep in mind that although sport psychologists may well enhance the experience of sport, bolster motivation, or improve elements of performance, they cannot guarantee successful outcomes. The outcome of a sporting contest often relies on factors outside of an individual athlete's control, including the performance of teammates and the opposition, the impartiality of officials, and environmental conditions. This is an important consideration to bear in mind regarding all aspects of sport psychology.

COMPONENTS OF PERFORMANCE

One of the first steps in planning a way forward involves determining how performance is controlled and examining its constituent parts. Performance in any sport is determined by a combination of three main elements: *physical conditioning* for competition, *skill level,* and *psychological readiness* to compete.

The relative importance of these factors differs considerably from sport to sport. For instance, cross-country skiers rely heavily on physical conditioning but devote less time to the actual skills involved in skiing. In contrast, top golfers, who need constant practice to keep their skills razor sharp, can perform well with relatively low levels of aerobic fitness. Similarly, developing stamina is much more important for a marathon runner than for a trap shooter. Trap shooting, however, involves very precise skills that require more practice than the relatively straightforward and repetitive skill of running efficiently.

The element of performance that makes demands of all sportspeople equally is the psychological readiness to compete. Without mental toughness, no athlete can be considered suitably prepared for competition. Yet many people enter the sporting arena having given very little thought to mental preparation. It is a component of performance often left to chance; you might feel up for it, but then again, you might not!

The great irony associated with the lack of attention to psychological readiness is that athletes, coaches, and fans invariably attribute lackluster performances to psychological factors rather than physiological or biomechanical ones. If even a small fraction of the time athletes spend on physical conditioning and skills training were devoted to improving their mental approach, they would at least be giving themselves the chance to avoid the frustration of inconsistency. This book explains how performance in sport is affected by mental factors and includes a range of psychological techniques that you can learn and practice, the first of which we demonstrate in exercise 1.2 on page 8.

Exercise 1.2
An Applied Sport Psychology Technique to Get You Started:
The Standing Long Jump

We have used this exercise many times in lectures and public presentations to demonstrate how sport psychology techniques can assist performance. Ask a friend or a coach to read the following instructions to you one by one and follow them carefully:

1. Perform a gentle stretch, particularly of the major muscles in your legs.

2. Mark a line on the floor ensuring that there is at least 6 yards (about 6 meters) clear in front of you. Stand just behind the line with your feet shoulder-width apart.

3. Perform a standing long jump (i.e., bend your knees and propel yourself forward to land on both feet), jumping as far as you can (see figure 1.1). Have your friend or coach place a marker to the side of where your heels landed.

4. Repeat this process a few times so that you are properly warmed up.

5. Now place another marker a few inches beyond your current best effort to give you a specific goal to aim for. Before you jump, close your eyes and visualize yourself reaching the target distance.

6. When you have seen yourself achieving this improved distance in your mind's eye, take another jump. Measure the distance between the best of your earlier trials and the post-visualization trial. You may well find that you have jumped a significant distance farther.

Figure 1.1 Jump as far as you can and have a partner place a marker to the side of where your heels landed.

Photo courtesy of Sally Trussler, Brunel University photographer

When we start working with an athlete or a team, we often present a picture of the "performance pie" (see figure 1.2) as a general introduction to the notion of psychological readiness. This is a very simple but illuminating way to assess the time you devote to each of the three main components of performance: physical conditioning, skill level, and psychological readiness. Your performance is essentially the sum of these three components. Go ahead and rate in percentage terms how much time you devote to each of them.

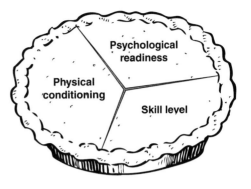

Figure 1.2   The performance pie.

If you are like the majority of the athletes that we encounter, the time you devote to your psychological readiness is minimal. Usually athletes report that they devote only 5 to 10 percent of their time to psychological readiness, and the work they do is often fairly sporadic and unstructured. This is surprising given the high psychological demands of sport and the fact that mental preparation has been shown to be just as important as physical and tactical preparation.

The great thing about psychological readiness is that it can be enhanced almost anywhere, at any time. In this book we present techniques such as goal setting (chapter 2) and mental rehearsal (chapter 7) that can have a positive effect on performance and can be carried out on the bus, in a waiting room, or before you go to bed.

Also, when you are suffering with an injury, although your skills practice and physical conditioning may need to be curtailed, the development of your psychological readiness can continue. There are few genuine boundaries to practicing and honing mental skills. Take advantage of this freedom and ensure that your psychological readiness is on a par with the other two components of the performance pie.

In the following sections we detail some of the training principles that underlie physical conditioning and explain key elements such as strength, speed, stamina, and suppleness. Next we describe the nature of skill and how skilled performance can be enhanced through effective feedback and practice schedules. We then highlight the main aspects of psychological readiness.

Physical Conditioning

No matter how much you practice psychological skills, you will not get very far in any sport that involves running, jumping, stretching, twisting, lifting, pushing, pulling, dodging, or throwing without physical conditioning. This refers to how well prepared your body is for the demands you will place on it. Physical conditioning is not the main focus of this book, so we touch upon it only very briefly. If you would like to read further about physical conditioning, there are literally hundreds of books on the subject. One that we often recommend to athletes is *High-Performance Sports Conditioning,* edited by Bill Foran.

Improvements to physical condition are based primarily on the overload principle. This principle holds that the capacity to respond improves only when the demand placed on the body increases. Therefore, as you gradually increase the amount of work normally demanded of your body, you correspondingly increase its ability to perform at higher levels of work. In essence, your physical conditioning depends on how much, how often, and how vigorously you train.

With increased levels of training, the body adapts to a new reality and becomes better conditioned. Even everyday activities such as brisk walking, gardening, and doing housework make people fitter if they exceed their present levels of activity. Whatever your current level of physical conditioning may be, if you start to train more regularly, for longer, or with greater intensity, your capacity for work will increase.

If you are like most athletes, you are probably well along the way to being physically conditioned and may just need to step up a gear or organize your activities a little better to make significant performance gains. The better physically conditioned you get, however, the harder it becomes to make further improvements. At elite levels of performance, you will make relatively small gains from year to year.

Another important principle of physical conditioning is that of specificity. This has to do with training the muscles you use primarily in your sport to enhance your performance. For example, although a sprinter might need to do lots of running to improve her 100-meter-dash performance, if she does this at her 800-meter pace, she would not improve a great deal.

Sprinters are far more likely to complete repetitions in the range of 30 to 300 meters to increase their speed. Nonspecific training can actually have a detrimental effect on performance. If our sprinter trained regularly with a middle-distance squad, her 100-meter time would likely get worse and she would become utterly frustrated because the many hours she devoted to training would not bear fruit. Specificity is a cornerstone of a good training regime.

The popular notion that a fit person should resemble a particular shape and be able to perform certain tasks is only half true. Consider the people on page 11. Which one do you think is the fittest?

Well, in a way they all are! Paula Radcliffe is the fittest for running long distances, Usain Bolt is the fittest for sprinting, Pyrros Dymas is the fittest for lifting weights, and Beth Tweddle is the fittest for performing gymnastics.

Physical conditioning is specific to the nature of your performance, and any conditioning work you undertake should be designed to meet the requirements of your sport. Broadly speaking, physical conditioning is comprised of four main elements: strength, speed, stamina, and suppleness—the four Ss. Most sporting events require some degree of all four, but referring back to our four champions, distance running puts a premium on stamina, sprinting clearly emphasizes speed, weightlifting requires great strength and power, and gymnasts must be extremely supple.

When preparing for competition, you should think about which element of physical conditioning you are trying to improve and how this might best be achieved. The goal-setting exercises presented in chapter 2 can help you improve aspects of physical conditioning. This is an example of how your psychological approach can enhance your physical development.

Distance runner Paula Radcliffe, sprinter Usain Bolt, weightlifter Pyrros Dymas, and gymnast Beth Tweddle. Who is the fittest?

Skill Learning and Development

Athletes often misunderstand this component of performance and use the term *skill* interchangeably with terms such as *ability, talent,* and *technique.* When watching a sporting event, youngsters often exclaim, "Wow! Did you see that skill?" referring to an impressive action on the field of play.

We cannot actually "see" skill. Skill is intangible, and the term refers to the capacity to produce a desired result consistently and with efficiency of time and effort. What the kids are seeing is *performance*, not skill, but the two are often thought of as one and the same. A high level of skill makes successful performance more probable but does not guarantee it.

We should emphasize that a gap exists between skill level and performance level. One represents potential; the other represents production. All we can see is *skilled performance*, the manifestation of potential, and it is worth remembering that your performance, although undoubtedly the best indicator of your skill level, is a far-from-perfect measure of your skill.

Consider the skills of Argentinean soccer star Lionel Messi. If he pulls a muscle or twists an ankle, we could hardly expect him to produce a great performance. But has he lost his skill? Has it evaporated in an instant? Absolutely not! The skill remains, but the ability to perform has been temporarily impaired. Ability is the quality that makes a particular action possible. Providing no permanent damage has been done, the skills will flow again once the injury mends.

Skill is not necessarily a gift that is endowed on some very fortunate people and denied to others. Athletes do not inherit skills; they acquire them through systematic practice. Not even the prodigious Michael Jordan emerged from the womb reverse-dunking a basketball. Until he had mastered the simple skill of walking and the basics of hand–eye coordination, he was unprepared to attempt even a meager chest pass.

So how do we explain the skills of Sachin Tendulkar and Phil Mickelson, whose genius places them head and shoulders above most of their fellow cricket and golf professionals? Perhaps in the final analysis, the rare gifts of sporting virtuosos defy even the most rigorous scientific scrutiny, but, in theory at least, they are simply supreme examples of *ability trained to perfection.*

Sporting ability often emerges very early in life, in the form of general abilities such as balance, coordination, intelligence, a sharp eye, or a retentive memory. Such qualities equip a person for many sports because they are the bedrock on which skills are built. Intelligence is required to understand skills; memory is required to retain them once they are learned; and balance, coordination, and good eyesight all aid in their execution. Skill training, which involves molding and refining ability for specific activities, is certainly easier when these qualities are present, but natural ability is by no means essential for producing a competent athlete, as we will explain a little later in this chapter.

How Does Skill Develop?

Skill development involves understanding the relationship between what we want to achieve and the actions required to bring it about. For instance, a young athlete learning to throw a javelin soon realizes that by varying the position of his body, the angle at which the javelin is released, and the force that he applies, he can change the distance and direction it travels as well as the angle at which it lands. The way he learns is by comparing what he wanted to happen with what actually happened after each throw. A challenge for young athletes and novice performers is that they are often poor judges of how much they have learned.

An athlete's senses play a vital role in the learning process. Sight tells him whether the javelin flew as he intended it to. His sense of touch tells him how the action felt, and gradually he learns to distinguish between what felt right and what felt wrong. If the athlete manages to identify the errors correctly—and here he probably needs the experienced eye of a coach—he can modify his next attempt accordingly.

The more trials the athlete completes, the better he will understand the relationship between performance and outcome, and the more skillful he will become. Research tells us that experts become less reliant on visual feedback and know through just the feel of a movement whether they will achieve the desired outcome. For example, when a skillful golfer such as Karrie Webb swings a driver, at the moment of impact she knows from experience whether the ball will have the appropriate distance and direction.

In the early stages, a process of trial and error is an effective way of learning sport skills because it helps to develop a feel for right and wrong. When coaches guide athletes rigidly toward executing correct technique, they deny them the experience of judging their own movements and risk producing stereotyped, robotic, and therefore very predictable performers. Effective learning of skills occurs when activities are well defined and pitched at an appropriate level of difficulty. Coaches are needed to structure practices, motivate athletes and teams to persist at what can seem like mundane repetitions of drills, and provide appropriate feedback.

Exercise 1.3
Exploring Novel Practice Routines

This exercise is designed to get you to think a little differently about what you practice. In upcoming training sessions, try out the drills you write down in this exercise.

- Think of a remarkable skill that you have seen from a great exponent of your sport: perhaps an overhead kick in soccer, a devastating sidestep in rugby, or a bullet serve in volleyball.

- Jot down the constituent parts of the skill—what needs to happen and when. Also note competitive situations in which it can be executed.

- Now try to work out how you might mimic that skill; what sort of drills would you need to practice to pull it off with style and panache?

- Run your proposed drills by a coach or a very accomplished athlete from your sport and obtain some feedback. Integrate this feedback into your practice schedule.

- You can then use some of the principles of practice that you will learn in this chapter to organize precisely how you will master the skill and subsequently perform it in competition.

- Apply this approach to as many skills as you wish.

Photo courtesy of Mark Shearman

The Fosbury Flop revolutionized high jumping in the period following the 1968 Mexico Olympic Games.

We subscribe to the notion that coaches should focus on correcting just one aspect of technique at a time, particularly with young athletes; otherwise, the overload of feedback can inhibit progress. There should be ample opportunity for the repetition of a skill before it is executed in competition, and the coach needs to be sufficiently skilled to spot errors and provide corrective feedback as necessary. We also believe in maintaining considerable variety coupled with an element of unpredictability in practice sessions. To exhibit flair and versatility, athletes need some variability in practice; they should not be afraid to practice unconventional skills. Exercise 1.3 on page 13 encourages you to explore novel practice routines.

Without unconventional practice routines, the world would never have seen the Fosbury Flop, which revolutionized high jumping in the period following the 1968 Mexico Olympics. How many times have you seen an elite high jumper perform an Eastern cut-off, Western roll, straddle, or scissors technique? Probably never, unless you like to watch archive track and field footage. Perhaps you have never even heard of these techniques. That doesn't matter because the point is that Dick Fosbury changed high jumping forever by clearing the bar with his back and landing on his shoulders. His innovation fundamentally changed the way athletes and coaches approached the event.

Also, in the last two decades shot-putters have been experimenting with the rotational throwing technique, which replicates the footwork used for the discus throw. This came about when discus throwers tried out their well-honed footwork in the shot circle. In the last decade some athletes have used a cartwheel shot-putting technique to great effect—again a direct consequence of unconventional practice routines—although this approach was banned by the International Amateur Athletics Federation in 2007.

How Well Are Sport Skills Retained?

Compared to other types of skills, such as speaking in a foreign language and playing a musical instrument, sport skills are quite durable once the movement programs are established. Even with the minimum of practice, a reasonable level of proficiency can be maintained, particularly in those who have mastered their craft.

That is not to say that those who have learned a range of sport skills should get complacent. Indeed, the Chinese philosopher Lao-Tzu once said, "Learning is like rowing upstream. If you stop, you get pushed backwards." To stay at the top of your game, you must strive constantly toward improvement. Skills are dynamic—they evolve and change—which means that the suite of skills that bring success in one season may not necessarily be as effective in the next. Also, as you mature from the junior to senior ranks, you often need to develop a wider repertoire of skills.

Given that skill involves understanding *how* to achieve certain results, in theory, we should be able to retain it indefinitely. However, some factors make it unlikely that the ability to translate skill into performance will last forever. For example, aging takes its toll on our physical functioning; joints stiffen and muscle fibers deteriorate. Physiologists have estimated that about 50 percent of the decline in performance with advancing years is due to the effects of the aging process. For the most part, this is beyond our control. Nonetheless, the remaining 50 percent can be largely explained by the fact that we may no longer be using our talents.

In fact, aging and disuse of talents conspire to form a vicious circle. As we grow older, we increasingly lack the confidence to use our physical capabilities, which diminish as a result, which, in turn, further decreases our confidence to use them. In other words, when you fail to use your skills and physical abilities, in time you lose their strength, your stamina, your agility, perhaps your golf swing or table tennis backhand smash. In effect, your body gradually forgets skills unless you use them. So the message is clear: Practice is crucial in maintaining skills. Use them or lose them!

Practice Fundamentals

Effective practices need to be carefully thought out to suit your specific needs. Frequency, duration, intensity, and type of practice are all important factors in skill development and maintenance. With your coach, review your practice schedule often to ensure sustained improvement. If you are not making steady progress, something may be wrong.

Be wary of the old adage "Practice makes perfect," which is often bandied about by coaches and teachers. It is not strictly true. To begin with, is there really such a thing as a perfect performance? Probably not because something can always be improved. This is why sport is such an engrossing pursuit. For example, when Michael Johnson obliterated the world 200-meter record at the Atlanta Olympics with a time of 19.32 seconds, he told reporters that he stumbled out of his blocks and could have gone even faster!

Also, although practice is certainly the most important variable in developing skill, inappropriate practice has almost the same effect as no practice or could even result in a decrement in performance. Moreover, practice in the absence of a reliable source of feedback will result in little or no learning, because poor technique may be practiced repeatedly.

The adage would hold more truth if it read "Appropriate practice with reliable feedback makes better." Although this is a bit of a mouthful, the modifications are important. In terms of what constitutes appropriate practice, here are some initial pointers, which are complemented by more extensive guidelines later in this section.

- Skills that cannot be mastered in their complete form need to be broken down into their component parts, practiced separately, and gradually pieced together again. Be wary of dissecting skills to such a degree that the overall flow of the movement is lost.

- Do not sacrifice quality for the sake of quantity. Also, avoid overpracticing to the extent that you lose enthusiasm or when you are exhausted, unless you are doing so specifically to simulate match conditions (e.g., taking a penalty kick during extra time in a soccer cup final when you are physically drained).

- Practices should be realistic to ensure that the skills can be transferred to competitive situations. For example, athletes in highly interactive sports such as basketball, ice hockey, and rugby should use only unopposed practices in the early stages of developing a skill. Thereafter, the number of opponents should be gradually increased until the practice simulates (or exceeds) match conditions. In our experience, the earlier that opposition is introduced, the better, because strategies are hardwired during the learning process.

- Drills should balance speed and accuracy. In the early stages of learning, greater emphasis may be placed on accuracy, but to master skills, you must practice them regularly at full speed. The speed/accuracy trade-off is evident in tennis: Some players play very carefully weighted position shots, and others blast the ball at every opportunity. We often devise drills that require athletes to execute skills faster than they would in competition to make those skills instinctive (e.g., reaction tasks for fielders in cricket and baseball that require them to catch and throw balls in quick succession).

The question of appropriate feedback is also crucial to skill development. In the sporting context, feedback can be viewed as any information relating to skilled movement that may change future movement patterns, confirm the correctness of current ones, or motivate you to continue. As you perform skills, your senses are constantly bombarded with information regarding the nature of your performance.

In the case of badminton players, for example, every shot provides feedback. They can see where the shuttlecock lands; they can hear the sound of the shuttlecock on the racket; and they can sense the feel of the shot through their wrists, arms, and shoulders. Sight and hearing are not the only senses that aid learning, however; all senses contribute to the process. Your internal sense of feel plays a particularly vital role. This sense, which is referred to as *proprioception*, relates to whether your body is moving with the required effort and where various body parts are located in relation to each other.

Sportspeople talk a lot about getting the feel for a sport. This implies that performance depends on the information relayed back and forth between your limbs and brain. Interpreting this information accurately is part of skill learning. Any skill performed for the first time (particularly one involving an unfamiliar body position) will feel strange. An action involving rotation through more than one axis, as in a complicated trampolining move, is often completely disorientating. Quite simply, you will not understand the physical sensations, partly because they are unfamiliar and partly because they are too numerous and too fast for your brain to process effectively.

With repetition comes familiarity and eventually an understanding of those sensations that are important and those you can ignore. During the early stages of the learning process, information overload can render you completely unaware of important information related to performance. The novice golfer, for instance, will typically lift his head before the shot is completed, often quite unconsciously, because of a reflex that links head and shoulder movement.

A novice golfer with this problem may benefit from an observer pointing out the fault, although it is not certain that he would benefit. This is because novices require time and all their powers of concentration to sort useful feedback from irrelevant feedback. The observer may actually be making a hard job even harder! Research suggests that complete beginners may benefit from a clear demonstration followed by a period of uninterrupted practice to allow them to get a feel for the movement before they receive coaching.

Experienced players have a different problem regarding feedback. After repeating a movement many times over, much of the feedback received from the body becomes redundant and is ignored unless it feels very different. The movement will continue to feel correct unless it varies significantly. The problem here is that gradual changes to technique creep in undetected, allowing major faults to develop unnoticed. At this point the athlete must go back to earlier stages of learning and break down the constituent skills and put them back together again.

Acquiring the Right Skills

To achieve superior performance, you must analyze the precise demands of your sport across a wide range of situations so that you can develop an appropriate set of skills. Evaluate your strengths and weaknesses to ensure that you spend most of your practice time working on the weak parts of your game.

Too often athletes are tempted to continue doing the things they know really well and fail to iron out glitches in their game. Repeatedly practicing what they already know well keeps athletes in their comfort zones. Champion athletes have the common behavior of identifying and working meticulously on weaknesses in their game; they are fully prepared to come out of their comfort zones.

Just as a chain is only as strong as its weakest link, so you are only as good as your least-well-trained skills. Formerly one-paced long-distance runner Paula Radcliffe worked meticulously on developing a reliable sprint finish, and lanky England soccer player Peter Crouch practiced dribbling the ball day in and day out. These essential skills did not come easily to these sport stars, so an extraordinary effort was required to develop them.

Exercise 1.4 on page 18 will help you examine the range of skills relevant to your main sport. First, list all of the skills that are common to your sport in column 1 (Key skills). In column 2 (Current competence) rate from 1 to 10 how good you are in executing them (1 = *Completely inept*; 10 = *Absolutely outstanding*), and in column 3 (Enhancing the skills) jot down three things you can do every week to improve each skill that you did not rate at 10. If you wish, complete column 3 with a coach who can guide you appropriately. We have filled in the details of a basketball player named Amanda as an example of what you need to do. Complete the exercise on a blank sheet of paper.

Exercise 1.4
Skill Set Assessment:
Example of Basketball Player Amanda (Center)

Table 1.1 Amanda's Skill Set Assessment (Basketball)

Key skills	Current competence (1–10)	Enhancing the skills
Blocking	8	• Practice against players taller than me. • Integrate drill of blocking opposition fast break into training. • Complete reaction time exercise once weekly.
Rebounding	7	• Complete plyometric drills set by my coach twice weekly. • Integrate rebounding exercise into training. • Practice one-on-one against a much stronger player.
Jump shots	8	• Take 20 extra jump shots during each training session. • Have my technique biomechanically analyzed. • Visualize the ball swishing just before shooting.
Dribbling	9	• Dribble during warm-up jog. • Dribble more with left hand in training. • Practice dribbling drills with eyes closed, with thick gloves, and with a light medicine ball to increase difficulty.
Layups	8	• Practice approach from left side twice as much as from front and right. • Run feigning drill against opposition. • Practice approach tricks in front of mirror in aerobics studio.
Breaking	6	• Work out five new variations with the point guards. • Analyze footage from last three games to see how mistakes are creeping in. • Practice speed drills set by conditioning coach as part of warm-up.
Free throws	7	• Practice with noise of crowd played over the PA system. • Take 10 at the end of each training session when I am heavily fatigued. • Visualize the technique just before going to bed each night.

Once you have completed this exercise, the next step is to integrate the enhancement drills tightly into your practice routines and, eventually, to make each key skill automatic.

Making Sport Skills Automatic

To become an accomplished performer, you need to make the suite of skills required for your sport operate automatically. This means that you can execute the skills with little conscious effort (much like an aircraft on autopilot) and make them technically correct or highly efficient. Such automaticity affords you the luxury of being able to process and act on information from a number of sources.

To execute skills automatically, you must understand them thoroughly. The contribution of a coach in providing appropriate feedback or demonstration is most important. Additionally, you must establish a feel for the movement through repetition so you can rely on instinct rather than having to think through the movement pattern. In fact, when skills are automatic, consciously focusing on movements is likely to severely disrupt performance. Research shows that this is particularly the case in high-speed sports such as squash or in floor routines in gymnastics.

Experts in skill development have concluded that the equivalent of 10 years, 100,000 hours, or over 1 million repetitions are required to make complex skills automatic in major sports such as American football, soccer, basketball, and cricket. Early research suggested that practicing a simple skill more than 150 times in succession resulted in a deterioration of performance. Hence, practice sessions should be scheduled in such a way that skill learning is not hampered by muscular fatigue and lapses in concentration. The trick is to move on to another skill or another facet of preparation before performance begins to deteriorate. Smart practice is often superior to long practice!

Once you are able to execute skills automatically, it is important to ensure that you keep gradual changes in technique in check. Otherwise, critical faults can develop and go undetected. When you pay too little attention to technique, minor changes can become deeply ingrained and, over time, prove difficult to eradicate.

Professional golfers, for example, have told us of their frustrations in having to "take a swing apart" because of glitches that have emerged during competition. What they mean by this is that they return to the constituents of the swing and relearn them, slowly piecing them together and hopefully ironing out any faults as they go. This process can be painfully slow and, at times, demoralizing. The important message is that you should pay close attention to technique and seek regular feedback from a coach; prevention is much better than cure. Your coach should aim to deal with one technical fault at a time and provide feedback that you can easily understand and act on.

A winning mentality includes knowing where to find the expertise to fine-tune skills. In the absence of an available expert, ask a friend to film your performance and then watch this recording followed by watching a DVD of an expert performing the same skill. This should help you identify critical errors, although it is not as effective

The Beauty of Automaticity

Albert Fabris is an opening batsman who has long since mastered the skill of making firm contact with the cricket ball on almost every delivery. He can simultaneously scan the field to gauge exactly where to dispatch the ball, anticipate how the pitch might affect the bounce, notice the idiosyncrasies of the bowler to predict the type of delivery, and observe the positions of the fielders.

as having a knowledgeable coach on hand. One of the main benefits of coaches is that they can devise practice schedules that enable you to develop and maintain skills.

Organizing Practice Schedules

If your goal is to make your sport skills silky smooth, then your practice schedule is a key consideration. This will be as fundamental to improving overall performance as weight training, flexibility work, or aerobic conditioning sessions.

Most sports require athletes to learn a variety of skills. Divers, for example, need to learn a number of dives with varying levels of complexity often from boards of different heights. Volleyball players need to learn how to serve, block, set, and smash. Racing drivers need to learn how to negotiate tight bends, how to brake without skidding or spinning, and how to overtake safely.

Practice schedules can be organized to optimize athletic performance in a number of ways. We explain the best-known methods and give some examples of how you might apply these to your sport.

Blocked Practice Versus Random Practice   One of the primary decisions is whether to practice individual skills in blocks until you master them, or several skills simultaneously in a random manner. This "blocked practice versus random practice" debate has been of interest to sport psychologists.

A *blocked practice schedule* allows you to focus on one skill at a time and involves completing all trials of an individual skill before moving to the next one. For example, in a two-week period a sprinter might learn start technique for three sessions, correct running form for four sessions, how to dip finish for two sessions, and how to receive and pass a relay baton for one session.

An alternative approach might be to work on all four of these skills in each practice session, but randomly, so that the sprinter never practices the same skill in two consecutive trials. This is known as a *random practice schedule*. With both schedules, the same number of trials of each skill is performed in the two-week period; however, the organization of the trials differs.

A pertinent question is, Which of these methods is more effective? Much research has been conducted in recent years to answer this question. Intuition might suggest that the blocked practice method is more effective because it allows athletes to concentrate on one type of skill at a time.

Although over a short period (two to four weeks) the blocked practice method does indeed facilitate greater learning, research shows that this does not apply to long-term skill development. Also, research has suggested that blocked practice can create a false sense of security or overconfidence in a particular skill, because the skill has not been practiced with reference to other important skills that may precede or follow it.

Random practice schedules allow you to retain skills for a longer time and make it easier to transfer these skills to a large number of situations. The reason is that random practice makes the practice environment less predictable and more challenging by requiring the brain to process more information while progressing from drill to drill.

Also, when the time comes to execute a particular skill in a random practice, the brain has to find a solution; the performance is not as well ingrained as it would be following a blocked practice regime. This makes you more adaptable to changing situations such as playing in a variety of weather conditions, tackling opponents who employ unorthodox tactics, or performing in unfamiliar environments.

We suggest that you use blocked practice in the very early stages of learning a skill. As soon as you master the rudiments of that skill, progress to random practice. The time that you devote to blocked practice will depend on the complexity of the skill. Highly complex skills such as a triple salchow in ice dance require more sessions of blocked practice than less technically demanding skills such as a smash in badminton.

Part Learning Versus Whole Learning   Earlier we mentioned the importance of breaking skills down in the early stages of learning or when well-learned skills are not being executed successfully. Psychologists interested in learning methods have heated debates about the relative merits of part versus whole learning. We present the respective benefits likely to be gained from each approach and leave it to you to decide when to apply each.

A dilemma for many coaches and teachers is whether athletes learn skills best by breaking them down into their constituent parts or as a whole. This is a complex issue with many subtleties and contrasting opinions; in this section we touch on some of the key principles.

The *part learning* method works well on parts of a skill that require a great deal of thinking to process in the initial stages or that pose a particular difficulty during competition. For example, novice discus throwers begin by mastering a standing throw; they then throw the discus with a half rotation, a one-and-a-half rotation, and so on, until they accomplish the complete skill of two rotations while "running across the circle."

A skill that is difficult for rugby players to execute effectively in competition is the reverse pass, which can off-foot opponents and create a crucial opening. This skill, however, often breaks down against tough opposition. Getting a playmaker such as a scrum-half to repeat this skill over and over in practice while being hounded by an opposing forward can help to make it dazzlingly effective.

Part learning is also very useful when trying to master skills associated with an element of danger; for example, high diving, BMX tricks, and gymnastics routines. In such instances, the performer can build confidence by learning each element of the skill separately. When these separate parts are eventually joined together, the performer will have a far better idea of what is required to execute the whole skill successfully.

Part practice is also very effective when learning serial skills. In both codes of rugby, for example, a complex offensive play can be broken down to enable each player involved to fully understand his role and the specific contribution he will make to the play. Once each component part of the play is perfected, they are pieced together and performed at full speed.

Another good example involves batting in baseball. Youngsters play a variant of the full game known as T-ball, in which the batter hits the ball off a stationary tee at waist height. This eliminates having to anticipate the idiosyncrasies of a pitcher and a moving target, hence reducing the number of stimuli to which novice players have to attend.

An advanced performer is more likely to benefit from applying the *whole learning* approach to practicing sport skills. The reason is that such performers have enough experience to allow them to understand the links between skill components without the need to break a skill down; in essence, they can more easily *intellectualize* a set of skills. Also, through practicing whole skills, the transfer to competitive situations is more natural because less thinking about how to link the parts of the skill is required.

Helen Flicker:
A Show Jumper Pitching for Championship Success

Show jumping is a sport that requires the rider and horse to function in perfect harmony. Sometimes this partnership can be a somewhat unholy alliance. The sport is tough and can be very dangerous. Even the slightest lapse in concentration can have disastrous consequences for both rider and steed. Tackling a show jumping course is a skill that requires the rider to break down its constituent parts. Each part of the skill is practiced separately, and then the various parts are meshed into a seamless whole. Helen Flicker struggled with a highly demanding championship course, and her horse, Parsifal, was refusing some of the big fences. Helen's coach, Claire Fernhall, advised her to tackle one fence at a time repeatedly. Helen and Parsifal then tackled two fences—know as a double—consecutively; they then negotiated a combination (three fences) including a 5-foot (1.5 m) wall. They kept adding fences in practice until they could cover the course of 12 fences without a knockdown or refusal.

Even top performers have performance breakdowns or mental blocks related to particular aspects of a skill. Such glitches require the practice of one component of the skill over and over again using the aforementioned part-learning approach.

We recommend the whole learning approach for two other situations. The first is when a skill is continuous, which means that it is not possible or meaningful to break it down, such as cartwheels in gymnastics or a slam dunk in basketball. Each part of the skill interacts very closely with the next. The second is when a skill is self-contained and breaking it down reduces its coherence, such as serving in volleyball or taking a penalty kick in soccer.

Nature Versus Nurture

It is impossible to establish exactly what percentage of performance is determined by genetic makeup. Consequently, the long-running nature-versus-nurture debate continues to rage in sport psychology. Certainly factors such as height, build, and muscle fiber composition predispose us toward some sporting activities rather than others. British comedian David Walliams, for instance, may be an accomplished long-distance swimmer having swum the English Channel for charity, but he will never be a top powerlifter. On the other hand, considering good genes and bad genes as the be-all and end-all of future achievement is wrong.

Let's take the example of the legendary Tiger Woods. Some might believe that his prolific talent in striking a golf ball is God-given. Even a glance at his autobiography, however, suggests that nurture played a much bigger part than nature. Tiger's late father, Earl Woods, decided that his infant son would excel at golf. He maintained that the first step in leading an offspring toward sporting immortality is brainwashing. From the tender age of six months, Tiger would be sat in his high chair in such a position that he could not fail to view the hypnotic charms of Earl's pendulous golf swing. Unsurprisingly, before long, baby Tiger began to mimic his father's rhythmic movements. At seven months, Tiger was presented with his first putter.

Earl believed that the second step to greatness entails familiarizing a child with the essential tools and rudiments of a sport at a very young age. Tiger was hitting golf balls even before he could walk. By age one-and-a-half he was using a driver and striking the ball accurately to a distance of 80 yards—almost as far as some adult golfers. At the age of three, he beat his local club professional in a putting contest! As they say, the rest is history.

Over the years, we have enjoyed reading the biographies of many sporting greats, including Andre Agassi, Andrew Flintoff, Sally Gunnell, Lewis Hamilton, Kelly Holmes, Carl Lewis, Chris Hoy, Magic Johnson, Michael Johnson, Dan Marino, Jackie Joyner-Kersee, Michael Jordan, Andy Murray, Michael Owen, Paula Radcliffe, Wayne Rooney, Ian Thorpe, Shane Warne, and Jonny Wilkinson. Significantly, many of these biographies double as manuals of how to achieve sporting immortality. By studying the upbringing of such sporting virtuosos, we begin to see a clear pattern emerging. They have the commonality of very supportive parents who provided a good environment but also, in many instances, had some sporting ability themselves. They grew up immersed in what might be termed a *physical culture*, and their involvement in sport was given constant positive reinforcement. Moreover, their parents knew when to let go of the reins and hand their talented youngsters over to top coaches so they might fully explore their potential.

Mike Agassi Nurtures a Tennis Superstar

Mike Agassi noticed a special kind of alertness in the eyes of baby Andre. He hung a tennis ball over his crib, and Andre patted it back and forth all day long. Like many tennis dads, he was a first-generation immigrant to the USA, looking to provide for his family in any way he could. The pro tennis tour seemed like an ideal route to the American dream. Mike Agassi had already represented Iran as a boxer in the Olympic Games at the tender age of 17. In the USA, he was Chicago Golden Gloves champion for three years in succession. Deciding to change tracks, he went to work as a tennis pro in Las Vegas, where he designed serving machines that would fire balls at a higher-than-normal speed and laid a makeshift tennis court in his back garden.

Andre, the youngest of four children, had a racket taped to his hand as soon as he could walk. He was serving overarm on a full-sized court at age two. By age 10 little Andre was regularly winning tournaments in California and playing against the likes of Michael Chang and Pete Sampras. When Andre reached age 13, Mike Agassi realized that he had imparted the sum of his tennis knowledge. His protégé was packed off to Nick Bollettieri's academy in Florida, where, following two years of tuition, Andre turned pro. By age 18 he was ranked number three in the world.

I did not know life away from tennis. It's kind of like a tortured soul, you know, you have a choice but you don't have a choice. There are times when you look forward to quitting and times when you don't imagine ever possibly doing anything different.

—Andre Agassi

Much research has examined the concept of the athletic personality. Are there psychological traits that distinguish elite athletes from nonelite athletes, strikers from defenders, individual sport players from team sport players, starters from nonstarters? A psychological trait is a genetic factor that causes a person to behave in a certain way across situations. For example, an athlete with a strong aggressive trait may exhibit hostility toward family members, authority figures, teammates, team officials, and the media, as well as opponents. Traits are stable and enduring personality characteristics.

The many studies looking at the athletic personality generally provide inconclusive results. Players who do not have what is supposedly an ideal personality can be extremely successful. Take the example of American tennis player John McEnroe. He was a three-time Wimbledon men's singles champion and winner of another 74 singles titles but had an extremely volatile character. We will examine McEnroe's approach in some detail in chapter 6.

The main trends to emerge from 40 years of research into personality in sport are, first, that athletes differ significantly from nonathletes: Athletes are more self-confident, outgoing, competitive, independent, objective, and intelligent, and less anxious. Second, positions in team sports require different personality types, but these predominantly have to do with concentration style. So, for example, a fly-half in rugby will be able to scan the field of play very effectively and make quick decisions. A tight-head prop, on the other hand, will tend to have a narrower focus and possibly be less flexible in decision-making ability. Chapter 6 has more information on concentration styles.

The third trend to emerge from sport personality research is that athletes at different competitive levels tend to differ, but only when extremes are compared. So elite athletes differ from club-level athletes, but not from national-level athletes. Also, the further one progresses in sport, the more alike personality types become. Hence, elite athletes are more similar to one another than novice athletes are.

Elite sport appears to attract people who are tough-minded, extroverted, emotionally stable, and highly self-motivated. Some athletes are introverted and emotionally unstable, although this does not prevent them from reaching the highest echelons of sport. There is quite a weak relationship between personality traits and success in sport. There is a much stronger relationship between psychological state (how one feels at a particular point in time) and sporting performance. We explore this relationship in chapter 5.

The important thing to note is that you must make the most of your natural talents. There is great potential performance within all of us, very little of which is ever realized. For example, physiologists acknowledge that only a small percentage of our potential strength is ever used at any one time. Rarely do more than 50 percent of our muscle fibers fire off during any voluntary muscle contraction, which leaves a huge untapped reserve of strength. Exceptional circumstances sometimes allow us to reach in and harness these reserves. There are many documented instances of mothers lifting cars to save their trapped babies.

At the 1968 Mexico Olympic Games, Bob Beamon somehow summoned up enough power to long jump 29 feet, 2 1/2 inches (8.90 m); nearly 18 inches (0.46 m) farther than anyone had ever jumped before and farther than anyone believed possible. Indeed, defending Olympic champion Lynn Davies of Great Britain told Beamon, "You have destroyed the event!" Beamon never got within 2 feet (61 cm) of this distance again. It wasn't until 23 years later, at the 1991 Tokyo World Championships, that fellow American Mike Powell managed to surpass the mark set by Beamon. This is a remarkable length of time for a track and field record to remain intact, and even to this day exceptional feats in the sport are referred to as Beamonesque. In advance of London 2012, Beamon's mark remains the Olympic record.

Although it may not be possible to call on these hidden reserves of strength at will, the simple acknowledgment of their existence should convince anyone of the possibility of performing far better than the present level of achievement. The four-minute mile was once an impossible dream; now the world's top runners are closer to three and a half minutes. It is a disservice to talk of our absolute limits, and we can easily shackle ourselves to mediocrity or impose artificial boundaries for achievement. In reality, we may all be limited by our genetic makeup, but the greater limitation comes from succumbing to the *belief* that we are limited (see chapter 3). To scale new heights, we must reach for the stars. That way, we might at least touch the moon.

Psychological Readiness

We have established that physical conditioning and skill development require a highly systematic approach. Top sportspeople devote endless hours to relentless practice in the justifiable belief that their performance will improve. But what role does psychological preparation and mental practice play in the rich tapestry of sport performance? We know that when athletes are very similar in physical conditioning and skill level, mental state differentiates winners from also-rans. How exactly does the mind influence sporting potential and sporting performance?

One factor that we encounter often is athletes' acceptance of the psychological weakness in their performances with resignation. Lapses in concentration, loss of motivation, or feelings of lethargy are acknowledged with a shrug of the shoulders: "Oh well, hopefully I'll feel OK next time." Athletes are rarely so blasé about their fitness levels, mastery of skills, or nutrition and dietary supplements. They often leave absolutely nothing to chance and no stone unturned as far as these aspects of preparation are concerned.

A fundamental misconception is that psychology is a random performance factor. The main message of this book is that psychology is *not* a random performance factor. Psychological preparation for sport is just as readily attained as physical conditioning and skill development. All that is required is proper guidance and sufficient dedication. The main reason for learning psychological skills is to bridge the gap between athletic potential and athletic performance. Athletes who can control confidence, anxiety, concentration, and motivation can control performance.

Whether you can translate your potential into a corresponding level of performance depends on how resistant you are to disruptive forces. *Mental toughness* is a term that many athletes and coaches use to refer to this resistance. But mental toughness is more than that. It has to do with *coping better* than opponents with the many demands that the sport imposes (e.g., training, competition, lifestyle). More specifically, mental toughness involves performing more consistently and being better than opponents in remaining determined, focused, confident, and in control under pressure.

SUMMARY

In this opening chapter we have emphasized that the content of this book may be relevant to individuals both from within the sporting community and beyond, in other high-performance domains (e.g., business and performing arts). A central consideration for all performers is *consistency* and the reproducibility of skills under a variety of circumstances. There is a growing interest in the seminal influence of mental preparation on performance among those who aspire to excellence. We have highlighted that many athletes report devoting only 5 to 10 percent of their time to psychological readiness! As a discipline, sport psychology is a mix of science and art. Although there is now a strong scientific basis for sport psychology techniques, considerable scope remains for creativity in how particular techniques are applied to individual athletes and teams.

A large part of this chapter was devoted to the acquisition of skills that underlie high-level performance. Skill refers to our capacity to produce a desired result consistently and with efficiency of time and effort. It develops though a process of trial and error in which persistence, appropriate instruction, and constructive feedback are all essential elements. Athletes should be encouraged to explore novel practice routines, as these have the potential to revolutionize a sport or event; remember the classic example of Dick Fosbury in 1968. Sport skills are durable but also dynamic in nature, which means that they need to evolve and change from season to season in order for an athlete to remain successful and to progress.

Some guiding principles in the development of skilled performance include the following:

- Break down skills that cannot be mastered in their complete form and apply the part-learning approach.
- Use blocked practice mainly in the early stages of learning, as random practice allows you to retain skills for a longer time and makes it easier to transfer those skills to different situations.
- Avoid sacrificing quality for quantity when practicing skills, and be wary of overpractice.
- Make practices as realistic as possible so that they emulate competition conditions as closely as possible.
- Balance speed and accuracy in the refinement of skills by placing greater importance on accuracy in the early stages of learning.
- Place particular emphasis on developing the weak aspects of your performance.

Ultimately the goal for athletes and their coaches is to make sport skills automatic so that they do not require conscious processing to be executed successfully. Not all skilled performers are necessarily endowed with great technical ability, and the available evidence shows that nurture has played a considerable role in the development of many well-known athletes. In addition, 40 years of personality research in sport has shown that athletes tend to be more self-confident, outgoing, competitive, independent, objective, and intelligent, and less anxious than the general population. Regardless of your physical characteristics or personality traits, make the most of your natural talents, as great potential lies within all of us. This book will assist you in unlocking that potential.

Motivation

It's taken me 15 years to become an overnight success.

—José Mourinho, celebrated soccer manager and self-proclaimed "special one"

Motivation is an aspect of performance that fascinates sportspeople and their coaches the world over. Some say it is very important, and they are right. Some believe some people are more motivated than others, and they too are right. Some say that certain challenges motivate them more than others, and this is hardly surprising. Some believe that if athletes are not motivated for particular training activities or specific competitions, there is nothing they or their coaches can do about it. This is certainly not true. Although high self-motivation is a characteristic of many champions, it can be consciously manipulated to a degree.

Coaches are quick to notice that some athletes' motivation for various activities fluctuates at different points in the year or according to their moods. By understanding the principles behind such fluctuations, they can influence not only athletes' willingness to participate but also their determination to persist with drive and enthusiasm.

The term *motivation* comes from the Latin word "movere," meaning "to move," and describes the powerful inner force that activates us to direct behavior in a certain way. We often refer to this force by other names such as *get-up-and-go, zip, desire,* and even *oomph.* Sometimes, when the spirit prevails against great adversity, we call it *guts.*

Whatever we choose to call it, motivation is clearly an essential component of performance; without it, we are never psychologically ready to compete. Its impact is fundamental to our daily lives. A complete absence of motivation would mean inertia, no activity at all. This is a totally unnatural state for the human species, because we all possess a deep-rooted need to explore and master our environment to promote our own survival. Therefore, nobody is entirely devoid of motivation. What athletes sometimes need to discover is the key that unlocks their own motivational reserves. Unlocking these reserves helps them to fulfill their potential.

An understanding of how motivation is activated is useful. At every moment, we are faced with a dilemma given that life, with its infinite variety, offers a vast range of activities that compete for our time. If offered a choice, some people would play sport,

---

Murray's Marathon

When British tennis player Andy Murray stepped onto Centre Court for his fourth-round match against Stanislas Warwinka in the 2009 Wimbledon Championships, he didn't expect to be taken to a fifth set in the 86 °F (30 °C) heat. Rather than an easy passage into the quarterfinals, he was matched every step of the way by Roger Federer's countryman. To add to the problems of playing a dogged, overperforming challenger who had nothing to lose, he was surprised to find that when the new roof was drawn over the court, he did not like the glare of the lights and had trouble focusing on the ball. Not only this, but the closed environment also caused the shrill noise of the crowd to reverberate, making it even harder to concentrate.

As a result of the extreme heat and humidity, Murray was on the verge of collapse after every game in the fifth set. Nevertheless, in keeping with his high seeding, he won the points that mattered for a famous victory that kept a nation out of their beds and set him on course to his first-ever Wimbledon semifinal. It was the latest game ever played in Wimbledon history, and 12 million BBC viewers stayed up until 11:00 p.m. to watch the drama unfold.

---

some would lie on the sofa eating a large tub of Häagen Dazs and watching TV, and some would choose to read a book, as you are now. One person may tire of a chosen activity very quickly and decide to stop, whereas another may persist much longer. Likewise, one person may devote only minimal energy to the task at hand, whereas another may dedicate every scrap of energy to the activity.

These differences illustrate the three components of motivation:

- Direction, referring to the desire to pursue one activity over any other (i.e., where we direct out efforts)
- Persistence, referring to the tendency to continue an activity until a particular aim is fulfilled
- Intensity, referring to the amount of energy devoted to the activity

So, whereas one person may demonstrate a very intense attitude toward sport and persist doggedly until success is achieved, a second person may participate only halfheartedly and settle for something easier when the going gets tough.

DRIVING FORCES IN SPORT

Much has been written about the very complex phenomenon of motivation. The knowledge that we have to date suggests that people are not generally motivated toward every possible type of endeavor; rather, they are motivated to perform in specific domains to achieve very specific outcomes. A professional snooker player may not be motivated at all to play in a club championship but may be extremely motivated to play in a national championship. Also, although a young child may not be motivated to try hard in physical education lessons at school, the opportunity to play sport in a club outside of school hours may fill him with enthusiasm.

Motivation operates at many levels and has many influences. People have an underlying level of motivation that influences how they behave across a wide range of situations. A person who is motivated across a wide range of contexts is likely to succeed in many arenas, such as sport, business, and art.

You may well have known a clever classmate who appeared to be motivated for every class and was seemingly brilliant at everything. The former French soccer player Eric Cantona, for example, has been a successful poet, film and stage actor, producer, model, businessman, and commentator. People are also motivated to perform at high levels in specific contexts or domains. You might be extremely motivated to play lacrosse but not at all motivated to study mathematics, or vice versa (try exercise 2.1 to uncover what characterizes your motivation for sport). People tend to gravitate toward specific sports for the following reasons:

- They find the sport particularly interesting and rewarding.
- They are encouraged to participate in the sport by friends or family members.
- They feel competent in performing the skills integral to the sport.
- They are exposed to the sport from a young age.
- They have a social network within the sport.
- They use sport as a path to excellence.
- They find that sport promotes health and fitness.

Motivation also exists at a *situational level*—that is, how motivated you are at a particular point in time within a given context (e.g., if you are a basketball player, how motivated you are to take a free throw in the last 30 seconds of a game with the scores tied). Inevitably, your general motivation feeds through to your motivation in individual achievement domains, which, in turn, is reflected in motivated behavior at the situational level.

Many personality and environmental factors influence variations in motivation at each level. We will explore some of these influences to facilitate an understanding of the concept and explore how you and your support team might work toward enhancing your level of motivation.

Exercise 2.1
What Characterizes Your Motivation for Sport?

Reflect on how many of the preceding reasons characterize your motivation for the sport you play. Perhaps some additional motives got you involved. Reflecting on why you got involved in the first place is a good way to remind yourself of some of the really good points about being a sportsperson. In high-level sport, people sometimes become detached from these initial motives, and their enthusiasm can wane as a consequence. Being pressured by others or controlled by rewards is not as fulfilling as doing something for the sheer love of it. Establishing why you're involved in sport helps to avoid inner conflict, allowing you to aspire toward peak performance.

SELF-MOTIVATION

Psychologists describe self-motivation as a part of personality that is relatively stable and enduring. Self-motivation refers to how hard you typically persist or how tenacious you are. More specifically, it's about how you persist in the absence of encouragement from other people and inducements such as money, trophies, or public acclaim. Top sportspeople tend to be extremely self-motivated. They have an ability to overcome many types of adversity that are part and parcel of high-level sport: injury, illness, staleness, burnout, choking, and losing to seemingly lesser opponents.

Although psychologists think of self-motivation as relatively stable, there are many anecdotes of athletes changing their behaviors almost overnight and rising to the very top of their chosen sport. One such example was the 1992 Olympic 100-meter champion, Linford Christie, discussed below. The key thing to note is that a change in attitude and daily habits can have a dramatic effect on performance.

Having clear life goals gives you a sense of direction that can help you overcome problems with self-motivation. We explore various ways of setting goals later in this chapter. For now, take some time to measure your self-motivation. The questionnaire in exercise 2.2 was developed by a group of British researchers and is one of the best indicators of self-motivation to persist in training. It was designed specifically for the context of sport and physical activity.

Christie Goes From Zero to Hero—Olympic Hero

Until 1986, Linford Christie was considered an also-ran of the British sprint scene. He was a good club runner, but that's about as far as he seemed to want to go. He led a fairly laid-back lifestyle in west London playing dominoes, staying out late at parties, eating fast food, and every now and again, turning up for training, but really not giving his all.

In the autumn of 1985, coach Ron Rodden decided to lay everything on the line: "You either work or you go!" he told Christie. Rodden was frustrated with Christie's level of commitment and poor attitude toward training. That ultimatum heralded a new era for Christie and for British sprinting. In the indoor season of 1986, Christie won every championship he entered including a totally unexpected European 200-meter title. From that point, he won medals with clockwork regularity culminating in both Olympic and World Championship glory in successive years. In fact, Christie remains the oldest winner of the Olympic and World Championship 100-meter titles in history.

Christie's apparent lack of self-motivation took a dramatic turn for the better. Yes, the initial stimulus came from the coach, but Christie came to the realization that he had the talent to be the best in the world and that, without sustained effort, he would never achieve this. The principle here is that no matter what your psychological predisposition might be, with systematic application and effort, you can make massive improvements. How far you go relative to others will depend on the genetic predisposition you have for your sport. Christie was blessed with an innate talent that he only really capitalized on quite late in his athletic career.

Exercise 2.2
Self-Motivation Test

Please answer each statement using the rating scale given here:

NO!   no   between   yes   YES!

Here is an example:

	NO!	no	between	yes	YES!
I think that reading books like this one can be fun.				√	

OK, let's start! Check one box at the end of each line.

	NO!	no	between	yes	YES!
1. I am not very good at getting myself to do things.					
2. When I get bored, I switch to do something else.					
3. I can keep going at things even when they are tiring and painful.					
4. If something gets to be too much of an effort to do, I am likely to stop doing it.					
5. I am good at keeping promises that I make to myself.					
6. When I take on something difficult, I try to stick to it until it is finished.					
7. I am good at making decisions and keeping to them.					
8. I usually try to find the easiest way to do things.					
9. I don't like to work too hard.					
10. I am a lazy person most of the time.					
11. I work harder than most of my friends.					
12. I don't often let myself down.					

(continued)

	NO!	no	between	yes	YES!
13. I like to do things that challenge me.					
14. I change my mind quite easily.					
15. Things just don't matter much to me.					
16. I often work until I get tired out.					
17. I never force myself to do things that I don't feel like doing.					
18. It takes a lot to get me going.					
19. I really want to achieve things.					
20. I don't have much self-discipline.					

Adapted, by permission, from S. Biddle, D. Akande, N. Armstrong, et al., 1996, "The Self-Motivation Inventory modified for children: Evidence on psychometric properties and its use in physical exercise," *International Journal of Sport Psychology* 27: 237-250.

Scoring instructions:

Statements 3, 5, 6, 7, 11, 12, 13, 16, 19:

YES! = 5, yes = 4, between = 3, no = 2, NO! = 1

For the other statements (1, 2, 4, 8, 9, 10, 14, 15, 17, 18, 20) the scoring is reversed:

YES! = 1, yes = 2, between = 3, no = 4, NO! = 5

What does your score mean?

If you scored in the range of 20 to 40, you are probably the type of person who struggles even to get out of bed in the morning! If you are an athlete, you will be very hard pressed to get anywhere near your physical potential unless you have a major change of attitude and rethink what is most important in life.

If you scored in the range of 41 to 60, you are like most of the general population. You find it quite challenging to commit to things on a long-term basis, so you may well benefit from some well-structured goal setting (see the goals section later in this chapter). You might not specifically identify a lack of motivation as a hindrance to your performance, but there is certainly room for improvement in how you go about committing yourself to important tasks.

If you scored in the range 61 to 100, you are blessed with the high levels of self-motivation that typify most top sportspeople. Capitalize on this psychological trait to fully realize your sporting potential. If your score is above 80, you likely pursue your goals so doggedly that you might slip on other important aspects of your life such as showing care for friends and family. Be sure to keep any obsessive tendencies that you have in check to retain a balanced approach to life.

INTRINSIC AND EXTRINSIC MOTIVATION

There are two main sources of motivation. Generally speaking, motivation can come from the outside, such as the motivation to win medals, receive financial rewards, and attract attention from the media. This is known as external, or *extrinsic,* motivation because it involves participation in sport for some kind of reward that is external to the process of participation. On the other hand, athletes who participate because they enjoy the process—that is, they find sport interesting, stimulating, and enjoyable without being preoccupied by external rewards—are predominantly internally, or *intrinsically,* motivated. Exercise 2.3 will assist you in applying concepts of intrinsic and extrinsic motivation to your own sport participation.

Intrinsic motivation is closely allied to the fundamental motivation to learn and acquire new skills. The building blocks, or psychological needs, that underlie intrinsic motivation are the need to determine one's behavior (what psychologists term *self-determination*), the need to feel *competent,* and the need for *relatedness,* or to have meaningful relationships with other people. When these basic needs are satisfied, high intrinsic motivation results and athletes are stimulated by their participation in sport; they strive to learn new skills and improve their performance.

Many athletes and coaches ask us to identify the main difference between intrinsic motivation and self-motivation (which you assessed previously). Intrinsic motivation is about enjoyment and immersion in an activity, whereas self-motivation can involve an internal pressure to perform well, which is part of personality. Intrinsic motivation comes with a complete absence of any internal or external pressure to perform well. Most people can recall a time from their childhood when they were playing a game with friends that was so enjoyable that they were entirely engrossed in what they were doing; it didn't matter who won the game, and the time just flew by because they were having such a great time.

Our own research has shown that athletes who have the best motivational outcomes, such as persistence, a positive attitude, and unflinching concentration, tend to be both extrinsically and intrinsically motivated. Athletes who are predominantly extrinsically motivated tend to become discouraged when they do not perform to expectations and can experience a downturn in form. Conversely, athletes who are predominantly

---

Exercise 2.3
Extrinsic Versus Intrinsic Motivation

Reflect for a moment on what motivates you to be an athlete. Write down your ideas on a sheet of paper and study them. Most likely your list includes both intrinsic and extrinsic motives. For example, you might desire fame and fortune through your participation in sport, but at the same time, you may genuinely enjoy being involved in the day-to-day routines of training, strict diet, and competition. Such a mix of motives is typical of most successful athletes.

Now see if you can group your motives under two columns labeled *Extrinsic Motives* and *Intrinsic Motives.*

Competitive Buzz Without the Competition

An example of a sportsperson who typifies the high intrinsic/low extrinsic profile is the Formula 1 test driver Alexander Wurz. Known to motor racing fans as a colorful and articulate character, Wurz had a couple of seasons driving for Williams but chose to curtail his competitive driving career to be the test driver for Honda and, in 2009, for Brawn Formula 1. This gave him the opportunity to drive the cars day in and day out while still focusing on the technical intricacies of operating at race speed. Wurz was still around Formula 1 and indeed a focal point for the Brawn team. High intrinsic motivation is essential as he drives on his own while needing to maintain the levels of performance required in a competitive situation.

Thierry Bovy/DPPI/Icon SMI

Alexander Wurz decided he preferred testing Formula 1 cars to racing them.

intrinsically motivated often do not have the competitive drive to become champions. This is because they tend to enjoy mastering the tasks that comprise their chosen discipline, but they lack a strong competitive streak in their personalities.

What we have just said about the combination of extrinsic and intrinsic motives does not hold for young athletes, and in particular prepubescent athletes. Coaches should be aware that fostering intrinsic motives brings about the best psychological outcomes for children. Many parents are responsible for causing their offspring to drop out of sport prematurely because they place such an overt emphasis on winning that participation just isn't fun.

Coaches and parents should work together to create a positive motivational climate for young athletes. Research has shown that the motivational climate can be *performance oriented*, which means focused on social comparison and winning, or *mastery oriented*, which means focused on self-referenced goals and feelings of competence. The latter type of climate is by far better for young athletes. They need time to fully master the skills involved in their sport without the pressures of winning and constantly comparing themselves to others. Important lessons for children to learn are that increased effort enhances their performance and that sport is essentially a fun activity.

For adult athletes, high performance levels may be stimulated partly by the tangible rewards that sport provides, but still the emphasis should be on the fun associated with participation. On balance, it is much more important to be high in intrinsic motivation than to be high in extrinsic motivation. In the long run, extrinsic motivation is only effective when intrinsic motivation is high. Being driven solely by extrinsic motives is not psychologically healthy because the lack of intrinsic rewards can lead you to quit or seriously question your involvement. Having intrinsic motivation helps you get through dry patches in your career and keeps the emphasis on having fun. As the old Russian saying advises, you should take time to smell the roses!

Flow

The highest level of intrinsic motivation is known as *flow*. Flow is typified by complete immersion in an activity to the point that nothing else seems to matter. Hungarian psychologist Professor Mihaly Csikszentmihalyi has led much of the work in this exciting area, which has intrigued sport psychology researchers in recent years.

Flow occurs when there is a perfect match between the perceived demands of an activity and the perceived ability to meet the demands. During flow, you lose self-consciousness and become one with the activity. This creates a state in which you are intrinsically rewarded by the movement patterns involved. Flow is seen as the ultimate experience among the sporting community. Many athletes and coaches refer to flow as being "in the zone," "on song," or "in the groove." It is an optimal psychological state and a deeply pleasurable experience.

Flow can enrich your life and make you want to persist at your chosen disciplines with greater intensity. Many interventions designed to promote flow are detailed in later chapters of this book, but we have included some introductory flow exercises here. You will need a pen and paper to complete them.

Flow Tip 1: Create an Immersion Effect

Sit down in a place where you are unlikely to be disturbed. Close your eyes and take a few long, slow, deep breaths, inhaling through your nose and exhaling through your mouth until you feel completely relaxed. Recall a time when you were performing at the very peak of your ability, when everything just seemed to click into place. Spend a few minutes trying to recall every detail about that experience. When the experience feels really lifelike and you are entirely immersed in it, open your eyes and write down everything that characterized it: how you felt inside, what you were thinking, how other people were reacting to your movements, how you were controlling the environment, and so on. Likely, your mind was completely clear and you were focused entirely on the task at hand. Using your checklist, recall the feelings associated with peak performance and flow just prior to your next performance. Engaging in this process will enhance the likelihood of your entering a flow state.

Flow Tip 2: Plan and Chart Progress

We noted earlier how important it is to have clear goals. It is now widely recognized that the most effective way to set goals is to have some overarching objectives (e.g., winning an Olympic medal) that are underscored by numerous medium-term and short-term process goals. It is no coincidence that the secret to entering flow is to immerse yourself in the process of your activity. Over time, persistent focus on the process brings about successful outcomes such as winning Olympic gold medals. By *process*, we are referring to the nuts and bolts of your discipline—mastering the skills, working on your mental toughness, and attaining appropriate fitness levels.

We suggest that you keep a training or activity diary in which you list your major goals on the first page and strategize, review, and monitor your progress from day to day, week to week, and month to month on subsequent pages. Be sure to adjust your initial goals if they turn out to be either unrealistic or too easy. Many athletes like to check off goals achieved as they progress through each week because this gives them a sense of accomplishment. The next time you go into a training session, be sure to have recorded in advance exactly what you expect to achieve. Get into the habit of making brief notes before and after each training session to keep you firmly focused on the most important components of your performance. *Don't just think it, ink it!*

Flow Tip 3: Use Positive Self-Talk

Positive self-talk is one of the most tried and tested strategies among sport psychology interventions. It is used to maintain concentration and to induce optimal arousal. We use three types of self-talk in our work with athletes. The first type is known as *task-relevant self-talk,* and as the name suggests, it involves a focus on the task at hand. A professional boxer uses the statement *Guard up, chin down* to reinforce his posture. The second type is known as *mood-related self-talk,* which should affect the way you feel (see also chapters 3 and 5). A female rugby player came up with *Wham bam thank you ma'am!* to encapsulate the ease with which she would dispossess her opponents of the ball. The third type is known as a *positive self-affirmation statement.* The most famous exponent of this type was the great Muhammad Ali, who told himself "I am the greatest" so many times that even his opponents became convinced of it.

Flow Tip 4: Seeing Is Believing

All great achievers in history are characterized by having a clear vision of what they wanted to achieve; as the old Chinese proverb goes, "If you chase two rabbits, you will catch neither." Structured imagery, or visualization, is the key that will unlock your potential and turn your dreams into reality (see chapter 7 for more detail). Imagery allows you to see in your mind's eye the outcomes you wish to bring about. By recreating these outcomes using multisensory images (sight, sound, touch), you greatly increase the chance of attaining superior performance because images program muscles. The more vividly you can create images and the better you engage each of your senses, the more effectively you will prime your muscles for superior performance. This holds true in all spheres of human achievement.

NEED FOR ACHIEVEMENT AND FEAR OF FAILURE

Two aspects of personality can have a strong influence on motivation in competitive situations. They are usually referred to by the terms *need for achievement* (NA) and *fear of failure* (FF). NA refers to the degree to which we are naturally competitive and actively seek out the sort of challenge sport provides. FF refers to the way we view the possibility of defeat. Although no sportsperson ever enjoys losing, defeat is more damaging for some than for others. There are many for whom failure results in self-doubt and low self-esteem, and this can have a detrimental effect on motivation.

To understand yourself a little better, see how you compare to the types presented in figure 2.1. As an active sportsperson or coach, you may have little in common with types 1 and 2. Sport, after all, is highly achievement orientated. If you do recognize these characteristics in yourself, however, your commitment to winning may be less than total. Ask yourself why sport attracts you and what you hope to get out of it.

Many sportspeople have reasons for participating that do not revolve around achievement but are related to friendships, personal respect, and the sense of exhilaration associated with movement. There is nothing wrong with this. If your need for achievement is low, recognize it, accept it, and enjoy participation for reasons other than winning.

A well-known example of fear of failure leading to dropout involved the French 400-meter star Marie-José Pérec, who won Olympic titles over 200 and 400 meters at the 1996 Atlanta Olympics. There was media frenzy over the impending clash between Pérec and Australian golden girl Cathy Freeman at the 2000 Sydney Olympics. Pérec was coming back from injury and playing a constant cat-and-mouse game with the world's media. On the eve of the showdown with Freeman, Pérec claimed to have been stalked in her hotel and caught the first available flight home. She was not seen or heard from by the French Athletics Federation for six months following this incident, and then, she communicated via an intermediary so that her whereabouts would remain secret. She never competed again.

The example of Pérec cracking under pressure is a very extreme one. In most cases fear of failure results in some precompetition anxiety that dissipates once the action gets underway. The importance of talking through your fears with a friend or coach cannot be emphasized enough. Talking through a fear usually helps you see it in its true perspective and makes it much easier to deal with.

It is also possible to develop a fear of success, which involves anxiety about the consequences of winning. More is expected of a champion: higher performance levels, further victories, and an ability to deal with the media. The pressure of future demands and the exposure to public scrutiny can result in some athletes settling in just below the top level rather than really striving to be number one in their chosen sport. Also, some people harbor an unconscious fear that if they fulfill their dreams, there will be nowhere to go; they believe that it is always better to travel than to arrive. The media

Figure 2.1 Need for achievement (NA) and fear of failure (FF) influence motivation for competition.

has suggested that former British tennis star Tim Henman may have suffered from a fear of success. Despite his talent and range of shots, he never quite managed to fulfill the hopes of the home crowd by winning the Wimbledon All England Tennis Championships. The mantle of British number one has almost been like a chain around the neck of a string of tennis players because of the very high expectations of the British public and media.

Try exercise 2.4 to assess your own need for achievement and fear of failure. Most likely, you do not fit comfortably into any of the four categories. Perhaps your need for achievement and fear of failure levels are moderate. In this case you have much in common with millions of other normal, well-adjusted people (although we do not mean to imply, of course, that any of the four types are maladjusted in any way!).

You can begin to address your own motivation by recognizing and bolstering the weak links in your motivational chain. Even if you decide that some problems are related to personality, many will be caused by situational factors, which you can change once you identify them. Remember the example of former Olympic 100-meter champion Linford Christie (see page 30).

Exercise 2.4
Assessing Need for Achievement and Fear of Failure

Estimate your own need for achievement and fear of failure levels below.

If you see yourself as type 3, then motivation for competition will not be a major problem for you. You love to win but realize that losing is not the end of the world. You are likely very persistent and enjoy taking calculated risks. You may not find training challenging enough, and therefore, effective goal setting, which is explained later in this chapter, may be necessary to maintain your self-motivation through the long hours of practice.

Type 4 people are very common in sport. Often they have a lot of talent and excelled in sport as youngsters, when losing was virtually unknown to them. As a result, failure became difficult to handle. Anxiety about losing, loss of motivation, and in some cases severe depression can combine to cause underachievement among adult athletes of this type. Fear of failure causes many athletes to drop out because competition becomes too unpleasant and seemingly unrewarding.

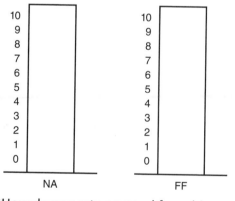

How do you rate on need for achievement and fear of failure?

From C.I. Karageorghis and P.C. Terry, 2011, *Inside sport psychology* (Champaign, IL: Human Kinetics).

HOW ANALYSIS OF THE OUTCOME INFLUENCES MOTIVATION

After any contest, we experience an immediate emotional response based on whether we won, lost, or tied. This can be anything from feeling "high as a kite" to feeling "gutted". It is very natural for us to feel pleasure when we win and disappointment when we lose. We also experience other emotions such as satisfaction and dissatisfaction that may be heightened by how we feel about the outcome. If we believe we won as a result of effort, the result may be pride. If we see defeat as a result of poor effort, then a sense of shame may result.

Because we naturally defend our egos, we tend to claim the credit when we win by attributing victory to our own effort and ability, but we like to shift the blame for defeat to things beyond our control such as bad luck, poor refereeing, and adverse weather conditions. We attribute causes to events to make sense of the world in which we live, and the explanations we give ourselves affect not only our emotional reactions but also our future motivation.

It is important to understand that the outcome of the contest is within your control. Those who believe that failure is an inevitable result of their poor ability typically react to losing situations with a shrug of the shoulders and a comment such as, "What's the point?" or, "Why am I doing this?" This leads to lower levels of effort and reduced motivation. Eventually, such people tend to either give up or stop experiencing sport as rewarding.

To avoid feelings of helplessness and to foster the unshakable belief in ability that characterizes true champions, you should learn to perceive failure as the result of some temporary factor. Such a factor might be poor form or bad luck, but a controllable factor such as insufficient effort or an incorrect mode of training is more likely to motivate you to rectify the problem because you will believe that you can do something about it.

London Marathon Phenomenon

The London marathon provides a classic example of success for all. Why would more than 35,000 people compete in a race that only one person can win, unless each had his or her own criterion for success? Before any race, marathon runners set many goals. Finishing the course regardless of the time it takes is one goal, and so it should be. A second goal might be to finish in a certain time. The quality of the run may also be important. "Did it feel good?" "Did I use my upper body effectively?" or "Did I judge the pace well?" may be questions runners ask themselves. The finishing position is almost irrelevant to all but the most elite runners. Individually and collectively, runners come away from the race feeling a sense of achievement. This is due, in part, to the feeling of communion with other runners that such mass participation events provide, although a sense of achievement also comes from having fulfilled some or all of their predetermined objectives. Few people can actually complete a run of 26 miles, 385 yards (42.2 km) and feel bad about themselves.

Believing that you are a success or a failure affects your sport performance in many ways. A belief that you are a failure immediately causes you to lose self-confidence, inhibiting your style of play and possibly even leading to you choosing another, less depressing activity. On the other hand, seeing yourself as a success brings contentment, improved confidence, and the motivation to persist with the activity that brings about these feelings. Fortunately, sport can provide enough opportunities for success to enable you to get your fair share. Your perception of your success belongs to you and nobody else. Use it to best advantage. The trick is to learn to recognize personal success and to capitalize on it.

DEMOTIVATION AND SLUMPS

Athletes at all competitive levels experience a reduced level of motivation, or *demotivation,* at some point in their careers. This is often associated with a slump in performance. It would be nice to think that all of the good advice in a text such as this one apply equally to every athlete, but the reality is that this is not the case. For example, we talk a lot about goal setting in sport psychology, but some athletes are just not goal-setting types. They do not enjoy either setting goals or working toward them. Rather, they enjoy the experience of sport and just want to see where it takes them without having any particular vision or predetermined path. Some athletes even revel in the uncertainty of sport. Also, achievement is not important for everyone; for some, the participation and camaraderie associated with sport carry greater significance than achievement.

Demotivation sometimes occurs when athletes get injured or have a run of poor performances. Such experiences diminish confidence, and a downturn in motivation may be one of the outcomes (see also chapter 3). From an early age, athletes need to learn that sporting careers are typified by peaks and troughs. Although gradual progression is common for children and adolescents, in early adulthood the pressures of college, relationships, and work often conspire to redirect focus away from sporting achievement and toward other things. Also, at this stage an athlete is likely to become a small fish in a big pond just as he has grown accustomed to being a big fish in a small pond. Inevitably, performance levels plateau and sometimes even decline a little.

In such circumstances, it is important to adhere to the *processes* that are likely to enhance both confidence and motivation. Motivation is very closely related to confidence because when we believe we can achieve a particular end, we are truly motivated to pursue it with vigor and enthusiasm (see chapter 3). So, creating small challenges based on your current performance level will help to lift you out of a motivational trough. We are referring to some of the bread-and-butter aspects of any sport such as basic speed, flexibility, agility, strength, endurance, and reactions. Once these basics begin to show improvement across the board, an increase in motivation is more likely.

Gender differences in sport motivation have been clarified during the past 30 years of research. A critical age for girls is 14 to 15 years, when there are many competing demands on their time and they have usually become aware of the opposite sex. The sport dropout rate among girls in this age group is very high—six times what it is for boys. This is unfortunate because, according to the Women's Sports Foundation (USA), high school girls who participate in sport are less likely to experience an unwanted pregnancy, are more likely to get better grades in school, and are more likely to graduate than girls who do not participate.

Coaches and parents should be mindful of the sociocultural norms that may send the message to young women that sport is not a worthwhile pursuit. Girls can be given sport-related gifts for birthdays and Christmas, be taken to watch major sporting events involving women where they are likely to find positive role models, and be provided with more social support to persist with sport into adulthood. Overcoming societal pressures on women is not just a matter of reading about motivation strategies, but more about a seismic shift in attitudes. For example, labeling a young girl a tomboy because she enjoys playing soccer attaches unnecessary connotations to her participation. We need to support and celebrate women's involvement in sport with particular emphasis on the early teenage years.

The motivational techniques presented throughout this chapter will not necessarily result in continuous improvement in performance levels at every point in your career. A performance plateau, for example, needs to be managed carefully by a coach or support team. It could indicate that you have reached a high level of performance that is difficult to sustain. Also, it is actually possible to continue improving aspects of performance without any corresponding improvement in performance levels. For example, in track and field, when a sprinter is taught to relax in full flight, his times will initially slow down a little or remain static. When the idea of relaxation truly clicks in and he is able to relax his arms and shoulders without conscious effort, this is when his performance can improve markedly.

A long-term injury poses one of the biggest threats to motivation. Often, there is uncertainty as to whether the injury will heal sufficiently to allow you to return to or surpass the preinjury level of performance. In these instances, focusing on things that can be done to facilitate rapid healing of the injury, rather than worrying about what might happen if it doesn't fully heal, is the key to recovery.

Setting small day-to-day targets for rehabilitation activities can offset a potential postinjury slump. The mood regulation strategies presented in chapter 5 might help you if your mood (and then motivation) suffer as a consequence of injury. Moreover, during periods of injury, coaches and team managers should help you feel like an integral part of the team. Chapter 3 provides specific examples of how this might be facilitated.

Beating Slumps Through a Change in Environment

The daily rigors and grinding routines of sport can make you feel demotivated or prompt a slump. Most people have heard the phrase "A change is as good as a rest." In reality, the benefit of change lies in the fact that it creates new motivation. Research in industrial psychology has demonstrated that the motivation and productivity of workers increases when their work environment is altered. Similarly, when professional athletes complain of becoming stale, they take themselves off for a while to do something completely different, and then return with their batteries recharged and their motivation restored, raring to go once again.

Jason Cairnduff/Action Images/Icon SMI

Former England cricket star Andrew Flintoff recharges his batteries by playing golf.

Cricketer Andrew Flintoff plays golf, Formula 1 driver Jenson Button goes fishing, and tennis player Andrew Murray enjoys go-carting. The high-altitude training that has been fashionable among international runners such as Paula Radcliffe may well be beneficial as much for providing a fresh and stimulating training environment as for its physiological benefits.

Whereas English soccer teams such as Arsenal might wind down in the West Indies, the likes of you and us will probably be forced to make more modest breaks in routine. This does not prevent us from reaping the benefits of the change, though. Simple changes are often all that are necessary. Rugby players might try American football or Australian Rules football, and so dispel those repetition blues that are so common during training. As consultants to an international tennis academy, we find that when the young tennis players cease to fire on all cylinders, an impromptu game of three-on-three basketball usually restores their enthusiasm.

The same principle applies to you as an individual. If training is getting you down or you feel demotivated, try a temporary change of scene. It could turn out to be the breath of fresh air that gives you renewed impetus and vigor. Athletes too often become obsessive about their training routines, pursuing quantity at the expense of quality because they are afraid that a missed session will damage their program. In fact, training that has become too arduous can cause the damage. As a general rule, remember that overtraining can do more harm to your performance than undertraining can.

MAXIMIZING MOTIVATION

We have covered the multifaceted nature of motivation, discussed how to assess different aspects of this important "energy source," and provided examples illustrating how athletes can sometimes be highly motivated and, at other times, extremely demotivated. When motivation slumps or is at a less-than-optimal level, athletes and coaches need techniques that can give it a boost. In this section we provide a series of strategies that we have found to be very effective during our many years of working with athletes.

Goal Setting

Setting goals is the process of defining clear objectives. It involves determining what you intend to do and how well you intend to do it. This also directs attention toward a particular activity and provides notice that a certain level of persistence and intensity of effort will be required. Whether done consciously or subconsciously, people routinely set goals for themselves in many areas of daily life. When a person makes a simple plan of the day's activities or writes a list of jobs that need doing, she is setting goals. If an athlete aims for international honors or sets a target of winning a particular competition, he is setting goals.

The concept of achievement is based entirely on setting goals. Fulfilling objectives often results in a sense of achievement. Falling short of objectives may well result in a sense of failure. How clearly defined are your sporting goals at this point? Your ultimate goals may have their roots in your childhood dreams of future glory. Some children dream of kicking the winning goal in the Australian Football League grand final or hitting the homerun that wins the World Series, whereas others dream of hitting a championship-winning volley at Wimbledon or leading the 400 meters in front of a full house at the Stade de France.

Such fantasies often continue into adulthood and become the foundation of ambition and self-belief. These goals, no matter how casually established, may set you on a specific path, but the all-important persistence and intensity with which you pursue them will depend on the quality of your goal-setting skills. Close attention to detail and frequent monitoring of goals are the keys to success.

You should consider setting goals for all aspects of your sporting life, from fitness work to skills training, from mental skills development to actual competitions and even to your long-term career development. The former Italian soccer star Gianluca Vialli once said that "every aspect of sport is a competition against yourself." For maximum effort in training, set objectives and try to beat your personal best performances in each activity, be it a bench press, a two-mile (3.2 km) time trial, or saving penalties.

You will get the best out of yourself by setting realistic but challenging goals every time you practice. Not only does this promote a sense of achievement, but it also provides a clear focus for each session.

Starting the Process

At present, the prospect of sitting down to mastermind your progress toward a far-off sporting triumph might daunt you. The list of sacrifices, the degree of effort, and the range of skills to be mastered can quite easily appear overwhelming. Like the winning tape that seems to evade the 800-meter runner, so the path to an ultimate goal can appear to be an endless road riddled with potholes and barriers.

If this resembles your own situation, take heart from the wisdom of American civil rights activist Ralph Abernathy III, who said, "When the escalator to success breaks down, take the stairs." Remember that the most unproductive time is spent worrying about all the things that need doing. You can only achieve one thing at a time, so you should learn to devote all your effort to the most immediate goal and temporarily forget about what lies beyond. The most immediate goal when starting out is to identify the destination. It may lie only a modest distance along the road of sporting achievement, or it may be a long and ambitious journey. Whatever you decide to aim for, the process is the same:

- Decide exactly what you wish to achieve.
- Identify the obstacles that are preventing your progress.
- Decide what is necessary to help you clear those obstacles.
- Establish specific goals to help you tackle obstacles one by one.
- Stay focused on the present; you cannot change the past, and the future can only be made better by what you do right now.

Certainty about your destination and the clarity with which you see the barriers will strengthen your determination to make progress.

Try completing exercise 2.5. At this stage you are only creating the bare bones of a plan, just the first step forward. Think carefully about what you want to achieve. Aim for something that is a challenge but within the bounds of possibility. Write it

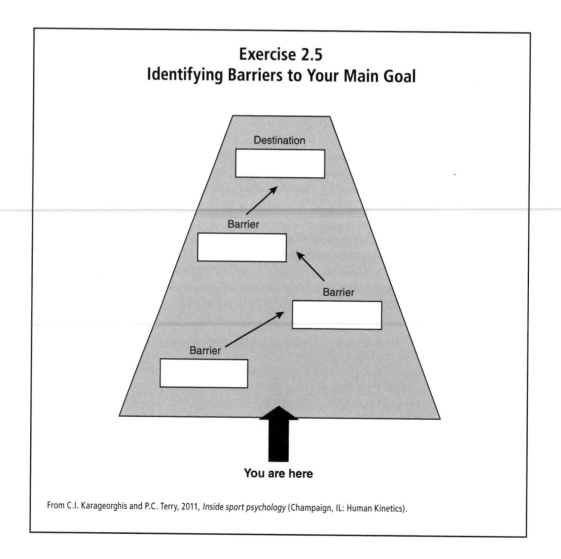

Exercise 2.5
Identifying Barriers to Your Main Goal

Destination

Barrier

Barrier

Barrier

You are here

From C.I. Karageorghis and P.C. Terry, 2011, *Inside sport psychology* (Champaign, IL: Human Kinetics).

down in the Destination box. Now express in your own terms the things you believe stand in your way. Write them down in the Barrier boxes. Try to be specific, but don't sweat over it for too long because you will have a chance to alter and refine your plan as you learn more about effective goal setting.

Goals for Reaching Your Destination

Once you have established the direction in which you are heading, you should start to consider specific objectives. The immediate temptation may be to establish goals in terms of winning contests. Although winning may be the ultimate objective, putting too great an emphasis on this type of short-term goal risks damaging both motivation and confidence. This is particularly important for young athletes.

Anyone with the solitary goal of winning a particular contest develops fixed attitudes about success and failure (success is about winning, losing represents failure). This is a guarantee of failure at some stage because nobody can win all the time—not even sporting greats such as Kelly Slater, Venus Williams, or Valentino Rossi. People who have this attitude are much too hard on themselves, even if they have absolutely prodigious physical talent.

It is more constructive to set goals that relate to things that contribute to winning but can be controlled directly. Such goals include fitness, effort, technical aspects, and general strategies, which all allow for achievement regardless of the result. Again, remember to keep winning in perspective: That is, find something to reflect positively upon that is unrelated to the outcome of the sporting contest. Goals that are independent of the outcome of individual contests are an important means of maintaining motivation when the result may be going against you.

To set effective goals, you must have a clear picture of your playing characteristics. For instance, if your sport happens to be tennis, you will need to assess each aspect of performance on its own by assessing the relevant skills in a systematic and detailed fashion. You should evaluate the serve, forehand groundstroke, backhand groundstroke, high volley, and so on. You will then need to do the same for each element of fitness (speed, strength, stamina, suppleness), aspects of your mental approach (concentration, confidence, staying cool under pressure), and performance strategies (approaching the net, court position, footwork).

Using the examples in exercise 2.6 on page 46 as a guide, complete a brief analysis of your own performance. If necessary, adapt the main headings to suit your sport. Avoid being general in your comments; be as specific as necessary. As the example indicates, you should use objective tests to assess performance wherever possible, but otherwise, rate yourself on a scale of 1 to 10. Eventually, you will need to complete this exercise more thoroughly, at which point you should seek help from a coach or someone who knows you well as a player and as a person in order to assess your performance characteristics accurately.

Once you have completed the analysis, identify the performance elements you would most like to improve. Multiple goals are most effective, so try 6 to 10 elements at first. Now decide how much you want to improve each element and by when. Make sure these goals challenge you but remain realistic. As a guide to help you decide how much improvement to aim for, try to raise your standard so that the best performance you have achieved so far for any particular item will be an average performance by the time you reach the end of the program. For instance, if you hit 60 percent of your free throws as a basketball player, work to improve your average to 70 percent.

Exercise 2.6
Performance Analysis Score Sheet

Example of a Completed Performance Analysis Score Sheet

Name: James Borg		Age: 19
Sport: Basketball		Standard: Collegiate
Skills	**Test**	**Time/score**
Dribbling	On-court dribble slalom	46.2 s
Passing	Percentage that are successful	85%
Rebounding*	Percentage taken	50%
Free throws	Percentage converted	80%
Layups*	Percentage converted	70%
Defending	Number of steals per game	4
Fitness		
Agility	Court shuttles	32.3 s
Speed*	30-yard dash	3.8 s
Strength	Bench press (3 reps max)	198 lb (90 kg)
Power*	Vertical jump	24 in. (62 cm)
Flexibility	Sit and reach	+1.6 in. (4 cm)
Mental approach		
Pregame nerves*	Scale 1–10	6
Confidence	Scale 1–10	8
Controlled aggression*	Scale 1–10	5
Focus	Scale 1–10	7
Strategies		
Court position	Scale 1–10	9
Fast break*	Scale 1–10	6
Footwork*	Scale 1–10	7
Assists	Scale 1–10	8

Performance Analysis Score Sheet

Name:		Age:
Sport:		Standard:

Skills	Test	Time/score
Fitness		
Mental approach		
Strategies		

From C.I. Karageorghis and P.C. Terry, 2011, *Inside sport psychology* (Champaign, IL: Human Kinetics).

How long you keep your goal-setting program is up to you, but it should be long enough to allow for a reasonable improvement but not so long that it feels endless. In practice, this usually means between two weeks and three months for most elements of performance. Within the program, of course, you will have goals for each performance assessment in addition to the final goal(s) of the program.

The most difficult part of a goal-setting program is deciding how the improvement can be achieved. For young athletes, in particular, relatively simple goals that can be easily measured are advantageous. As far as mental approach is concerned, the answers are in this book, but consult your coach as to which specific training methods will bring about the desired improvement in your skills, strategies, and fitness. Once you embark on this program, it is very important to keep full and accurate records.

Goal-Setting Principles

This is a good time to recap some of the important points. To get the most out of setting goals for yourself, remember the principles that govern their effectiveness. The acronym SCAMP may help you.

S: *Specific.* Avoid setting vague goals such as *improvement*. Specify how much you want to improve and how you can measure it. Predict the extent of your improvement and work hard to achieve it.

C: *Challenging and controllable.* Goals should remain within the realm of possibility, but you need to challenge yourself. Research has shown that specific, challenging goals produce better performance than easy goals or no goals at all. Also, try to keep your objectives within your personal control. Too many athletes use winning rather than personal performance as a reference point. Winning is controlled partly by someone else's performance. You have almost total control only over your own performance. Even losing efforts can and should result in goal attainment.

A: *Attainable.* Avoid burdening yourself with an impossible goal. All goals should relate to where you are now, and you should aim to improve yourself step by step. If your goals prove to be unrealistic, then reassess them.

M: *Measurable and multiple.* The sense of achievement is greatest, and motivation is enhanced most, when progress can actually be seen. Goals should therefore be expressed in a form that can be measured by an objective test. Failing that, you can use a subjective rating scale of 1 to 10. Remember that multiple goals increase the probability of achievement. Checking off items achieved on a list of things to do can provide a good feeling. Every training session should include smaller goals that contribute to some final objective.

P: *Personal and progressive.* The goals you set must relate to you as an individual. Decide what you want to achieve; don't borrow other people's goals. This will enhance your commitment to your objectives. Further, think through your goals so that they address various facets of your performance that will contribute toward your long-term objectives.

By now, you should be ready to design your own performance enhancement program, or PEP. This will allow you to chart your improvement and accept personal responsibility for your own development in sport. These are important steps on the road to fulfilling your potential.

Have a look at the example in exercise 2.6 carefully before you design your PEP. Note that weaknesses, which are priorities for improvement, are identified on the performance analysis score sheet with an asterisk (*). These baseline scores act as a benchmark against which you can measure improvement. Discuss your PEP with your coach, and then write it down. Our example shows weekly goals that encourage gradual progression toward a realistic target over a three-month period. If you discover as you go along that your final target is too high or low, you can reassess it.

Performance Profiling

Performance profiling is a technique developed by British psychologist Richard Butler, based on the approach of humanistic psychologist George Kelly. In the 1950s, Kelly maintained that how people view critical aspects of themselves in relation to their specific circumstances (their version of reality) determines how they behave. Performance profiling is a very useful way to identify strengths and weaknesses in performance. The profile can be used as a starting point for more detailed goal setting or give you a push toward devoting more time to your particular weaknesses. The performance profile is easy to complete. Exercise 2.7 provides a profile of a female soccer player that we worked with, along with a blank profile for you to complete.

Exercise 2.7
Performance Profile

Begin by identifying the qualities that are most important for high-level performance in your sport, as we did for the female soccer player example shown on page 50. Try to come up with a fairly exhaustive list of qualities that are entirely personal to you and embrace mental, physical, and tactical aspects of performance. From your initial list, choose the eight most important qualities; then label each of the eight segments of the blank dartboard on page 51 with these qualities. Next, rate yourself on a scale of 1 to 10 by shading the area that represents your score. Finally, list the three lowest-scoring qualities at the top of the dartboard. These are the areas that you will most need to focus on. Remember that your sporting performance is only as good as the weakest links in your performance profile.

As you develop your skills, revisit the performance profile, perhaps every one or two months, and shade in sections to represent genuine progress that you have made. The performance profile is a quick and easy way to identify strengths and weaknesses and to monitor your progress. Our female soccer player got all of the segments of the dartboard up to 9s and 10s within a year and then managed to represent her country, thus achieving one of her long-term goals.

(continued)

Priority Areas to Work On
- Mental rehearsal (3)
- Kick power (4)
- Aggression (4)

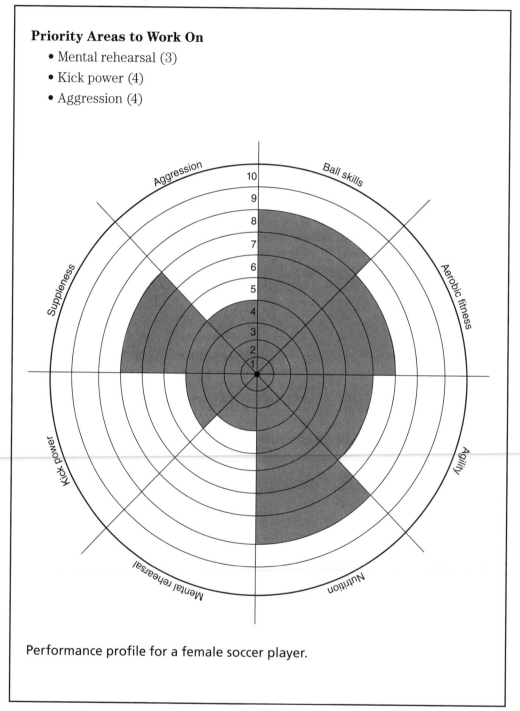

Performance profile for a female soccer player.

Priority Areas to Work On

-
-
-

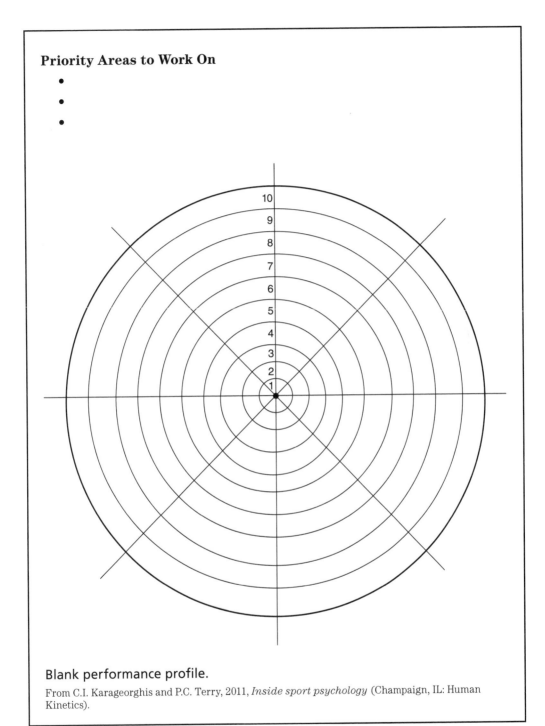

Blank performance profile.

From C.I. Karageorghis and P.C. Terry, 2011, *Inside sport psychology* (Champaign, IL: Human Kinetics).

Token Rewards

Token rewards are small prizes that have little or no actual worth but symbolize achievement; they can have great value for athletes. Player of the Year awards, the house colors given in some British schools, even Olympic medals are all token rewards and carry tremendous honor and prestige. Coaches can use token rewards to motivate teams of players or groups of athletes.

As consultants to an international tennis academy, one of our responsibilities was to improve the speed and agility of some of the finest young tennis players in Europe. Speed drills are by their very nature repetitive, and to be effective, they must be performed at very close to maximum effort. Motivation is an inevitable problem in these situations, and token rewards offer a simple but very effective solution.

To make the speed drills more rewarding, we started to award gold, silver, and bronze medals to the first three players in each drill. In actuality, no prizes were awarded; the winners were simply announced to the group. The effect was immediately noticeable. This simple system resulted in maximum effort because all the participants knew that their efforts were being noted and rewarded. Most important, the imaginary medals soon gained status among the group to the extent that the athletes themselves kept a close count of medals won. This system appeals to the person deep within the inner psyche who dreams of Olympic glory.

It is very important that everyone has a chance to capture a share of the glory. Remember that competition motivates only those who believe they have a chance of winning. In a small group, all players usually believe they have a chance of finishing in the first three. In the case of an imbalance of talent, relays are a useful option. Carefully pairing or grouping the players can facilitate the arrangement of teams of approximately equal ability. By manipulating the groupings and varying the events, it is usually possible to ensure that everyone wins something.

At the end of each session, we awarded Man or Woman of the Day status to the player who performed best relative to ability. We tried hard to share this around while keeping the system fair. Usually, we could work out who got the popular vote by listening to the players' comments to one another. After a year of using this system, the prestige attached to Man or Woman of the Day was remarkable.

To be successful, such a system requires consistency above all else. The trainer must be judge, referee, and commentator all in one. Enthusiasm is infectious, and any player who is cynical about the scheme will become enthusiastic once he or she wins a medal. Coaches should make a fuss of those who show the greatest personal improvement, regardless of whether they are the best. To make token rewards an effective way of increasing motivation, consider the following guidelines, and try to remember the acronym SCORE:

S: *Simplicity.* Keep the structure of the system relatively simple. A very simple reward system that is run well is more effective than one that is difficult to understand. Complexity often results in confusion, which defeats the object of the reward system.

C: *Consistency.* Leaders must be seen to be fair. Favoritism or inconsistency in applying the reward will kill its effectiveness. Remember, everybody wants a fair chance of winning.

O: *Observation.* Everyone must be assured that effort will be noticed. This encourages those who are really trying and discourages those who might otherwise think they needn't bother. Observation can ensure more action and less loafing.

R: *Reward.* Keep the reward in perspective. Remember that only public recognition of achievement is necessary; the reward needs no actual worth. We all worked hard to win gold stars in elementary school, and the same principle applies to older children and adults.

E: *Explanation.* Explain to all concerned precisely what you are seeking to improve, and then highlight the exact reward system being used; for example, "For every fitness test on which you beat your score from last month, you get 1 point. The person who accumulates the most points is Fitness Star of the Week." The explanation needs to be given in very clear language so that there are no ambiguities.

It should be clear to you by now that improved performance is closely related to increased effort. In fact, your education in the art of winning requires that you realize just how much performance depends on effort. But do not use up effort aimlessly. Motivation grows as effort is rewarded. Setting goals will demonstrate that improvement is taking place and will leave you in no doubt that your efforts are paying dividends.

Before you proceed, be sure to complete the exercises in this chapter, or at the very least, make a contract with yourself that you will fulfill these tasks by a set time in the next few days. Taking charge of your own progress is an important step forward. The next, vital step toward a winning mentality is to believe, no matter how unlikely it seems at times, that your success in sport is directly controllable by your decisions and your actions.

Additional Motivational Strategies

As you study the motivational strategies that follow, be aware that although all these techniques should help, there is no single cure-all for low motivation. Give different strategies a try until you find the one that is right for you. Don't expect miracles. Try to find the acorn that one day may produce the mighty oak, and remember that learning how to use goal setting, personal contracts, and token rewards effectively is a skill that requires much effort to perfect.

You may be one of those sportspeople who have, as yet, failed to apply themselves in training. Motivation can receive a significant boost just by acknowledging the absolute necessity of sustained effort. Sometimes technical skills need to be deconstructed, and you have to accept that performance may falter a little for a short while. Once you master the technical intricacies, however, there is often a massive boost to performance.

Success in sport tends to elude those who do not work for it. One of the world's greatest decathletes, Roman Šebrele of the Czech Republic, despite his supreme natural gifts, worked harder than anybody, training many hours a day, week after week, year in and year out. He also dealt with many setbacks in his career. For example, in 2007, while training in Potchefstroom, South Africa, the right edge of his shoulder was pierced by a javelin thrown from a distance of 60 yards (55 meters). Even if you cannot match his dedication and resilience, ask yourself whether your current level of effort in training really deserves the reward of winning performances. If you believe that it doesn't, then resolve to do something about it.

Admittedly, resolving to increase work and actually achieving it are two different things, but clearly that resolution is an important prerequisite. The point we are making here is that all the motivational strategies in the world will not help you if you have no real desire to be helped. You must decide what you really want to achieve in sport and then plan a logical progression toward that goal with the help of your support team (coaches, conditioning expert, physiotherapist).

Personal Contracts

If your motivation for a particular element of your program is very low, you can try making a formal contract with yourself (see the examples in exercise 2.8), thereby exploiting your inherent sense of duty and obligation. When we make appointments, we usually try to keep to them, and the more formal the commitment, the more likely we are to honor it. For instance, if we arrange to meet someone in a particular place, at a particular time, on a particular date, we are far more likely to actually get to see that person than if we simply agree to meet sometime next week. By formalizing

---

Exercise 2.8
Personal Contracts

Example 1

I, the undersigned, do hereby promise that I will devote every Monday and Wednesday evening, from 5:30 to 7:00 p.m. for a three-month period commencing September 15, to circuit training at the Queen Elizabeth II Sports Centre.

Signed: _____

Witnessed: _____

Date: _____

Example 2

I, the undersigned, do hereby promise to devote 10 minutes at the end of each day to practicing the four mental skills that I need to improve.

Signed: _____

Witnessed: _____

Date: _____

the arrangement, we are making a contract with ourselves and booking a particular time. Most of us abide by such contracts, even if they subsequently prove to be a bit inconvenient.

This system works equally well in enhancing motivation for sport. For example, if you have difficulty knuckling down to serious fitness training, you could try committing yourself to a written contract like those shown in exercise 2.8. Alternatively, if there is another aspect of sport to which you wish to increase your commitment, you can use these examples as a guide for a very specific contract. Someone close to you should witness the contract, then place it in a prominent position so that you are frequently reminded of your commitment. You can enter such appointments into a diary to avoid double-booking or having other, less important events take precedence.

Once you have fulfilled a contract, you can reward yourself in some small way, perhaps by taking a day off or enjoying a favorite meal. You can then make another, perhaps more challenging contract with yourself. Do not make your obligations *too* demanding; self-imposed demands must always remain realistic. Above all, it is vital that you fulfill your original commitments; otherwise, the impetus will be lost. With each contract fulfilled you will gain a sense of achievement, and gradually commitment will grow to the point at which you will no longer allow yourself to break a contract. The goal is to create a snowball effect in which the fulfillment of each task generates greater and greater motivation for the next task.

Training Partners

Training partners help to fulfill a basic psychological need, the need for socialization, belonging, and friendship. As the metaphysical poet John Donne wrote, "No man is an island." We all have a desire to interact with our fellow men and women. There are many benefits to having a training partner.

In keeping with the concept underlying personal contracts, partners formalize a program, because we tend to keep appointments that we make with others. Partnerships provide a sense of moral obligation to turn up for a particular session and to be punctual. Further, a training partner can provide encouragement to complete that 10-mile (16 km) run or grueling weight training session even when your mood isn't quite right. The verbal encouragement that a training partner can provide is a key motivational force that cannot be overlooked.

A training partner can make a session much more fun and a lot less arduous. You will likely have a great deal in common with your training partner, so you can exchange ideas, share problems, and crack jokes to help the time pass more pleasurably. The banter that typically takes place between training partners should not be underestimated as a motivational force in its own right.

Having a training partner adds a little bit of friendly rivalry to each session, which enables you to constantly push toward higher performance levels. Invariably, the two of you will have different strengths and weaknesses, so you can use your strengths to help your partner overcome her weaknesses, and vice versa.

A training partner can provide physical support such as spotting during weight training or holding harnesses during resistance runs. She can also provide technical support by timing repetitions, keeping a record of performances, and providing feedback. These are some of the many benefits of having a good training partner or group of training partners.

Many of the athletes with whom we work choose to have different training partners for different aspects of their training. For example, former UK hammer champion William Beauchamp works out with a powerlifter for his weight training regimen, joins a bobsledder for speed drills, conducts plyometrics with a triple jumper, and does throwing practice with other top British hammer throwers. This ensures that he is challenged optimally in each component of his training.

Finding the right training partner often requires time and patience. You may not have a great deal of choice, particularly if you live in a remote area where very few people engage in your chosen sport. Nevertheless, even if there are not people around who participate in exactly the same sport, there will certainly be people who might be aiming to develop the same fitness components and skills. It is not at all unusual to see rugby players training with sprinters or triathletes training with swimmers. Use the following principles to make a short list of appropriate training partners for either your entire preparation program or parts of it.

Choose somebody who

- you really get along with and can confide in;
- is in the same age group as you;
- is a good listener;
- has similar physical characteristics to you;
- you admire for his or her dedication;
- lives fairly close to you; and
- will encourage you even when your motivation is low.

Training partners provide motivation as well as a helping hand.

SUMMARY

Motivation is a force that lies within each of us to a greater or lesser degree. High achievers in sport are characterized by very high levels of underlying motivation; they have superior self-motivation coupled with a high need for achievement. Focusing on the day-to-day tasks that have to be mastered should be the primary consideration for any athlete or coach. Moreover, enjoying the mastery of tasks and the developmental process is one of the cornerstones of success. Enjoyment involves being intrinsically motivated, or motivated by the love of a sport. Extrinsic motivation relates to participating to obtain a reward or to avoid some kind of negative consequence.

Research has shown that top athletes tend to exhibit a combination of intrinsic and extrinsic motivation. It is critical that athletes participate for intrinsic reasons in the early stages of their sporting careers but also stay in touch with the fun and personal satisfaction derived as they grow older and the number of potential rewards increases. Those responsible for young athletes should seek to promote a mastery climate by supporting their charges in the pursuit of self-improvement and de-emphasizing social comparison. Children need to have fun while experiencing sport, and competitive outcomes should remain of secondary importance. Both parents and coaches need to remain mindful of this.

To be your best, you should set measurable and detailed goals that you review on a daily basis in a training diary, and with a coach or training partner. The goal-setting exercises and other motivational techniques covered in this chapter will develop the direction, persistence, and intensity components of motivation. For most athletes, the persistence component requires the most attention. Persistence, or tenacity, as it's sometimes called, will help you overcome adversity, beat motivational slumps, and work on the weaker parts of your game.

The examples in this chapter illustrate that motivation can certainly be improved, but you must have the underlying will to improve. You should seek optimal challenges that always stretch your mental and physical abilities. That way, you are more likely to experience the ultimate consequence of motivation—in fact, one of the most sought after of human experiences—flow.

3

Self-Confidence

I am the greatest. I said that even before I knew I was.

—Muhammad Ali, three-time world heavyweight boxing champion

People who are confident seem to be able to make things go their way. They appear to be the masters of their own destiny and can often turn the faintest opportunity into a successful outcome. They are typified by a resolve to keep going even when things are not going in their favor. Similarly, athletes who are high in self-confidence are more readily able to turn sporting potential into superior performance than those who are not. Because of this, confidence is a much-sought-after attribute in the world of sport.

When confidence is flagging, minor obstacles and setbacks can have an inordinate effect. When a slight adversity is not viewed in its proper perspective, poorer performance is often the result. Sport provides such a multitude of challenges that a positive mental attitude is an essential prerequisite for success. Almost every athlete we work with comments on the importance of a positive mental attitude in reaching superior performance. A loss of confidence can be as damaging to performance as a twisted ankle and can sometimes take much longer to recover from. Learning to maintain a state of self-confidence is a critical challenge on the road to a winning mentality.

Explaining the concept of self-confidence is barely necessary because it is a state that all sportspeople revel in. It is so palpable in some people you can almost reach out and touch it. Self-confidence is reflected in the way they look, the things they say, the way they walk, and in their style of play. The athlete of the 20th century who perhaps most clearly personified confidence was heavyweight boxer Muhammad Ali. As Cassius Clay, the brash young Olympic champion of 1960, he coined the phrase "I am the greatest" and thereafter carried an aura of greatness with him. He repeated the affirmation so frequently and with such conviction that eventually even his opponents believed him.

Ali had razor-sharp wit to complement his dazzling boxing skills, and he gave the world some of the most famous statements on sport confidence. Although we do not advocate that athletes try to emulate Ali's boastful approach, we have used a few of his great one-liners to exemplify some of the principles explained in this chapter. We

> # Rumble in the Jungle
>
> When Ali fought to regain his heavyweight crown for a second time against George Foreman in the famous Rumble in the Jungle of 1974, on paper he certainly wasn't the greatest. Fortunately for Ali, heavyweight contests are not decided on paper. Foreman, the world champion–elect, was thumped to the ground in the eighth round. This victory was as much a consequence of Ali's invincible reputation, unshakable belief, and dogged determination as it was of his boxing skills. Self-confidence is like faith: a belief exists even though the available evidence does not always support it.

hope they will resonate with you as much as they do with us, but remember that Ali's personality-based confidence and big talk are just one aspect of confidence. More important is developing a sense of confidence to master a specific set of circumstances or challenges. Big talk is often just an expression of arrogance; an inner sense of control is what really determines performance outcomes.

THE CONFIDENCE–PERFORMANCE CONNECTION

Confidence can be defined as the certainty that you are equal to the task at hand as a result of an absolute belief in your ability. Double Olympic and world champion rower James Cracknell put it like this: "The reason I am confident is that I know my worst is better than anybody else's best." Similarly, when sprinter Michael Johnson was not selected for the American team and controversially given a wild-card entry into the 400 meters at the 1997 World Athletics Championships, he won the final in what was for him an unspectacular time of 44.12 seconds. He told the press, "I can be good when I'm good and good when I'm bad."

You probably know someone whose self-belief has this unshakable quality, whose ego resists even the severest misfortunes. In such people, confidence is as resilient as a squash ball; the harder the blow, the quicker they bounce back. One secret of this quality is a realistic attitude toward performance. Acknowledging that bad performances are inevitable from time to time maintains the proper perspective when they do occur. This strengthens the resolve to pursue sporting goals.

Confidence is both a trait (a stable element of personality) and a state (how a person feels at any given moment in time). Therefore, in one sense, confidence is considered a part of personality; the self-esteem of some people is more resilient than that of others. Some athletes tend to think the worst of themselves; others are more generous in their self-perceptions. Some are prone to anxiety; others are more carefree. Although these tendencies can change given time, they will certainly not change overnight. Some people will always be more confident than others by nature. Fluctuations in confidence that are not necessarily related to personality reflect state-like qualities. These fluctuations are dictated by circumstances and your reactions to them; it is this ebb and flow of confidence that you can learn to control.

Anne-Marie the Trampolinist

Anne-Marie is a trampolinist who, according to her coach, has a very bright future on the international circuit. She walks tall and expresses herself very articulately, always with a knowing smile. Anne-Marie is forthright and not easily swayed by others in her opinions and attitudes. She is the kind of person who, no matter what situation she finds herself in, takes control and produces a successful resolution. She once managed to get an entire national squad moved from a hotel situated next to a nightclub into a quieter guesthouse a little down the way, and at no extra cost! When the chips are down, Anne-Marie can deliver across a wide range of challenging situations; she simply loves to test herself.

Lately, Anne-Marie has been coming up against some very stiff opposition and facing defeat. This is unusual for her; when she was coming through the ranks, defeat was a rare occurrence and then was only associated with genuine off days. Now, she has begun losing even when performing at the top of her game. The short string of defeats has led to low confidence in competitive situations. This is an unusual feeling for Anne-Marie and not something she can easily counter. Nevertheless, in her everyday life, she is strong-willed, confident, and outgoing. Her trait confidence has remained high, as expected, but her competition-specific (i.e., state) confidence has plummeted.

Anne-Marie's example demonstrates the specific nature of confidence. To be full of confidence or totally devoid of confidence in *all* situations, or *all* of the time, is rare. People generally have more confidence in familiar surroundings where they feel most at home. For example, Anne-Marie felt more confident in the trampoline clubs near her home than she did in foreign arenas.

Even people who are normally the very epitome of confidence can lose it in an unfamiliar environment. Imagine Prince Charles hanging on to the end of a pole about to propel himself toward a 6-meter-high bar, or Steve Hooker, World and Olympic pole vault champion, on the back of a pony with polo stick in hand. It's a fair bet that the unfamiliar circumstances would cause their self-assurance to desert them.

In the same way, a successful athlete like Anne-Marie who suffers a run of bad results for the first time, a prolonged period of poor form, or recurrent injuries, may perhaps experience a disturbing reaction. A new reality emerges that must be faced up to and coped with. In all sports the pendulum of success swings toward athletes one moment and away from them the next. Too often this pendulum can have an undue effect on their confidence.

Ideally, confidence should remain stable across a wide range of circumstances. One aspect of any sporting outcome is luck, and Lady Luck will not shine on the same athlete every day. A confident athlete will accept the odd bad result without harboring any unnecessary self-blame. Legendary American football coach Vince Lombardi once explained that confidence when you're winning isn't real confidence. Everyone is confident when they're winning. Real confidence occurs when athletes are losing but are still able to maintain self-belief, or when they learn from their failures or mistakes and move on. Use exercise 3.1 on page 62 to assess your own situational confidence.

Exercise 3.1
Situational Confidence

Divide a clean page into two columns. Label the first column *Confident Situations* and the second *Situations of Doubt.* In the first column, list all of the situations or circumstances in your sport in which you feel completely confident. Conversely, in the second column, list the situations or circumstances that sometimes cause your confidence to wane. Clearly identifying the situations that make you feel uneasy is the first step toward building your confidence. We will come back to this list later in this chapter, but for now it should have just served to increase your awareness of areas in which you can improve.

Although we have established that confidence is a very important attribute, being overconfident, arrogant, or cocky can have negative consequences. It is critical that self-confidence be founded on ability. If your sureness stretches beyond what you are truly capable of, your competitors will pounce on an opportunity to rattle you. The annals of sporting history contain many examples illustrating that although self-confidence is the guardian angel of performance, arrogance can be its nemesis (see Thunder in Africa).

I've missed more than 9,000 shots in my career. I've lost almost 300 games. Twenty-six times I've been trusted to take the game-winning shot and missed. I've failed over and over and over again in my life. And that is why I succeed.

—Michael Jordan

Young athletes often experience a downturn in confidence when they lose. Some youngsters attain mini-celebrity status in their local area, becoming the proverbial big fish in a small pond. They may have matured early or had very pushy parents and, as a consequence, achieved a great deal of success in the junior ranks. When they move into the senior ranks, it is an entirely different story; the challenges are far greater. These mini celebrities need to learn how to take a defeat from more experienced or stronger opponents and bounce back.

The keys to continued success are to reevaluate goals and have realistic expectations. The techniques provided in this chapter complement those presented in the early part of chapter 2. To achieve a greater sense of stability in confidence, both young and adult athletes must know exactly what causes it to fluctuate.

The vast majority of athletes know that self-confidence enhances performance. Even under strict laboratory conditions, it has been demonstrated many times over that manipulating confidence either up or down has a significant effect on sport performance.

Thunder in Africa

Too much confidence can have a catastrophic effect on performance. A highly talked-about example of this from heavyweight boxing is the bout dubbed "Thunder in Africa," which took place in April 2001. The British heavyweight and undisputed world champion, Lennox Lewis, put up all three of his world title belts in a contest against relatively unknown American Hasim Rahman. Despite the fact that the contest was to be held in Soweto at an altitude of 6,000 feet (1,828 m), Lewis adopted a rather blasé attitude toward preparation and flew in just 10 days before fight day. Rahman, on the other hand, took four weeks to properly acclimatize.

Lennox Lewis avenges an earlier defeat from Hasim Rahman.

In round 5, Lewis was dancing around the ring with his hands down, while smiling and ridiculing Rahman. One right hand was all it took to send Lewis crashing to the canvas in a fight he was expected to win with consummate ease. One moment of carelessness and it was all over. The BBC's long-serving boxing commentator, Harry Carpenter, described it as the greatest upset he had ever seen in professional boxing.

Twenty-seven years previously, George Foreman had done the same against a 32-year-old Muhammad Ali in the Rumble in the Jungle. Even the all-time greats cannot afford to become complacent and drop their guard. Foreman, who happened to be a spectator at the Lewis–Rahman fight, said, "Lewis made the mistake of actually believing all the hype about his invincibility." Respect must always be maintained for opponents, and even more so in contact sports in which pain is the sole reward for complacency.

The epilogue to the Thunder in Africa story is that, fortunately for Lewis, Rahman displayed similar arrogance prior to their rematch seven months later in Las Vegas, USA. Rahman's prefight jibes rattled Lewis, who said, "He showed a lot of disrespect . . . he's going to pay fight time." Lewis was determined not to make any mistakes this time. He dominated the fight from the outset, and payback time came in round 4, when he hit Rahman with such a ferocious left hook that his head bounced when it hit the canvas.

A classic research study used an arm wrestling task to examine the effects of manipulating confidence. Experimental subjects were paired with someone they thought to be either significantly weaker or stronger in arm strength and asked to wrestle. Amazingly, in 10 of the 12 contests, the physically weaker participants won because they *thought* they were stronger. The experiment showed that the expectation of success had a stronger association than actual physical strength with arm wrestling performance.

Confident athletes are more highly motivated in terms of the persistence and intensity with which they respond to a challenge. The athletes involved in the arm wrestling experiment were persuaded that their competitors were weaker than they actually were, and the resultant confidence enabled them to beat objectively superior opponents.

The same phenomenon can occur in a team situation. Teams in which the players exhibit high self-confidence also tend to perform at superior levels and have a greater tendency to come back from behind. Prior to their victory over traditional rivals Cambridge University at the 2004 rugby union varsity match at Twickenham Stadium, the Oxford players wrote a short statement to each member of their team indicating what they most admired about his game or mental approach. These were collated in an envelope for each player, which was opened a couple of hours before the match. The team's high *collective efficacy* helped them to turn around an 11-7 half-time deficit to win 18-11.

Collective efficacy is defined as the team's collective expectation for a successful outcome. It is based on individual team members' assessments of their team's capabilities. A soccer striker who rates his belief in his ability to score 30 goals in a season is assessing self-efficacy, or his self-confidence in a specific set of circumstances. If he rates his belief in the team's ability to score 100 goals in a season, he is assessing collective efficacy. Research shows that collective efficacy is a much stronger predictor of a team's success in sports that involve a high degree of player interaction, such as soccer, basketball, and hockey, than in sports in which the team's performance is more a function of individual member performance, such as golf, track and field, and wrestling.

Confidence causes psychological barriers to crumble. Weightlifters have been shown to perform better when they believe that the bar holds less than it actually does. This phenomenon has been exploited by coaches who have helped weightlifters lift heavier weights by convincing them that the barbell held a weight they had already lifted. Similarly, in the training session preceding a major championship, high jump coaches sometimes inform athletes that they have cleared more height than they actually have. This method, called *false feedback*, is a powerful tool for coaches and training partners if used sensibly and sparingly. Clearly, giving false feedback repetitively is likely to backfire, resulting in athletes losing confidence in both their performance and the integrity of the coach.

When high confidence results in successful performance, the exhilaration that athletes feel is tinged only by the knowledge that all good things must eventually come to an end. The surfer's immediate thought when she completes a successful ride is, "How quickly can I find another big wave to ride?" In the same way, all successful athletes are hungry for further competition in which to demonstrate mastery of their discipline. Conversely, when there is a lack of success and confidence problems ensue,

Teresa the High Jumper

Teresa is a 29-year-old high jumper who has been representing her club and winning regional championships regularly since her mid-teens. Throughout her career, Teresa's performances have been consistent but never outstanding in terms of national standards. Her personal best of 1.69 meters (5 ft 6½ in.) dates back to her 24th birthday. She has been getting close to that in recent seasons, although she will need a jump in excess of 1.70 meters (5 ft 7 in.) to make an impact at the forthcoming Swedish national championships in Stockholm.

Teresa's coach suspects that she experiences a mental block when attempting heights close to her personal best, which causes her to become overanalytical at critical moments. In short, Teresa is a "choker." The coach has kept a careful record of Teresa's progress in training in terms of weights lifted, sprint time-trials, performances in plyometric drills, and so on. The progress she made during winter training suggests that Teresa has the potential to exceed her personal best by several centimeters.

Four days before the national championships, Teresa is performing her final jumping session. A tapering is planned for the remainder of the week to ensure that she arrives at the championships feeling fresh and energized. Her coach makes a point of checking the height of an elastic bar used for practice jumps prior to each trial. Teresa progresses to a point at which she attempts a height of 1.67 meters, just shy of her personal best. She clears it with ease, but following a "careful" check of the tape measure, the coach informs her that the height cleared was actually 1.69 meters, equaling her personal best. Teresa completes her warm-down on a real high, knowing that she is at the top of her game.

On Saturday at the Ullevi Stadium in Stockholm, Teresa keeps a clear head as the bar progresses beyond 1.65 meters. After clearing 1.67 meters comfortably, she opts to pass at 1.69 meters and reenters at 1.71 meters, putting her opponents under pressure owing to the countback rule. Teresa narrowly clears 1.71 meters on her third attempt. She feels elated having produced a lifetime best and a career-best sixth place in the national championship final. The tactic employed by her coach four days earlier, when he told Teresa she had cleared 1.69 meters, helped her to overcome a psychological barrier. Teresa's coach never revealed to her the use of that little white lie, realizing that he had a trump card to use again in the future.

athletes seek to break out of the downward spiral. Too often, the negative attitudes produced by low confidence lead to lethargy rather than the positive actions required to improve performance.

SOURCES OF SELF-CONFIDENCE

A great deal of research has been conducted on the sources of self-confidence. In this section we focus on the perspectives of two of the world's leading researchers in this area, both based in the USA, Professor Albert Bandura from Princeton University and Professor Deborah Feltz from Michigan State University. To begin our exploration of self-confidence, have a crack at exercise 3.2 on page 66. The confidence someone feels

---

Exercise 3.2
Spotlight of Excellence

- Imagine a huge spotlight beaming down on the floor 1 yard in front of you. The light beam is about 1 yard in diameter.

- Now think back to a time in your sporting career when you were performing at your best. Each movement you made brought about a successful outcome, and everything just seemed to click into place.

- See yourself inside the circle excelling. Imagine exactly what the *you* inside the circle is seeing, hearing, feeling, smelling, and tasting.

- Now step into the spotlight and become fully associated so that you are experiencing events through your own eyes and in real time. Again, notice what you are seeing, hearing, feeling, smelling, and tasting.

- Notice exactly what this feels like so you can try to reproduce it at will in the future.

---

during a particular activity or in a particular situation is generally derived from one or more of the following six sources, which are listed in descending order of importance:

1. Performance accomplishments
2. Vicarious experience
3. Verbal persuasion
4. Physiological states
5. Emotional states
6. Imagery experiences

Performance Accomplishments

Performance accomplishments is by far the most important source of confidence; it is what most athletes refer to when talking about confidence. When you perform any skill successfully, you generate confidence and are willing to attempt a task that is slightly more difficult. Skill learning should be organized into a series of tasks that progress gradually and allow you to master each step before progressing to the next (see chapter 1 for full details on skill learning).

In sports such as diving and gymnastics, in which performance relies very heavily on confidence, the progression to more difficult skills always depends on mastering the previous move. Personal success breeds confidence; repeated personal failure diminishes it. Learning, or sometimes relearning, what success feels like is a compulsory confidence-building lesson for all athletes who find themselves down in the dumps. The key is a planned, focused evolution of performance that builds on previous successes.

I've done it before and I can do it again.

—Muhammad Ali

Vicarious Experience

Watching other people perform successfully can bolster your confidence, especially if you believe that the performer closely matches your own qualities or abilities. In effect, you think, "If he (or she) can do it, so can I." All those who strive to lead by example use this principle. Team captains are often appointed on the assumption that their confidence will rub off on and inspire those around them.

Success Breeds Success

At the 2004 Athens Olympics, a great example of the success of others providing inspiration came when Kelly Holmes outstripped expectations to win two gold medals, the first at 800 meters and the second on the final night of the track program, at 1500 meters. Immediately after Holmes won her second gold medal, the Great Britain 4 × 100-meter relay team comprising Jason Gardener, Darren Campbell, Marlon Devonish, and Mark Lewis-Francis took to the track for a final in which they were the rank outsiders. The Brits, previously famed only for dropping the baton, romped home a whisker ahead of a formidable U.S. quartet to secure a third gold for the GB team. Significantly, each of the U.S. sprinters had won individual medals in either the 100- or 200-meter events at the Athens Games. The unheralded Brits attributed their extraordinary success to the mental boost they had received from earlier seeing their teammate Holmes win her second unexpected gold.

© Sport the Library

British sprinters Marlon Devonish, Mark Lewis-Francis, Darren Campbell, and Jason Gardener of Great Britain celebrate after winning the final of the Men's 4 × 100-meter relay at the 2004 Athens Olympic Games.

Verbal Persuasion

Verbal persuasion is a fundamental way of attempting to change the attitudes and behavior of others, including their self-confidence. In sport, coaches often try to boost confidence by convincing athletes that the challenge ahead is within their capabilities. You can reinforce this by repeating the message over and over to yourself as a form of self-persuasion. Although verbal persuasion can prove beneficial, it is not nearly as potent an influence on self-confidence as success. Nevertheless, you should not underestimate the force of your inner voice.

Saying things to yourself repeatedly and with conviction will eventually result in these messages entering your unconscious mind and influencing your behavior in a positive way. If a negative thought enters your mind, you can visualize a red stop sign and immediately replace it with a positive statement or image. This technique is known as *thought replacement*. Another tip is to state what you want in positive terms. Instead of saying "I don't want to lose this one" you can rephrase it to "I really want to win this one." By doing so you have clarified your goal rather than expressed your fear. Exercise 3.3 will help you to create positive self-talk statements, while exercise 3.4 on page 70 presents a fun way to demonstrate the power of self-talk in a team setting.

We need to add one crucial word of warning with regard to the use of positive self-talk. For athletes with low self-esteem who do not combine self-talk with some of the other main confidence-building techniques, the repeated use of self-talk can actually cause a decline in self-confidence. This is because repeating positive self-statements can spark negative counterstatements, which can set athletes on a downward spiral. In other words, a part of the athlete's mind might question and challenge the content of the repeated self-statements. Interestingly, a recent study from the University of Waterloo in Canada showed that, in a nonathletic group, repeated use of a positive mantra reduced self-confidence.

> *I figured that if I said it enough, I would convince the world that I really was the greatest.*
>
> —Muhammad Ali

Physiological States

The fourth source of self-confidence concerns the degree to which we are able to control physiological responses to stress such as muscular tension or butterflies in the stomach. Essentially, you need to learn to perceive the bodily sensations associated with competition as entirely normal and facilitative of performance. Chapter 4 examines how to deal with the symptoms of competition anxiety. In that chapter you will learn that excessive competition anxiety and some of the extreme bodily symptoms that it can provoke constitute almost the flip side of a confidence state. Particularly good techniques to look out for in chapter 4 for the control of physiological arousal are the five breath technique and progressive muscular relaxation.

Emotional States

Self-confidence is the emotional response of the body to various situations. If, for instance, you become anxious about a particular contest, your confidence will almost

Exercise 3.3
Positive Self-Talk

A good way to use your powerful inner voice is to use positive self-talk. This will affirm that you possess the skills, abilities, positive attitudes, and beliefs necessary for success. The statements you choose should be vivid and roll off the tongue, and you should prepare and practice them well in advance of competition. Most of all, they must be believable. Here are some examples from athletes we have worked with:

Striker in soccer: *Slot every chance.*

Boxer: *Chin down, guard up.*

Basketball player (for free throws): *It's just me and the basket.*

Ski-jumper: *My timing is always spot on.*

Judoka: *I'm as strong as an ox.*

Golfer: *I'm the king of the swingers.*

Discus thrower: *I'm the queen of the slingers.*

Middle-distance runner: *I always run my own race.*

Javelin thrower: *My arm is a catapult.*

Goalkeeper in soccer: *My goal is a fortress.*

Batter in cricket: *I'm here for the long haul.*

Rugby prop forward: *Steamroll the opposition.*

Sprinter: *I'm always one stride ahead.*

Tennis player: *My racket is a sweet spot.*

Crown green bowler: *I'm always jack high.*

Make your own list of four or five positive self-statements, and read them to yourself every night before you go to bed and every morning as you wake up. Through repeated use, they will become embedded in your unconscious mind, and positive thinking will guide your actions in sport and everyday life. Make a poster of your affirmations and put it on your bedroom wall so that you can see it as you lie in bed. You can change your affirmations over time as and when your priorities change. Some athletes like to combine major outcome goals such as winning an Olympic medal along with their affirmation statements, because this gives them a clear sense of direction.

Exercise 3.4
Exercise for Team Coaches:
Demonstrating the Power of Self-Talk Using Muscle Testing

This exercise involves two people: a coach and athlete, two teammates, or training partners. The athlete being tested decides on a very specific target for an upcoming competition or practice (e.g., a better free-throw percentage for a basketball player or a faster 30-yard-dash time for a rugby league player).

The exercise runs over eight steps:

1. The athlete holds his or her arm straight out to the side and parallel to the ground. The arm is kept as stiff as possible.

2. The tester stands facing the arm, one hand on the athlete's shoulder and one on the wrist of the extended arm (see figure 3.1).

3. The tester makes a baseline measurement by seeing how much downward force is needed to push the hand about 6 inches (15.2 cm).

4. In test 1, the tester asks the athlete to say and think, "I don't know whether I will be able to [throw the hammer 73 meters (80 yards)—or whatever the goal might be], but I hope I can."

5. The tester applies downward force to the athlete's wrist and notes how much pressure is needed to push it down 6 inches or so (15.2 cm).

6. In test 2, the tester asks the athlete to say and think, "I will try to [throw the hammer 73 meters—or whatever the goal is]." Again the tester pushes the wrist to determine whether more or less force is needed to push the arm down by the same amount.

7. In test 3, the tester asks the athlete to say and believe, "I will [throw the hammer 73 meters—or whatever the goal is]." For most athletes, the progression from self-doubt to belief will produce a stronger arm in each case.

8. Go back to the first statement to demonstrate the use of language. Try another tester if the athlete thinks that you are varying the force applied to the wrist. This will serve the purpose of convincing two people of the power of self-talk.

Figure 3.1 Muscle testing technique.

Photo courtesy of Sally Trussler, Brunel University photographer

certainly be diminished. Sometimes this happens when athletes return from injury. Often the importance of the occasion creates self-doubt. Maintaining confidence, therefore, is partly the result of controlling thoughts and emotions. Learning relaxation and concentration skills can be particularly helpful. Hence, there is very close connection between this source of self-confidence and the mental techniques presented in the exercises of chapters 4 and 6.

Imagery Experiences

Imagery experiences relate to recreating multisensory images of successful performances in your mind. Such mental representations make the mastery of a particular task or set of circumstances far more likely. Chapter 7 is devoted to imagery experiences and the related topic of self-hypnosis; in that chapter you will find many examples of how to use imagery to bolster your self-confidence.

ASSESSING CONFIDENCE

Psychologists have developed numerous questionnaires to assess athletes' confidence. In this section we present a measure known as the Sources of Sport-Confidence Questionnaire, which was developed by Professor Robin Vealey of Miami University in the USA to assess sources of sport confidence. The questionnaire has 43 items that relate to nine aspects of confidence. These are explained here to enable you to interpret the results of exercise 3.5 on page 72.

Mastery involves performing well, improving and achieving personal goals.

Demonstration of ability entails demonstrating ability, or showing off, and gaining favorable social comparison by beating others.

Physical and mental preparation involves feeling physically and mentally prepared with an optimal focus for performance.

Physical self-presentation refers to gaining confidence from believing that the run of the game or breaks in the situation are going in your favor.

Social support concerns the support of coaches, team officials, teammates, peers, fans, family members, friends, and significant others.

Coach's leadership concerns your perception of your coach's ability to make the right decisions and lead effectively.

Vicarious experience involves gaining confidence from watching a friend or teammate perform successfully.

Environmental comfort refers to factors such as the degree of comfort with the playing venue and being at ease with the officials presiding over the contest.

Situational favorableness relates to the perceived strength of the opposition, the playing conditions, the opportunity to perform prematch rituals, and so on.

After you have completed exercise 3.5, you should be able to identify the conditions most likely to make you feel confident. You can then work on aspects within your control at upcoming competitions but also develop coping strategies for aspects outside of your control, such as playing at a particular away venue or unfavorable officials (see also chapters 4 and 5 for guidance).

Exercise 3.5
Sources of Sport-Confidence Questionnaire

Think about a time when you were very self-confident in your sport, and think about the types of things that made you confident in those situations. Consider how important each of these sources was in creating this feeling of self-confidence. (Check one box for each item.)

	Not at all important				Of highest importance		
I usually gain self-confidence in my sport when I	1	2	3	4	5	6	7
1. Master a new skill	❏	❏	❏	❏	❏	❏	❏
2. Improve my performance on a skill	❏	❏	❏	❏	❏	❏	❏
3. Improve my skills	❏	❏	❏	❏	❏	❏	❏
4. Increase the number of skills I can perform	❏	❏	❏	❏	❏	❏	❏
5. Develop new skills and improve	❏	❏	❏	❏	❏	❏	❏
6. Win	❏	❏	❏	❏	❏	❏	❏
7. Demonstrate I am better than others	❏	❏	❏	❏	❏	❏	❏
8. Show ability by winning or placing	❏	❏	❏	❏	❏	❏	❏
9. Know I can outperform others	❏	❏	❏	❏	❏	❏	❏
10. Prove I am better than opponents	❏	❏	❏	❏	❏	❏	❏
11. Show I am one of the best	❏	❏	❏	❏	❏	❏	❏
12. Keep my focus on the task	❏	❏	❏	❏	❏	❏	❏
13. Psych myself up	❏	❏	❏	❏	❏	❏	❏
14. Know I am mentally prepared	❏	❏	❏	❏	❏	❏	❏
15. Stay focused on my goals	❏	❏	❏	❏	❏	❏	❏
16. Prepare myself physically and mentally	❏	❏	❏	❏	❏	❏	❏
17. Believe in my ability to give maximum effort	❏	❏	❏	❏	❏	❏	❏
18. Feel good about my weight	❏	❏	❏	❏	❏	❏	❏
19. Feel I look good	❏	❏	❏	❏	❏	❏	❏
20. Feel my body looks good	❏	❏	❏	❏	❏	❏	❏
21. Get positive feedback from teammates	❏	❏	❏	❏	❏	❏	❏
22. Know I have support from others	❏	❏	❏	❏	❏	❏	❏
23. Am told others believe in me	❏	❏	❏	❏	❏	❏	❏
24. Am encouraged by coaches and family	❏	❏	❏	❏	❏	❏	❏
25. Get positive feedback from coaches	❏	❏	❏	❏	❏	❏	❏

	Not at all important				Of highest importance		
	1	2	3	4	5	6	7
26. Receive support/encouragement	❑	❑	❑	❑	❑	❑	❑
27. Believe in my coach's abilities	❑	❑	❑	❑	❑	❑	❑
28. Know coach will make good decisions	❑	❑	❑	❑	❑	❑	❑
29. Know coach is a good leader	❑	❑	❑	❑	❑	❑	❑
30. Trust in coach's decisions	❑	❑	❑	❑	❑	❑	❑
31. Feel coach provides good leadership	❑	❑	❑	❑	❑	❑	❑
32. See successful performances	❑	❑	❑	❑	❑	❑	❑
33. Watch another athlete perform well	❑	❑	❑	❑	❑	❑	❑
34. Watch a teammate perform well	❑	❑	❑	❑	❑	❑	❑
35. See a friend perform successfully	❑	❑	❑	❑	❑	❑	❑
36. Watch teammates at my level	❑	❑	❑	❑	❑	❑	❑
37. Perform in an environment I like	❑	❑	❑	❑	❑	❑	❑
38. Follow certain rituals	❑	❑	❑	❑	❑	❑	❑
39. Feel comfortable in my environment	❑	❑	❑	❑	❑	❑	❑
40. Like environment I'm performing in	❑	❑	❑	❑	❑	❑	❑
41. Get breaks from officials	❑	❑	❑	❑	❑	❑	❑
42. See breaks going my way	❑	❑	❑	❑	❑	❑	❑
43. Feel everything is "going right"	❑	❑	❑	❑	❑	❑	❑
44. Self-suggested source: _____	❑	❑	❑	❑	❑	❑	❑
45. Self-suggested source: _____	❑	❑	❑	❑	❑	❑	❑

Scoring the Sources of Sport-Confidence Questionnaire

To summarize responses from the questionnaire, total the scores for each group of items, referred to as a *subscale*, and then divide by the number of items in the subscale to produce a mean score. The higher the score, the more your self-confidence is derived from that particular source. For example, a score of 6 for mastery and a score of 2 for social support would indicate that your sport confidence is derived more from mastery than from social support. This might prompt you to recreate some conditions, such as achieving some key performance indicators in the last training session before competition, to help you feel confident. The items that correspond to each subscale are as follows:

Mastery (items 1–5)

Demonstration of ability (items 6–11)

Physical and mental preparation (items 12–17)

Physical self-presentation (items 18–20)

Social support (items 21–26)

(continued)

Exercise 3.5 *(continued)*

Coach's leadership (items 27–31)

Vicarious experience (items 32–36)

Environmental comfort (items 37–40)

Situational favorableness (items 41–43)

If you have come up with self-suggested sources of sport confidence (see bottom of questionnaire), first see if they fit into any of the existing categories. If they don't, then you might create another category of your own into which they do fit. Score your own subscale in the same way as you scored the others.

From C.I. Karageorghis and P.C. Terry, 2011, *Inside sport psychology* (Champaign, IL: Human Kinetics). Adapted, by permission, from R.S. Vealey, S.W. Hayashi, M. Garner-Holman, and P. Giacobbi, 1998, "Sources of sport-confidence: Conceptualization and instrument development," *Journal of Sport & Exercise Psychology* 20(1): 54-80.

It is worthwhile noting that Professor Vealey and her colleagues did find some significant gender differences in the importance of certain sources of sport confidence. For example, female athletes perceived physical self-presentation and social support to be more important contributors to sport confidence than did their male counterparts. Other research has shown that females generally have lower self-confidence than males particularly when involved in masculine-type tasks. When females participate in feminine-type tasks such as dance or netball (a predominantly female sport), the trend is reversed. This is indicative of the important influence of situational and task characteristics on athletes' confidence. It reinforces the discussion in chapter 4 of gender differences in anxiety.

THREATS TO CONFIDENCE

Only a man who knows what it is like to be defeated can reach down to the bottom of his soul and come up with the extra ounce of power it takes to win when the match is even.

—Muhammad Ali

When you lose confidence, you may feel as though your control over the situation has been taken away. You may switch from feeling like the puppeteer to feeling like a puppet; before you understand how it happened, someone else seems to be pulling the strings. Numerous factors pose threats to confidence; an understanding of them can help you maintain a positive mindset for performance.

Many athletes comment on the relationship between confidence and time. Those who are very confident feel as though they have unlimited time to perform skills, as though they are operating in a dreamy, slow-motion world with time to observe, time to think, time to decide, and time to act. As confidence seeps away, time starts to rush by. All actions feel hurried and ill-performed, attention wavers, and fluidity disappears. Time can also seem to pass quickly when confidence is high; a sporting experience is so rewarding that everything clicks into place and events seem to flash by in an instant—much like a flow experience (see chapter 2).

Loss of confidence also allows fear to creep in. This fear may be no more than the brief thoughts of physical injury that flash through the minds of high divers, or the rugby full back's fleeting image of another broken nose as he prepares to dive on the ball at the feet of opposition players. In some sports, the merest hint of fear might be enough to end careers because total concentration on the task at hand is required. Former Grand Prix driver David Coulthard, now a BBC TV commentator, said: "Danger is an occupational hazard in our sport. We can't have a series of low-speed corners, because that's not what Formula 1 is about." When the stakes are high, confidence in your ability is paramount.

If you are returning to sport after even minor injuries, lost confidence can significantly affect your performance. Going on to the football ground with even a slight hamstring strain can make you feel like a knight trying to do battle with a piece of armor missing. More often than not, a second-rate performance or a further injury will be the result.

Lack of confidence in your physical condition is another potential threat to performance. If you have been injured, you must resist the temptation, with the aid of your coach, to return to competition too soon. Allow your rehabilitation program to follow its full course. If you don't, your body has its own ways of catching you out. Rehabilitating confidence after injury requires delicate handling (see exercise 3.10 later in this chapter).

Perhaps even more damaging to your performance than the fear of physical injury is the fear of evaluation that accompanies a loss of confidence. You may find yourself inhibited because of apprehension that others will view your performance unfavorably. Teammates and coaches are especially important here. If they are caring and sensitive

Nigel the Ice Hockey Player

Nigel is a goalkeeper for a well-known ice hockey team. His bravery in making tough challenges on opposing forwards has resulted in a long list of minor injuries. In a recent, more serious incident, Nigel was hit on the head by an opponent traveling at high speed and sustained a broken jaw. During his time in the hospital, the team coach ensured that Nigel received at least one visit from each of his teammates and the team officials. Some even chose to make several visits. On leaving the hospital, Nigel's movements were restricted by the pain associated with the broken jaw; however, the coach prescribed some very gentle exercises Nigel could do with other players recovering from injury. After a few weeks, Nigel was invited to team meetings and to share his opinions on match tactics. He also sat on the bench at games.

Nigel was eased back into competition very gradually with specially designed drills, and the coach instructed his teammates not to make any moves in training that might aggravate his injury. The coach also instructed some of the most respected members of the team to give Nigel some positive affirmations to rebuild his game confidence. They were told to do this in a subtle way so that their comments would appear perfectly natural to Nigel. As soon as the injury healed, after about two months, Nigel was reintegrated into the team for the last few games of the season. It was as though he had been on the team all along. In fact, he *had* been on the team all along—just not in his usual role.

people, they will be supportive when you are going through a difficult period. Coaches and team managers should maintain close contact with athletes when they are injured.

As well as being a trying time that causes great frustration, injuries can also result in your being marginalized from the group because you are not part of its day-to-day activities. Doing as much as possible with the team is important to maintain a high level of cohesion and team spirit.

The influence of family and friends, opponents, and sometimes spectators and the media can quite easily make a confidence problem worse. Many professional soccer players have had their confidence shattered and performances ruined by taunts from spectators and cruel press reports. In the 2008/2009 UK Premiership season, Arsenal player Emmanuel Eboué was continually heckled by certain sections of the Gunners' support after a string of lackluster performances. In a match against Wigan Athletic, he was substituted after coming on as a substitute himself and was visibly upset by the crowd's euphoric reaction to his departure. Early in 2009 Eboué won huge respect among the Arsenal faithful by lifting his performance levels considerably and maintaining his dignity by forgiving the fans who rebuked him.

Remember that fear itself is the greatest villain. An overactive imagination may lead to poor self-confidence. The great New Zealand cricketer Sir Richard Hadlee was known to use the self-statement "Fear is negative, desire is positive." Have you noticed that when confidence is low, opponents always appear bigger or faster or stronger than they really are? Keep in mind that your imagination is a powerful ally. Muhammad Ali pointed out that "The man who has no imagination stands on the earth. He has no wings. He cannot fly." But you must keep your imagination on a tight rein, especially when interpreting personal events.

It is important to bear in mind that any occurrence is neutral, lacking in form or significance, until *we* attach meaning to it. The interpretation of all events, sporting or otherwise, is a personal process. Stand in a crowd of spectators at any sporting event and you will see different people attach entirely different meanings to the same occurrence.

For example, when a neck-high tackle occurs in rugby, most people grimace, grit their teeth, and even gasp in sympathy with the player being tackled, whereas a small minority chuckle because they find such dangerous incidents amusing. Essentially, how you interpret each element of your participation in sport is entirely up to you,

One Event, Multiple Interpretations

People can attach entirely different meanings to the same event in sport. When British sprinter Darren Campbell won a silver medal at the 2000 Sydney Olympics, he crouched on one knee at the end of the race and shook his head in disbelief. So delighted was he with his performance that he thanked God and savored the magic of the moment. The interpretation of members of the Greek press, who were focused on their gold medalist Kostas Kenteris, was that Campbell shook his head in disappointment owing to his defeat to the Greek champion. They even accused him of poor sportsmanship! Here is an example of one set of events, but two vastly differing interpretations. This is an all-too-common phenomenon in the world of sport that afflicts both observers and performers.

but you should realize that your imagination may have the greatest effect on your emotions and confidence. You can turn this to your advantage by always using your imagination to search out strengths in yourself and weaknesses in your opponents that you might exploit.

All players have doubts and fears, although some may be good at hiding them. Everyone is human and susceptible to fear, fatigue, and indecision. Any time you spend thinking about your opponents should be focused on ways to counter their strengths and exploit their weaknesses. Knowing the main weaknesses of an opponent helps you strategize and use tactical rehearsal (see chapter 7), which will give you a distinct advantage in any sporting contest.

Exploiting Weaknesses in Your Opponent

Danny enjoys an occasional game of snooker with Noel, who is an old school friend. In terms of the skills involved in potting balls and judging angles, Noel is far superior to Danny. However, there are weaknesses in Noel's mental approach to the game that Danny can easily exploit to clinch the odd undeserved victory.

Very occasionally, Danny uses a series of preplanned techniques to psych Noel out. If he were to use the techniques consistently or systematically, Noel would soon catch on to what Danny is up to, and his ploys would be ineffective. Here are just a few of the ploys that Danny uses to manipulate Noel's confidence or break his flow:

- While walking up the stairs to the snooker hall, Danny tells Noel that he managed to practice two or three times that week.
- Danny doesn't congratulate Noel on his truly skillful pots, but only when he makes a really lucky pot.
- Prior to a challenging pot at a critical point in the match, Danny chalks his cue quite vigorously to throw off Noel's concentration.
- While Noel is making a good break, Danny congratulates him on the sequence of pots and encourages him to add up his break total; this diverts Noel's focus from the skills involved to the score, which nearly always curtails his break.
- Danny stands immediately opposite Noel while he is cuing and adopts an impatient body posture, sometimes holding his cue like an AK-47. This communicates at a subconscious level that Danny is eager to return to the table.
- When Noel is showing a run of good form, Danny breaks his flow by either offering him a beer (which he never refuses) or by changing tactics to playing tight safety shots, which slows the game to a snail's pace and thoroughly frustrates Noel.
- If Noel gets into a potting rhythm and begins to run away with a frame, the next time Danny is at the table, and long after the opportunity to win the frame has passed, he looks for a snooker to stall Noel and prevent him from building confidence in his potting ability.
- When Noel wins a frame, Danny intonates that Noel was lucky rather than skillful.

Now make a detailed list of *legal* ploys that you can use to psych out opponents, or even a particular opponent, and then try them out in competition. Remember to keep these techniques as subtle as possible.

BOOSTING CONFIDENCE

Diagnosing the problem is the first step to any cure. Following are some of the symptoms of poor self-confidence to help you identify it:

- Belief that defeat by a superior opponent is inevitable
- Belief that control has slipped from your grasp
- Feeling that time is against you while you are performing
- Fear of physical injury
- Fear of disappointing people who are important to you
- Fear of disappointing spectators
- Feeling that you are not immersed in the *here and now*
- Failure to produce your best in crucial situations
- Reduced persistence and lower expenditure of effort
- Acceptance of limitations that may or may not exist

The following section outlines a series of simple but effective exercises to set athletes and coaches moving in the right direction.

Step 1 is to identify the precise circumstances in which you lack confidence. Self-exploration is always the first step toward regaining control over your performance. Sit down and make yourself comfortable. Recall a time when your confidence was at a low ebb. What were the exact circumstances? Now is the time to use the list that you made in exercise 3.1 to help you remember situations that sometimes undermine your confidence. What negative thoughts did you have? What sparked them? How frequently did they occur? Were they related to something you did or something your opponent did? Spend a few moments reliving the experience using all of your senses.

If, for some reason, you are unable to recall in detail exactly how your confidence was drained, the next time you are in competition, tune in very carefully to your thoughts, feelings, and actions, and then make notes afterward. Once you can recall the situation vividly, you are ready to complete exercise 3.6, the Self-Confidence Analysis Record (SCAR). By the time you have finished this, you will already have begun to break down the barriers to renewed confidence. Once you understand the process by which confidence dries up, you can gradually regain control of this process and start to reverse it. Read through Douglas the cricketer's SCAR answers before completing exercise 3.6 for yourself.

Step 2 involves identifying your personal associations with a deep sense of self-confidence. Write down a word or the name of any person, character, animal, or object that you associate with confidence. It can be anything you like; you will not have to justify the logic to anyone else. What qualities does he, she, or it have that truly represent what you are aspiring toward?

Athletes from the same sport tend to choose similar images to represent confidence. For example, sprinters might mentally reenact the graceful image of a gazelle in full flight, swimmers may see themselves as dolphins gliding

---

Exercise 3.6
Self-Confidence Analysis Record (SCAR):
Douglas the Cricketer

1. Describe a recent sporting situation that caused your confidence to decline.

   I was fielding in an important local derby and was really focused. Somehow I missed three catches in a row, which is very unusual for me.

2. Write down any details about the situation that seemed important.

   I began to doubt myself even though, in most games, I wouldn't miss a single chance. I had this recurring thought that I couldn't catch the cricket ball, that I was useless. Foolishly, I kept looking down at my hands as if they had let me down.

3. What did you imagine was going to happen?

   It was enough that I was down on myself, but what really concerned me was how my teammates would react and, even more, the reaction of the team coach. I kept thinking that I would probably lose my place on the team.

4. How did that make you feel?

   I felt really down and out, like I wanted a big hole to open up in the ground and swallow me. Most of all, I was full of guilt and felt as though I'd let people down.

5. Note any other negative thoughts that passed through your mind. Express them any way you like. Use a single word or a detailed description, or even a picture if you prefer.

   I began to worry about what my parents might be thinking in the stands. I saw myself sitting on the reserves' bench for the next match. I thought I'd blown my chances of starting on the team.

---

effortlessly through the water, and weightlifters might use the image of a large brown bear lifting fallen logs with consummate ease. Ask athletes in your sport whom you consider to be very confident what images they like to use. You may glean some useful information from them that you can apply to your own psychological preparation.

I am the astronaut of boxing. Joe Louis and Jack Dempsey were just jet pilots. I'm in a world of my own.

—Muhammad Ali

Step 3 involves recreating the confident scene in your mind with full attention to detail. Refer to the visualization exercises in chapter 7 (exercises 7.6 and 7.7 in particular) and adapt the instructions in exercise 3.7 to suit your own requirements. You may need to ask a close friend or your coach to read them to you while you sit comfortably with your eyes closed. Alternatively, you can make your own digital recording of the 12 steps. Be sure to always speak slowly, clearly, and in a soft voice.

The best way to record details is to describe both the circumstances and your feelings, speaking aloud into a digital voice recorder. Concentrate on describing what is happening and the phrases and images that best encapsulate this feeling. Use them to complete exercise 3.8, in which you summarize "the winning feeling." Use the example as a guide as you fill in the blank boxes.

Step 4 requires turning any negative thoughts or obstacles into positive challenges. The route planner shown in exercise 3.9 on page 84 will help you regain confidence step by step by employing the goal-setting skills you learned in chapter 2.

Step 5 is the point at which you begin to develop a sense of control over the proceedings. You do this by actively seeking challenges, turning negatives into positives, and finding a little bit of success in all that you do. Gaining confidence

---

Exercise 3.7
Recreating the Confident Feeling

1. Relax and try to recreate a feeling of complete confidence.
2. Picture yourself preparing to perform.
3. Notice the sights, sounds, and atmosphere of the scene. What are you wearing? What colors can you see? Are there any distinctive noises or smells?
4. Look at your opponent(s). How does your opponent appear? How does your opponent make you feel?
5. You are performing very well indeed. Pick out what is especially good about your performance.
6. Notice the score or outcome, the way you are moving, and the way you feel.
7. You are performing as well as you possibly can and are feeling very confident. You are a tough opponent for anybody when you feel like this.
8. Notice how intensely focused you are and how relaxed your body feels.
9. Who or what do you remind yourself of when you perform like this?
10. Imagine yourself performing like this for a few more moments. Everything is easy.
11. In a moment, you will let the scene fade, but before you do, pick out any other details that seem important to you.
12. Now, slowly return to a state of full awareness.

Exercise 3.8
The Winning Feeling

The winning feeling (example)

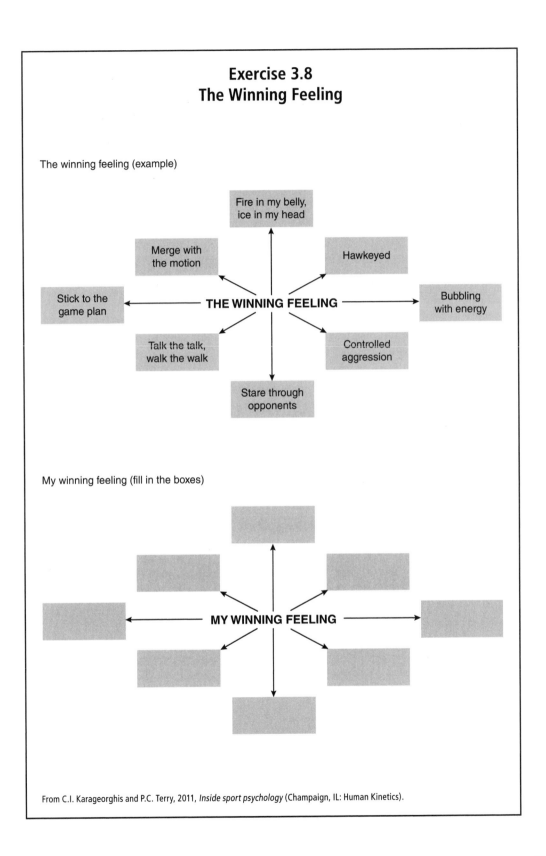

My winning feeling (fill in the boxes)

From C.I. Karageorghis and P.C. Terry, 2011, *Inside sport psychology* (Champaign, IL: Human Kinetics).

comes most readily through achieving a series of bite-sized goals. Eventually, these goals merge together, and before you know it, you have overcome what once appeared like a major barrier (see exercise 3.9 for an example). Obstacles are often psychological, which is why achieving a series of small goals helps you through psychological barriers.

Before you complete exercise 3.9, read through case study 1. This will give you some ideas to help you identify the precise attitude you wish to achieve and the specific obstacles you need to overcome. If you cannot identify four barriers, this is not a problem; the fewer obstacles the better. If you have more, just list them on your route planner and tackle them one by one.

Case Study 1: Brad the Football Player

Brad was a very talented quarterback who could throw a football 50 yards with pinpoint accuracy. He had just been drafted to the NFL and revealed during consultation that he had recently become reluctant to take the snap when opposed by hulking defensive linemen. On several occasions, Brad's hesitation had resulted in his being sacked while trying to complete a pass to his wide receivers. Both his rib cage and his pride had taken a bruising each time this happened. The demoralization Brad felt had started to spread to the rest of his game, and his form slumped. Brad feared that his teammates were also beginning to lose faith in him.

Brad's self-confidence analysis revealed that he believed that his physical build (typical of a quarterback, he is quite lean but agile and quick) exposed him to harm against bigger and stronger opponents. He had begun to believe that his size and strength were not equal to the task. About 18 months before this, he had sustained quite a serious rib injury in just this kind of situation, and although the injury had long since cleared up, the self-doubts lingered. The attitude Brad once had toward taking the snap in these situations had gradually slipped away. He appeared both hesitant and inhibited. Four barriers stood between Brad's current attitude and the renewed confidence he was aiming for:

- How he viewed his strength
- How he viewed his size
- His negative attitude toward the snap
- How he interpreted recent attempts to take the snap

Strength   Brad's confidence in taking the snap and withstanding challenges while passing the ball was being affected adversely by the belief that his strength was inadequate. Logically, if he could improve his strength, he would feel better equipped for the challenge and therefore more confident. Consequently, we devised a specific weight training program aimed at a 10 percent overall strength gain over a three-month period. This was prepared in consultation with his team's strength and conditioning coach.

Size   Brad clearly could not make himself as big as some of the defensive linemen trying to sack him. What he needed was to change his interpretation of the situation. We agreed that instead of thinking "They are big, I am small", Brad should think "They are big and slow; I am smaller and much more agile." To achieve this, he visualized a variety of scenarios in which his superior speed helped him to evade bigger and slower defenders to complete the pass. He complemented this with a three-month program of agility drills alongside his weight training program.

Negative Attitude Toward the Snap   Brad visualized the incident in which he had sustained the rib injury and also recent occasions in which the opposing defense had steamrollered him. In each case, he visualized the situation but changed the script so that he took the snap and completed the pass without hesitation, resulting in a successful outcome. He identified that his hesitation had given his opponents time to gather momentum. This was the key factor that had made passing more difficult.

To restore Brad's controlled attitude toward passing, we returned to his personal images of confidence. He had used an eagle as an image that conveyed confidence. Further prompting revealed that a bald eagle was a particularly evocative image for Brad, representing the power and dominance he wanted to restore as well as the ability to scan the entire field of play. The predatory nature of the bird was integral to reversing Brad's feelings of being victimized on the field. He controlled the game.

We suggested that for a three-month period Brad place a picture of a bald eagle on his bedroom wall. For five minutes each day he was to visualize himself as an eagle to the tune of "Sunset (Bird Of Prey)" by Fatboy Slim. When faced with an opportunity to strike, the eagle did so without any hesitation. It was afraid of no other creature, big or small, and Brad visualized what it felt like to have that attitude. "I am the eagle" became an effective self-statement that he used to instill self-confidence.

By the end of the three-month period, Brad had made significant strength gains, he was reassured that his speed gave him an advantage over the hulking defensive linemen, and he was showing a more determined attitude toward taking the snap and passing. In short, his confidence had been not only restored but also bolstered.

Now you must select the appropriate strategy for clearing each of your own obstacles. Examples of the sorts of problems you may be faced with and the sorts of solutions that will help overcome them follow. You may need to implement more than one of these techniques to help you along the road to full confidence. If you are willing to persevere, you will get there in the end. An old Chinese proverb states, "One who moves mountains begins by carrying small stones."

Confidence in Preparation

Winning has been called the science of total preparation, and confidence certainly grows from the belief that you are fully prepared for the task ahead. Conversely, if you have doubts about the thoroughness of your preparation for a particular contest, your confidence will suffer. Total preparation refers not just to fitness, diet, and skill development but also to what might be called the logistics of competition.

Timing is a crucial aspect of logistical preparation: time to travel, time to eat, and time to prepare both physically and mentally for the contest. Your confidence can be left in tatters if you make a mess of the arrangements and are left short of time to prepare. Forward planning and thoroughness will add an edge to your confidence.

A much-publicized example of logistical problems playing havoc with precompetition preparation came at the 1996 Atlanta Olympics at which the Great Britain rowing team was hoping for a medal bonanza. During the first week of the Games the buses used for transporting athletes to their competition venues had consistently failed to turn

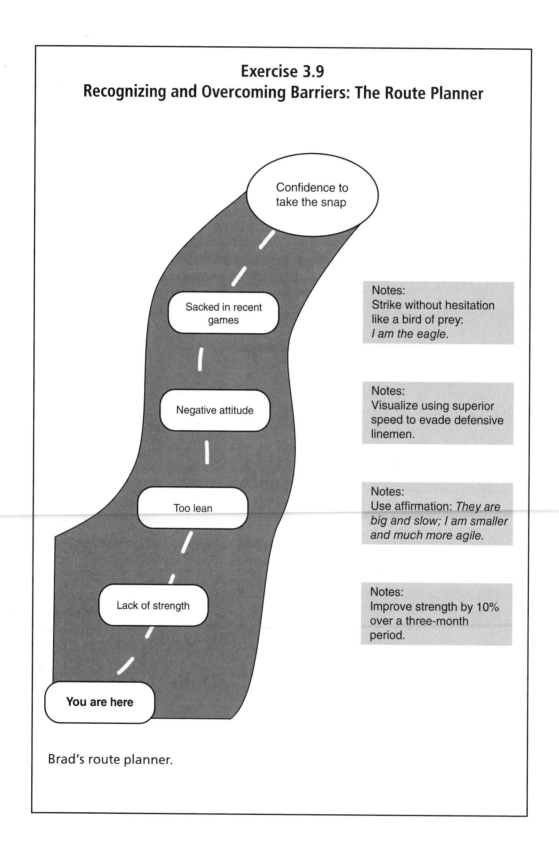

Exercise 3.9
Recognizing and Overcoming Barriers: The Route Planner

Confidence to take the snap

Sacked in recent games

Negative attitude

Too lean

Lack of strength

You are here

Notes:
Strike without hesitation like a bird of prey: *I am the eagle.*

Notes:
Visualize using superior speed to evade defensive linemen.

Notes:
Use affirmation: *They are big and slow; I am smaller and much more agile.*

Notes:
Improve strength by 10% over a three-month period.

Brad's route planner.

up on time. Veteran British rower, Oxford graduate Alison Gill, became so concerned about missing her event that she commandeered a bus bound for the hockey stadium, grabbed the driver by the scruff of the neck, and demanded that he detour to the rowing venue at Lake Lanier. The incident received widespread coverage in the British press.

Always remember the well-known maxim of the seven Ps: *Proper Planning and Preparation Prevents Pitifully Poor Performance.* Perhaps the British rowing team should have allowed much more time to reach the venue. The epilogue of the story is that the team officials relocated several of the rowers to accommodations that were much closer to Lake Lanier.

Aside from logistical issues, there is also the question of clothing and equipment. The well-known tennis couturier of the 1960s, Teddy Tinling, used to boast: "Players dressed by me have an advantage over opponents." The number of Wimbledon champions among his clients may have proved him right. Think for a moment about how you respond to an opponent who truly looks the part.

It is remarkable how much looking good can contribute to feeling good. Muhammad Ali used to make great psychological capital from boasting about his handsomeness ("Man, I'm pretty") while often branding his opponents as ugly (most famously, Joe Frazier before the epic "Thrilla in Manila" of 1975). Such taunts play on the human disposition to equate beauty with higher worth and optimal functioning.

These are all good reasons to give some thought to your appearance in competition. Using the best-quality equipment you can afford will move you another rung up the confidence ladder. Smart clothing and good-quality equipment often are an integral part of the winning feeling that top-class athletes describe.

As a final example, we worked with a competition aerobics athlete who took great pride in his appearance and always used a self-statement that he had lifted from the hit Eddie Murphy comedy film *Trading Places*: "Looking good, feeling good!" he would say aloud before going into competition. This also gave his teammates a lift, because he said it with such panache. Keep an ear out for similar phrases that you can use effectively as part of your preparation.

Changing Attitudes in Golf

One of the solutions to unfavorable playing conditions is a change in attitude. One way to do this is to create positive challenges. For example, the first author worked with a Scottish amateur golfer who told him during an initial consultation that "My approach shots miss the green 65 percent of the time when it's raining." The author suggested that he revise his attitude to "My challenge is to improve upon the 35 percent of approach shots that land on the green when I play in the rain." As you can see, there is absolutely no difference in the facts running through the player's mind, and the situation has not changed. Using this simple technique, the author created a positive challenge that improved the average of approach shots landing on the green during wet conditions to 55 percent.

Give yourself such realistic challenges to enhance both confidence and motivation. Never underestimate the extent to which attitude affects performance; always adopt a realistic but positive attitude.

Confidence in the Conditions

Adverse weather conditions, certain surfaces, and particular locations can cause low self-confidence. This is usually related to previously unsuccessful performances in identical or similar circumstances. For instance, the Brazilian tennis star Gustavo Kuerten, despite being a former world number one, was not at his most confident on grass; he never progressed beyond the quarterfinals at Wimbledon. Similarly, most golfers with a high handicap do not relish playing when it's windy.

Your prejudices against certain conditions may be based on logic (e.g., "I have had insufficient practice on grass courts."), on myth (e.g., "Mud is the great equalizer in sport."), or on pure superstition (e.g., "That stadium is a jinx."). Whatever underlies your belief that conditions are unfavorable, the effect is always the same: low confidence. This, in turn, allows tension and anxiety to creep in, and poor performance can be the consequence. You may then blame defeat on the unfavorable conditions rather than the effects of lowered confidence. This makes the problem even worse the next time around.

Confidence After Injury

Any injury serious enough to prevent you from competing can be regarded as a threat to confidence. The after-effects of injury range from slight tentativeness, which disappears soon after you get back into competition, to genuine dread of further physical harm, which stays with you long after the physical damage has healed. Often, the effect is subtle and takes only the edge off one small aspect of your game, which results in you shying away from certain challenges. The danger is that this fear can infect your general confidence. Choosing the most suitable strategy to recover your confidence after injury depends on how the injury occurred. Case study 2 deals with confidence shaken by an unpreventable accident.

Case Study 2: Kylie the Netball Player

Kylie was a 6-foot-1-inch (185 cm) netball player who suffered a badly twisted ankle while rebounding under the opposition's net. Her foot landed on a teammate, and her ankle turned over sharply. It was the sort of fluke accident that happens in sport from time to time. One month later, her physiotherapist confirmed that the ankle was fully recovered, but Kylie's confidence was still very shaky. She knew that there was little danger of the same thing happening again, but she was very reluctant to rebound. Her attention was clearly divided between taking the ball cleanly and landing safely. Consequently, her rebounding, which had been a very strong feature of her game, lost its former effectiveness.

The strategy we used to overcome this problem was threefold. First, Kylie continued the strength rehabilitation program set by her physiotherapist for an additional two weeks to rebuild her confidence in the strength of her ankle. Second, she used a combination of visualization and physical practice to gradually desensitize her fears about rebounding. Third, she developed positive self-statements to reinforce her progress.

Desensitization involves being exposed gradually to a situation that causes fear or concern and gaining confidence at each stage before moving on to the next. Fear is monitored numerically along the way. Kylie was instructed to visualize herself rebounding successfully for a few minutes and then give another fear rating out of 10. The process was repeated during physical practice.

Kylie started by mentally rehearsing rebounding without opposition. Initially, she rated this as 7. After a few minutes' rehearsal, she felt more at ease with the situation, and her rating dropped to 5. She then practiced this physically for 10 minutes, after which her fear rating was down to 2. Kylie progressed in this fashion over a period of five days until rebounding in a game situation had a fear rating of only 1. The results of this program are shown here.

Kylie's Desensitization Program to Restore Her Confidence in Rebounding

Mental practice	Rebounding alone	Rating: 7 down to 5
Physical practice	Rebounding alone	Rating: 2
Mental practice	Rebounding one on one	Rating: 8 down to 5
Physical practice	Rebounding one on one	Rating: 3
Mental practice	Rebounding two on two	Rating: 6 down to 4
Physical practice	Rebounding two on two	Rating: 3
Mental practice	Rebounding four on four	Rating: 5 down to 3
Physical practice	Rebounding four on four	Rating: 2
Mental practice	Rebounding seven on seven	Rating: 4 down to 2
Physical practice	Rebounding seven on seven	Rating: 1

To reinforce her growing confidence, Kylie also devised positive self-statements related to her problem. During the first week, she used the statement "Moving on up" and the song of the same name by M People, which helped her sustain the belief that her ankle was regaining strength. At the end of the second week, her self-statement became "Reach for the rim" to the accompaniment of the Jesse Johnson tune "Jump For It" from the soundtrack of the hit movie *White Men Can't Jump*. This indicated that her positive attitude toward rebounding had returned in full and that the accident had been forgotten.

The strategy of desensitization is best for injuries sustained in circumstances beyond your control. An alternative strategy is effective when evasive action or an adjustment to technique could have prevented your injury. This strategy is referred to as changing the script; as the name implies, it involves visualizing the situation

---

Exercise 3.10
Changing the Script

1. Visualize the situation in which you were injured.
2. Replay the scene several times noticing exactly what happened.
3. Identify the exact circumstances that caused the injury. What could you have done to change this outcome?
4. Now rehearse the situation but change the script so that the outcome is different.
5. Continue rehearsing this new outcome until you feel confident of being able to cope with the original circumstances.

in which the injury occurred but reexperiencing it with a different outcome. Brad in case study 1 used this technique. Once you have identified the key to the outcome and practiced the new script sufficiently, the memory of the original outcome becomes blurred and forgotten. Exercise 3.10 contains instructions for changing the script.

SUMMARY

We hope that this chapter has demonstrated that confidence is not solely in the hands of fate. Confidence inevitably fluctuates in response to events and circumstances, but you can maintain the flow of confidence while countering the occasional ebb with appropriate strategies. We have encouraged you to take greater control over how confident you feel in sport. To this end, a good exercise in self-awareness is the completion of the Sources of Sport-Confidence Questionnaire (page 72), which can provide details on which aspects of confidence are most pertinent to you.

According to Professors Albert Bandura and Deborah Feltz, there are six main sources of self-confidence which are arranged here in a hierarchy of importance:

1. **Performance accomplishments** equate with recent form and are the strongest contributor to sport confidence.

2. **Vicarious experience** entails experiencing success through a friend or team-mate.

3. **Verbal persuasion** comes from coaches, teammates, significant others, and yourself.

4. **Control of physiological states** prevents excessive bodily anxiety from disrupting performance (see also chapter 4).

5. **Emotional states** need to be regulated so that your mindset is optimal for competition (see also chapter 5).

6. **Imagery experiences** are multisensory images of successful performance in the mind that prepare you for competition (see also chapter 7).

To generate or restore self-confidence, first identify the factors that are causing your confidence to wane. Second, establish personal images of confidence along with the precise nature of your "winning feeling." Third, perform a visualization exercise to fully experience the desired self-confident state. Fourth, along with your coach(es), formulate a plan to turn negative obstacles into positive challenges. Finally, a feeling of personal control over proceedings is the bedrock of confidence. You can facilitate this by achieving a series of small tasks that collectively help you overcome any major barriers to confidence.

Ideas for promoting confidence range from the simple principle of thorough preparation to the techniques of desensitization and changing the script. We have also elaborated on how you can adopt a can-do attitude, act confidently, use positive self-statements, and dress for success.

A book can cover only a small selection of the situations that crop up in sport. It is up to you to extract the most relevant details from this chapter and adapt them to your own needs. Confidence is just as important as ability in sport. Accordingly, you and your coach should spend time finding the technique that stops any downward shift in confidence and puts you firmly back on the road to ascendancy.

Anxiety

There is no room in your mind for negative thoughts. The busier you keep yourself with the particulars of shot assessment and execution, the less chance your mind has to dwell on the emotional. This is sheer intensity.

—Jack Nicklaus, widely regarded as the greatest golfer of all time

High anxiety often causes people to perform well below their usual standard in any performance domain. For many athletes, anxiety manifests as an all-too-familiar feeling of worry, tension, apprehension, and fear. In fact, in sport, anxiety could be considered public enemy number one. When a competitor freezes in the big moment or commits an inexplicable error, anxiety in one of its many guises is very often the root cause.

Sport is littered with the broken dreams of those who wavered when they most needed to be in control of themselves and the situation at hand. Consider the penalty shootout, a strategy used to decide tied games in major soccer competitions, which provides heart-stopping moments for all concerned. The burden of responsibility often results in spectacular misses by players who are unable to handle the pressure.

When former England soccer captain David Beckham hacked the ball way over the crossbar during a penalty shootout against hosts Portugal in the quarterfinals of the 2004 European Championships, the only possible explanation was that the pressure got to him. The England team lost 6-5 as a consequence of that miss, and Beckham was inconsolable. Put yourself in his shoes, and just for a few seconds, imagine the isolation of that moment in which he was carrying the hopes of the entire nation. Even as a spectator, the tension was unbearable. What causes experienced professionals to choke at such critical moments?

Choking is an extreme symptom of anxiety that occurs when athletes focus excessively on the execution of skills rather than allowing them to flow automatically, without conscious effort (see chapter 1). Sport commentators often use the word *choking* to describe a sharp decline in an athlete's performance.

In reality, anxiety is not tangible; it simply involves a *perceived* imbalance between the skills you have and the demands of a particular sporting situation. The precise

Zuma Press/Icon SMI

England soccer captain David Beckham was distraught after missing from the penalty spot against Portugal in Euro 2004.

impact of anxiety on your sporting performance depends on how you interpret it. If you accept anxiety as a normal psychological reaction to competition, it will be less likely to disrupt your performance.

What is your reaction when anxiety inhibits your performance at the brink of success? Do you just shrug your shoulders and hope it doesn't happen again, or do you resolve to do something about it? Perhaps, finally, a solution is at hand.

KNOW YOUR FOE

Anxiety is a natural response that the human species has evolved to promote its survival in the face of threats in the environment. It comes in preparation for the well-known biological response of fight or flight first described by Walter Cannon in 1915. Sport competition promotes similar psychological and bodily responses even though, in most sports, there is little threat to survival. The threat is more likely to your *self-concept,* or how you perceive yourself.

Sport produces a wide variety of stressors. A stressor is a situation, event, or demand that has the potential to disrupt our equilibrium; it often triggers a reaction known as the *stress response.* When we are stressed, the sympathetic nervous system, which controls up- and down-regulation of all living organisms, is activated. Common bodily feelings relating to fight or flight include an elevated heart rate, increased muscular tension, and a release of adrenaline.

Sport provides a number of stressors, including having to work hard when the body is drained of energy, competing against seemingly unbeatable opponents, and often baring emotional frailties to the world. On the other hand, sport offers an opportunity to grow, push back personal boundaries, and liberate the body and the mind simultaneously.

The stress associated with sport, in itself, is not damaging. Indeed, stress is defined as the nonspecific response of the body to any demand (stressor) made of it. The implication is that stress can be a very positive influence; what some people call stress, others may call challenge. The key point is that when we perceive stress as negative, anxiety can result. Therefore, much depends on how you view the demands placed on you and your capacity to meet them.

In addition to providing challenge and stimulation, sport also provides much uncertainty. At the precise moment the Olympic shooter squeezes the trigger, or the professional golfer swings a club, the outcome is unknown. The stressors or demands of sport are therefore closely linked with its inherent uncertainty. Perhaps this is why sport has such universal appeal; it is a theater of unpredictability. Sport draws large audiences because we love to predict the future and then watch to see our predictions either confirmed or dashed.

Because of this combination of stress and uncertainty, sport can be interpreted as either a challenge or a threat. One athlete may be motivated by the challenge and relish the uncertainty, whereas another may be disturbed by it and feel anxious. Anxiety is an emotion characterized by feelings of worry and tension that, in sport, may be brought on by a host of doubts—about the outcome, about ourselves, about safety, and about what others might think.

Gender is an important variable in the prevalence of competition anxiety, and coaches and parents should be mindful of its influence. Research has shown consistently that across all age groups, females are generally more anxious than males. That is not to deny the existence of very confident female athletes and male athletes who are paralyzed by fear, but on the whole, female athletes require greater social support than their male counterparts to deal with anxiety.

One of the reasons advanced by psychologists to account for this gender difference is the fact that females tend to take on more social roles than males do (e.g., child rearing, caring for seniors, running the home) and accordingly have more to think about. Also, female athletes make more frequent and intense social comparisons. Such comparisons are influenced by media representations of women that emphasize slimness, beauty, and femininity as desirable attributes. Some psychologists have suggested that asking women to participate in activities that might be considered gender inappropriate, such as high-contact sports or lifting heavy weights, can trigger an anxiety response.

SPORT PERFORMANCE AND ANXIETY

British sport psychologist Graham Jones developed a view of competition anxiety that has become very popular among coaches because it is both logical and easy to understand (see figure 4.1 on page 92). In essence, Professor Jones' view is that our *perception* of our ability to control our environment and ourselves determines the stress response. Hence, if you believe you can cope in a particular sporting situation, you will tend to strive to achieve your goals with positive expectations of success. Having positive expectations will help you be more confident and therefore more likely to perform at your best (see also chapter 3).

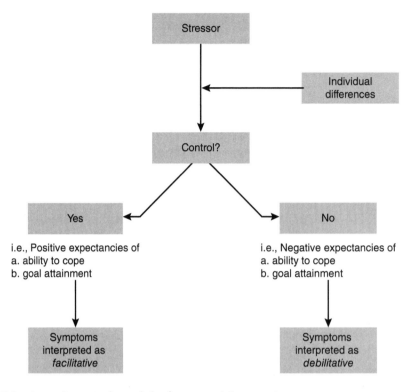

Figure 4.1 Jones' control model of competition anxiety.

From G. Jones, 1995, "More than just a game: Research developments and issues in competitive anxiety in sport," *The British Journal of Psychology* 86(4): 449-478. Reproduced with permission from *The British Journal of Psychology* © The British Psychological Society.

If you believe you can meet the challenge of a particular stressor, such as a tough opponent or difficult weather conditions, you will interpret symptoms of anxiety (butterflies in the stomach, elevated heart rate, sweating) as *facilitative* of, or helpful to, your performance. Conversely, if you believe you do not have control over the situation, that your opponent is too good, or that the wind will disrupt your game, then you will interpret the same symptoms as *debilitative* of, or likely to impair, your performance. This interpretation is then likely to become a self-fulfilling prophecy, and your performance will suffer.

The extent to which you can expect to control competition stressors depends on factors that are specific to you, such as your personality, upbringing, and experiences. These are known as *individual differences* because they make each one of us unique.

Because the presence of anxiety depends on your perceptions, it is a very personal and unpredictable phenomenon. It will tend to occur if you believe either that the demands of the task have increased or your ability has decreased. Anxiety may be no more than a fleeting moment of dread when, as an outfielder in cricket, you find yourself under another high catch having dropped a previous one, or it may develop into a long-term aversion toward a particular situation, such as a fear of facing a spin bowler after a series of failures. In either case, self-belief has been shaken and has tipped the balance toward anxiety, although the actual demands of the task remain the same. To understand the process fully, look within yourself to discover exactly why you react the way you do.

To put Jones' model into context, let's take the example of a female downhill skier. Looking down from the top of a difficult run, she compares the demands of the hill with her own perceived skill level. If she feels in control and is convinced that the run is within her capabilities, she will interpret any nervousness as normal and likely to help her to execute the run successfully. If, on the other hand, she doubts her ability to negotiate the course, she may perceive the hill as threatening and her feelings of anxiety as likely to hinder her performance.

As self-belief declines, the perceived demands of the task grow in equal measure. When things are going badly, the task appears progressively more demanding. Targets appear to shrink, and events speed up. In such circumstances, rational thought often proves very difficult and instinct takes over. The effect on performance, especially when fine muscle control and a clear head are essential, often proves catastrophic.

Two British sport psychologists, Lew Hardy and John Fazey, developed what they termed a catastrophe model of anxiety. Their model helps to explain the sharp declines in performance that occur when physiological arousal, typified by elevated heart rate and muscular tension, is coupled with worry and negative thoughts. Athletes excel when their physiological arousal is at an optimal level, but their performance declines markedly when it gets too high. For performance to reach a peak once again, physiological arousal needs to be reduced significantly. Figure 4.2 illustrates how during high levels of thought-related anxiety, correspondingly high levels of physiological arousal cause a sharp decline in performance.

More recently, Professor Hardy emphasized the importance of self-confidence in avoiding the negative effects of anxiety on sport performance. He suggested that self-confident athletes are more likely to avoid the catastrophic effects of competition anxiety for longer periods of time. The catastrophe model underlines the importance of

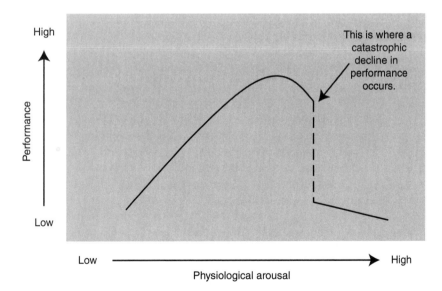

Figure 4.2 Effect of physiological arousal on performance during high thought-related anxiety.

Adapted, by permission, from R.S. Weinberg and D. Gould, 2007, *Foundations of sport and exercise psychology,* 4th ed. (Champaign, IL: Human Kinetics), 90.

being self-confident and maintaining a positive attitude toward competition. Chapter 3 offers suggestions for how to offset some of the potentially adverse effects of anxiety.

Sport presents a vast array of stressors with which you must learn to cope. On certain occasions, you may have to compete in conditions of excessive heat and stifling humidity, or freezing cold and driving rain; at other times, you may be faced with extreme fatigue, illness, or even injury. These physical stressors have a profound but relatively predictable influence on performance, either by making the task more difficult, or by making you doubt that you are equal to the challenge. In addition several stressors of a psychological nature have a subtler, but equally real, impact on performance. We will explore these one by one.

Importance of the Event

Generally, the more important the contest is, the greater the stress will be and the more prone you will be to feeling anxious. Clearly, the final of an important tournament carries more stress than a preseason friendly scrimmage. Studies have shown that in national championships, around 66 percent of competitors experience anxiety symptoms; whereas in Olympic finals, this figure rises to around 99 percent. Some athletes are outstanding in regional and national competitions, but when it comes to

---

Soldati Rises to the Challenge and Falls to Victory

One of the most remarkable U.S. female athletes of recent years is Olympic diver Kimiko Soldati. Her life story is characterized by a constant fight against adversity and misfortune. Soldati was forced to retire from a promising career in gymnastics at age 14 by a knee injury. She made the difficult transition to diving but endured a string of serious injuries that blighted her progress and necessitated a series of painful operations. One of Soldati's biggest emotional hurdles was the loss of her mother to breast cancer the summer before her senior year at high school.

Having established herself as an NCAA champion, Soldati blew her chances of going to the 1996 Atlanta Olympics by tearing a biceps muscle at the U.S. trials. Shoulder injuries hampered her qualifying efforts for the 2000 Sydney Olympics. Hence, qualifying for the 2004 Athens Olympics was, at the age of 30, her last realistic chance to achieve her lifetime goal of becoming an Olympian.

In a contest decided by the last of five dives from the 3-meter springboard, the moment of that final dive was even more tense for her husband, family, and friends than it was for Soldati. Low scores for the second dive had threatened her Olympic hopes. It was all or nothing on the last dive, but Soldati kept her nerve and focused on "hitting the dive to make the Olympic team" (her words).

She scored 8s on a reverse 2½ somersault in pike position and finished first with 884.70 points. Had Soldati scored 6s for the last dive, she would have dropped from first to third and ruined her chances of going to Athens. When asked about the pressure in light of her advancing years, Soldati said: "I look at my age as an advantage. I'm a lot more emotionally balanced. I realize that diving is not who I am, it's what I do. It's hard for a lot of athletes to get there."

international competitions in front of large crowds, their performance levels fall dramatically; the lamentable performance of the England soccer team at the 2010 FIFA World Cup is a good case in point. This emphasizes the need to "play the game and not the occasion"—a favorite expression of soccer coaches.

Remember, though, that the importance placed on the event depends on how you view the situation. For example, a seasoned professional can become nervous before a comeback game following an injury. Doubts about whether the old skills will still be there, or whether the injury is fully healed, can make the occasion seem more important than a cup final in the eyes of the player.

Audience Effects

Research has shown that spectators can have a huge impact on athletic performance. In fact, studies of the homefield advantage show that teams playing at their home stadiums win, on average, around 56 to 64 percent of the time, depending on the sport. The impressive medal count of host nations during Olympic Games is also notable, in particular the record-breaking haul of gold medals won by Australia in Sydney (2000), by Greece in Athens (2004), and by China in Beijing (2008). Spain's 13 golds in Barcelona (1992) was also a record; it was as many as they had won in all other Games from 1984 onward!

The presence of even a single person can influence your performance, either positively by increasing your motivation or adversely by getting you flustered. This effect is associated with a basic human fear of being evaluated unfavorably. Chapter 2 addresses the influence a fear of failure has on athletic motivation.

Generally, a large audience (such as in the tens of thousands) exaggerates the effect on performance—either bringing out the very best in an athlete or causing an under-par performance. The supportiveness of those watching is also a factor, and this clearly contributes to the homefield advantage in team sports. Even in individual sports, athletes can be influenced by the crowd. In Beijing 2008, the gold medal–winning Hungarian kayaker Attila Sandor Vajda told reporters, "These Olympic Games, it's so nice . . . but not for European people." He was alluding to the cheering crowds that accompanied every Chinese athlete throughout the Games.

The homefield advantage is prevalent in most team sports but especially in professional soccer and ice hockey, sports in which home crowds have the reputation of being hostile toward visiting teams. Research has shown that supportive crowds tend to reduce the anxiety and increase the motivation of performers, whereas hostile crowds increase anxiety and often promote overtly aggressive behavior among players.

A situation in which a previously supportive crowd suddenly turns against a player, or a player suspects that an audience has started to judge him unfavorably, is especially likely to cause anxiety. Professional soccer players often become anxious at the prospect of returning to play for a new team against their former team, which frequently provokes hostility from the home fans. Experienced players may have no problem with such a "homecoming" and put in a game-winning performance to spite their former fans, but younger players need to be taught to cope with the likely taunts and abuse from the crowd. This can be done in part through simulation training, which we cover in chapter 6. As a general rule, audiences are more disruptive with less experienced performers or those who are not entirely confident in their skills and abilities.

Cantona Flies Off the Handle

A classic example of a hostile crowd sparking overt aggression involved the legendary French soccer star Eric Cantona during his playing days for Manchester United in the English Premiership. The occasion was an away game against Crystal Palace. Cantona was sent off the field of play for a dangerous tackle and, after a short protest with the referee, trudged sullenly from the pitch. One of the Crystal Palace fans ran down to the front of the grandstand and reputedly taunted Cantona with racist remarks. Most professionals would have ignored such hostility, but in this case, the taunts triggered Cantona into launching a high-flying kung fu–style kick at the fan. This example illustrates the profound effect that a hostile crowd can have on a player who is quite highly strung. Incidentally, Cantona received a lengthy ban and a hefty fine for his "moment of madness."

© Sport the Library

Eric Cantona loses control and launches an aerial assault on a Crystal Palace fan.

Emphasis on the Individual

Generally, participants in individual sports have been shown to experience more anxiety before, during, and after competition than participants in team sports. This is because the sense of isolation and exposure is much greater in sports such as gymnastics, tennis, and golf than in field sports. However, at times in team sports one player is stressed by being put momentarily in the spotlight. The batter in cricket, the shooter in netball, and the penalty taker in hockey or soccer are faced with moments of isolation when their individual contributions are placed under very close scrutiny. The stress is compounded because the success of the whole team depends on the contribution of one player. Former Great Britain Olympic field hockey captain Mark Pearn put it like this:

> *When you are up to take a penalty flick at a crucial time in the match, sometimes it feels as though the goal is shrinking while the goalkeeper is getting bigger and bigger. It's really quite freaky, and you need to stay extremely focused so as not to become disaffected by it.*

Sledging: Amiable Banter or Unacceptable Intimidation?

Sledging is a practice common in cricket, especially in Australia, where members of the fielding team make audible comments designed to break the concentration of, or provoke anxiety in, the opposition batters. Such comments are mostly good humored but often include a derogatory comment about some aspect of the player's performance or personal characteristics. Former Australian cricket captain Steve Waugh once described sledging as "mental disintegration" because it can gradually wear down a batter's resolve and generate sufficient anxiety to force an error. Often the batters will try to give as good as they get. In a classic sledging encounter in 1991, Pakistan batter Javed Miandad referred to burly Australian fast bowler Merv Hughes as a "fat bus conductor" during a break in the action. Shortly afterward, the bowler captured Javed's wicket, and as he ran past the departing batter, Hughes screamed, "Tickets please." There is frequent debate in cricket about whether sledging is an amiable form of gamesmanship or, when the banter becomes personally insulting, an unacceptable form of psychological intimidation.

Team players in possession of the ball are in essence solo performers, with both opponents and teammates judging their contributions in a similar manner. Many performers become acutely aware of this fact and feel threatened by it. In these situations, anxiety may show itself in many ways: an unwillingness to shoot for goal, a tendency to get rid of the ball quickly, or trying to do too much and losing the ball as a consequence.

Given the difference in anxiety levels between male and females athletes as discussed earlier, coaches and parents should note that when females are learning new skills, a decrease in the competitive element can reduce their anxiety. For example, a swimming coach teaching a young female athlete how to improve her block start would do well to do this individually rather than in front of the team, where the competitive element of trying to outperform the other athletes adds an unnecessary stressor.

Fear of Physical Injury

For the professional boxer, the possibility of getting hurt can be a genuine occupational hazard and a potential source of anxiety. Typically, this anxiety causes important changes in technique. Anxious boxers often lean too far forward, are clumsy in their leg movements, or fight very defensively; any of these reactions may result in the knockdown they dread.

Nonetheless, even in sports that carry an obvious risk of physical injury, athletes in competition can become more anxious about performing well than about injuring themselves. In apparently high-risk sports such as bobsledding, the threat of being assessed unfavorably or of letting the team down can far outweigh any fear of getting hurt. Jason Wing, a member of the British four-man bobsled team at the 1994 Olympic Winter Games in Lillehammer, Norway, expressed it like this:

Physical injury simply never concerned me. The fear of making an error that affected the team was ever present and did play on my mind.

Expectations of Success

The stress on competitors is probably at its greatest when they are favorites to win. Anxiety almost certainly contributed to Hicham El Guerrouj's poor showing in the final of the 1500 meters at his first Olympics in Atlanta, 1996. His form going into the Games had made him a genuine gold medal contender. Indeed, the press, his Moroccan compatriots, and track aficionados had proclaimed him a natural successor to former golden boy Saïd Aouita. Expectations soared, and the pressure grew accordingly.

When favored to win, a performer can easily magnify the task ahead. The hopes of a nation weigh far more heavily on a young man's shoulders than his own hopes and dreams. The race itself was a disaster. El Guerrouj's nervous performance bore all the hallmarks of "energy left on the warm-up track." He seemed to lack the spring in his stride and tactical mastery that had typified his earlier races. El Guerrouj got himself boxed in, became indecisive about making a move, and allowed his attention to become focused on Noureddine Morceli, the runner immediately in front of him. As a result, he clipped Morceli's heel at the beginning of the final lap and came crashing to the ground. Morceli went on to win the race, while El Guerrouj picked himself up off the ground to trail home in 12th position.

El Guerrouj also failed to win the 1500 meters at the 2000 Sydney Olympics having lost only two races since the previous Olympic Games and being a clear favorite once again. The Moroccan press tormented him for his inability to win an Olympic gold medal, despite the fact that he was a four-time world champion. This aptly illustrates the type of stressors with which elite athletes must learn to cope.

El Guerrouj eventually silenced his critics at the Athens Olympics of 2004. He showed tremendous strength of character in scoring a resounding double victory in the 1500 and 5000 meters. Each of these victories was made memorable by El Guerrouj's huge outpouring of emotions. The tears of happiness were testament to the torture he had endured in his two previous Olympic campaigns. El Guerrouj told reporters:

> It's amazing to think that in Sydney I was crying tears of sadness and here I am crying tears of joy. I'm like a five-year-old with a toy.

Unfortunately, it is not only the Olympic Games that cause high anxiety. During any contest in which an athlete senses a pressure to win, there is a potential threat to self-esteem. Athletes are only too aware that many people have invested time, effort, and money into their preparation. They may believe that the only way to repay this debt of gratitude to coaches, family, and perhaps sponsors is to win. Consequently, some athletes compete with a great burden of self-inflicted pressure, often having also set unrealistic goals for themselves. Psychologists call this type of pressure *introjection*, and it is not considered a healthy source of motivation.

Clearly, there can be many anxious moments in sport. Anxiety sometimes acts as the enemy within, an extra opponent that can ruin performance. As Confucius said, "It's not the mountain under your feet; it's the stone in your shoe that wears you down." And yet, clearly, sport ought to present multiple stressors. Sport would not be sport if the challenge wasn't there. There has to be some pressure; the key question for any athlete is, "How much anxiety is optimal?" Anxiety should not be perceived solely as an enemy; it is also a friend that can provide a gentle nudge toward peak performance.

STRESS SYMPTOMS AND RESPONSES

Stress can be the force that either stirs you into action or inhibits your performance. The determining factor is not so much the amount of stress but how much control you think you have over it. In fact, it could be said that stress results in two closely related but separate responses, a physical one and a psychological one.

Physical Response

Whenever the body is stressed, it automatically responds to prepare itself for action. Typically, we experience a rush of adrenaline, our breathing quickens, and our heart beats faster. This bodily reaction is what we referred to earlier as preparation for fight or flight, and it is an instinctive response to challenge or changes in the immediate environment. As a result, the body becomes alert and prepared to react, and feels less pain.

Many athletes and coaches call this physical response to stress *getting psyched up*; psychologists refer to it as *activation*. Either way, the result is stimulation of the mind and body to create an energized state that facilitates performance. The trick is to become sufficiently psyched up without becoming psyched out. It is wrong to believe, however, that the more psyched-up you get, the better you will perform. You need to discover your optimal level of activation, the level that will produce the best performance. This level varies greatly from person to person and from task to task.

Peak performance in explosive activities, such as powerlifting and shot putting, requires higher levels of activation than that in manipulative tasks involving fine muscle control, such as golf putting and snooker. Clearly, a powerlifter would need to psych up, and a snooker player would need to stay calm, but what about sports that fall between these two extremes? What is the correct activation level for netball or soccer or cricket or tennis? In these cases, it becomes much more difficult to generalize.

If you have ever been part of, or witnessed, a team psych up before a rugby match, you know just how ritualistic and aggressive psychological preparation can be. The Haka, which is performed by the New Zealand All Blacks on the rugby field prior to games, is a very public example of prematch preparation. At lower levels of rugby, the stomping and chanting and overt aggression that occurs in rugby changing rooms is similarly designed to raise activation levels in preparation for the battle ahead. The underlying assumption is that all rugby players require a high level of activation to perform at their best.

A fervent warm-up may prove extremely effective for many players. Sometimes, though, the activation level achieved does not match the requirements of the tasks to be performed or the needs of the individual players. For instance, in rugby, the fly-half performs a role that requires vision and judgment, and consequently, great fly-halves such as New Zealand's Dan Carter or South Africa's Morne Steyn tend to be the most relaxed players on the field. The excitement and aggression that might benefit a flanker or a prop forward would almost certainly diminish the fly-half's ability to make the right decisions.

The All Blacks' Haka

The All Blacks (New Zealand national rugby team) famously issue a Maori challenge known as the Haka just before the start of each game to reinforce their identity and unity. There is, however, an ancillary purpose to such collective bravado; in displaying unified strength, the All Blacks hope to intimidate their opposition. Although the Haka is undoubtedly a great spectacle for rugby fans, its influence on opposing teams is variable. Some teams have famously countered the Haka by turning their backs on the ritual, while others attempt to stare down the All Blacks in their own efforts to demonstrate strength and unity.

New Zealand All Blacks performing the Haka.

Optimal activation depends to an even greater extent on the player's personality. For instance, Richard Hill, the former England and British Lions flanker, whose playing position, in theory, demands a high level of physiological arousal, aptly illustrated his prematch preparation needs, when he said:

Throughout my experiences as a rugby player, I have not felt the need to shout and be aggressive in the changing room in order to improve my arousal for a game. I very much prefer to prepare as an individual, quietly contemplating my own performance and the contribution I need to make to the team.

In 1998 the Wales rugby team suffered a disastrous 61-16 defeat at the hands of England. In a subsequent game against Ireland in Dublin, prematch tension caused some players to become physically sick. A kind of domino effect occurred, in which this rather extreme symptom of anxiety spread among nearly half the team. This phenomenon demonstrates what most athletes would regard as an unhealthy level of anxiety. Some rugby players, however, regard vomiting as confirmation that they are sufficiently aroused for the ensuing physical contest.

Clearly, some people are at their best when excited and agitated, whereas others need to remain calm and composed to perform well. Ultimately, the only reliable way to determine your optimal activation level is to monitor your performance level in relation to your emotional state. The mental preparation questionnaire in exercise 4.1 will help you establish fairly accurately, using a process of retrospection (thinking about past experiences), the level of activation associated with your best performances.

Exercise 4.1
Mental Preparation Profile

Name: _____   Main event: _____

These questions are designed to help you reflect on your competitive experiences and develop your competition preparation plan.

A. Think of your best performance in recent seasons and respond to the following:

1. How did you feel just before performing? (Please circle.)

No determination to achieve goal	1	2	3	4	5	6	7	8	9	10	Completely determined
No physical activation	1	2	3	4	5	6	7	8	9	10	Highly physically activated
No worries or fears	1	2	3	4	5	6	7	8	9	10	Extremely worried or afraid
Mentally calm	1	2	3	4	5	6	7	8	9	10	Mentally uptight
No confidence	1	2	3	4	5	6	7	8	9	10	Completely confident

2. What were you thinking or saying to yourself, or focusing on, *just before* the competition?

_____

_____

_____

(continued)

3. What were you thinking or saying to yourself, or focusing on, *during* the competition?

_____

_____

_____

4. How much were you focused on the process of competing rather than the result of the competition?

_____

_____

_____

B. Think of your worst performance within the last two seasons and respond to the following:

1. How did you feel just before performing?

No determination to achieve goal	1	2	3	4	5	6	7	8	9	10	Completely determined
No physical activation	1	2	3	4	5	6	7	8	9	10	Highly physically activated
No worries or fears	1	2	3	4	5	6	7	8	9	10	Extremely worried or afraid
Mentally calm	1	2	3	4	5	6	7	8	9	10	Mentally uptight
No confidence	1	2	3	4	5	6	7	8	9	10	Completely confident

2. What were you thinking or saying to yourself, or focusing on, *just before* the competition?

_____

_____

_____

3. What were you thinking or saying to yourself, or focusing on, *during* the competition?

_____

_____

_____

4. How much were you focused on the process of competing rather than the result of the competition?

_____

_____

_____

C. Compare your responses from your best and worst performances, and then respond to the following by indicating how you want to feel in the future before and during a big competition:

1. How do you want to feel just before performing?

No determination to achieve goal	1	2	3	4	5	6	7	8	9	10	Completely determined
No physical activation	1	2	3	4	5	6	7	8	9	10	Highly physically activated
No worries or fears	1	2	3	4	5	6	7	8	9	10	Extremely worried or afraid
Mentally calm	1	2	3	4	5	6	7	8	9	10	Mentally uptight
No confidence	1	2	3	4	5	6	7	8	9	10	Completely confident

2. What do you want to think or say to yourself, or focus on, *just before* the competition?

_____

_____

_____

3. What do you want to think or say to yourself, or focus on, *during* the competition?

_____

_____

_____

4. How much do you want to focus on the process of competing rather than the result of the competition?

_____

_____

_____

5. Now spend a few minutes reflecting carefully on your answers. Think of strategies that you can use to help attain your optimal mindset, and write them down. Use these strategies in your upcoming training sessions, and then gradually introduce them into competitive situations.

_____

_____

_____

_____

_____

Adapted from T. Orlick, 1986, *Psyching for sport: Mental training for athletes* (Champaign, IL: Human Kinetics), 23-24. Used by permission of Terry Orlick (www.zoneofexcellence.ca).

Psychological Response

Research has shown that thought processes, or *cognitions*, tend to drive anxiety responses. Therefore, thought-related, or cognitive, anxiety often acts as a catalyst for the unwanted physical symptoms of anxiety. If you start to have doubts about whether a challenge is within your capabilities, if your self-talk is defeatist, or if your head is full of negative images, then there is every chance that your activation level will be pushed beyond its optimal point.

To reach an optimal psychological state, you need to understand your own natural responses and be sensitive to your bodily signals. Learning to handle the stresses of competition requires that you learn to read your thought patterns and physical responses and that you develop the skills necessary to find your ideal activation level. Stress management requires excellent self-awareness because if you know yourself well, you will better understand the roots of your anxiety.

ASSESSING AND RECOGNIZING ANXIETY

Anxiety is experienced by most people from time to time, but some people are much more prone to becoming anxious than others. Because this potential for anxiety is considered an aspect of personality, it will not disappear overnight. Psychologists call the tendency to become anxious *trait anxiety* to distinguish it from the anxiety response itself, which is called *state anxiety*. This is not to say that those who are high in trait anxiety are constantly in a nervous, tense condition, just that they experience the symptoms of anxiety more readily and often more intensely than those who are low in trait anxiety.

Most research suggests that athletes who are predisposed to feel anxious (high trait anxiety) are not necessary precluded from becoming champions, although clearly they do have a greater need to develop ways to avoid the negative effects of anxiety during performance. Research has also shown that more experienced athletes generally have less anxiety about competition. There are two plausible explanations for this—either sportspeople learn to cope effectively with the stresses of competition, or highly anxious athletes drop out of sport because competition is too unpleasant for them. Perhaps older and more experienced athletes are less anxious by virtue of their greater maturity and self-knowledge.

If you do not want to wait a long time for further experience to lessen your anxiety, then you must find a way to meet the challenge of competition anxiety. The first step is self-analysis. Exercise 4.2 is the Sports Competition Anxiety Test developed by Professor Rainer Martens at the University of Illinois. This simple test allows you to assess your predisposition to becoming anxious prior to and during competitions.

Exercise 4.2
Sports Competition Anxiety Test

Following are some statements about how people feel when they compete in sports and games. Read each statement and decide if you feel this way *hardly ever* (**A**), *sometimes* (**B**), or *often* (**C**) when you compete. There are no right or wrong answers. Do not spend too much time on any one statement, and do not look at the scoring instructions until you have completed the test.

	A	**B**	**C**
1. Competing against others is socially enjoyable.	❑	❑	❑
2. Before I compete, I feel uneasy.	❑	❑	❑
3. Before I compete, I worry about not performing well.	❑	❑	❑
4. I am a good sportsperson when I compete.	❑	❑	❑
5. When I compete, I worry about making mistakes.	❑	❑	❑
6. Before I compete, I am calm.	❑	❑	❑
7. Setting a goal is important when competing.	❑	❑	❑
8. Before I compete, I get a queasy feeling in my stomach.	❑	❑	❑
9. Just before I compete, I notice that my heart beats faster than usual.	❑	❑	❑
10. I like to compete in games that demand considerable physical energy.	❑	❑	❑
11. Before I compete, I feel relaxed.	❑	❑	❑
12. Before I compete, I am nervous.	❑	❑	❑
13. Team sports are more exciting than individual sports.	❑	❑	❑
14. I get nervous waiting to start the contest.	❑	❑	❑
15. Before I compete, I usually get uptight.	❑	❑	❑

Calculating Your Score

For questions 2, 3, 5, 8, 9, 12, 14, and 15:

A = 1; **B** = 2; **C** = 3

For questions 6 and 11:

A = 3; **B** = 2; **C** = 1

Ignore your answers for questions 1, 4, 7, 10, and 13.

Add up your scores to arrive at a total between 10 and 30. The higher your score, the more prone you are to competition anxiety. Using table 4.1, compare your score with those of other sportsmen and sportswomen. The scores indicate

(continued)

the percentage of males and females who are as anxious as or less anxious than you about sport competition. For example, if you scored 21 on the test, 69 percent of males and 42 percent of females are as anxious as or less anxious than you about sport competition. Remember that the ideal state is one of mental alertness and physical relaxation. Those who are not at all anxious may be insufficiently activated by competition to reach an optimal psychological state, whereas those who become very anxious may lose all physical relaxation.

Table 4.1 Sport Competition Anxiety Test: Normal Scores for Male and Female Athletes

Percentages		
Score	Males	Females
30	99	99
29	99	93
28	97	88
27	93	82
26	89	75
25	86	65
24	82	59
23	78	53
22	74	47
21	69	42
20	61	35
19	50	28
18	40	22
17	30	15
16	24	10
15	18	8
14	14	6
13	9	4
12	7	3
11	5	2
10	1	1

From C.I. Karageorghis and P.C. Terry, 2011, *Inside sport psychology* (Champaign, IL: Human Kinetics). Reprinted, by permission, from R. Martens, R.S. Vealey, and D. Burton, 1990, *Competitive anxiety in sport* (Champaign, IL: Human Kinetics), 53.

Anxiety can be recognized on three levels: by physical responses (*somatic* level), by particular thought processes (*cognitive* level), or by specific patterns of behavior (*behavioral* level). Table 4.2 lists some of the symptoms on each level. Use this as a reference for recognizing anxiety. As you can see, many of the somatic responses are only too obvious, but not all of them are a cause for concern. Increases in heart rate, respiration, and adrenaline production can be very positive influences on performance, but the appearance of further somatic symptoms, and the emergence of the cognitive responses listed, means that excitement has turned to anxiety and appropriate remedial action may be required. Symptoms across the three categories can be experienced concurrently, which means that you could, for example, feel irritable, have a dry mouth, and bite your fingernails all at once.

Table 4.2 Symptoms of Anxiety

Cognitive	Somatic	Behavioral
Indecision	Increased blood pressure	Biting fingernails
Sense of confusion	Pounding heart	Lethargic movements
Feeling heavy	Increased respiration rate	Inhibited posture
Negative thoughts	Sweating	Playing safe
Poor concentration	Clammy hands and feet	Going through the motions
Irritability	Butterflies in the stomach	Introversion
Fear	Adrenaline surge	Uncharacteristic displays of extroversion
Forgetfulness	Dry mouth	Uncharacteristic displays of aggression
Loss of confidence	Need to urinate	Avoidance of eye contact
Images of failure	Muscular tension	Covering face with hand
Defeatist self-talk	Tightness in neck and shoulders	Incessant talking
Feeling rushed	Trembling	Pacing up and down
Feeling weak	Blushing	
Constant dissatisfaction	Distorted vision	
Unable to take instructions	Twitching	
Thoughts of avoidance	Yawning	
	Voice distortion	
	Nausea	
	Vomiting	
	Diarrhea	
	Loss of appetite	
	Sleeplessness	
	Loss of libido	

ALLEVIATING ANXIETY

It is often said that pressure focuses the mind. This is all well and good as long as the pressure does not tense the body unnecessarily. To perform at your best, you need just the right amount of tension; too much will result in poor muscular control.

All skilled movement involves controlling the muscles that need to be tense and those that need to be relaxed (see chapter 1). For example, as you tense your biceps, the muscle fibers contract so that your arm bends. To straighten your arm, you tense the opposite muscle, the triceps. To hold your arm in a particular position requires that you balance the tension in the two muscle groups. This pairing of muscles occurs throughout the body so that all bodily positions are achieved through the delicate balance of tension and relaxation in pairs of muscles. So, if you contract your hamstring muscles at the back of your leg, the antagonist muscle group—the quadriceps at the front of your leg—will relax.

During movement the voluntary contraction of one muscle automatically causes the opposite muscle to relax. However, if a muscle contracts involuntarily, as a result of anxiety, the opposite muscle will also contract to maintain the equilibrium of the body. This means that severe muscular tension can build up simply by worrying. Unfortunately, the tension may go undetected until it brings about poor performance through rigid and awkward movements. If you have ever attempted to perform delicate skills immediately after a heavy weight training session, you understand how much excessive muscle tension interferes with fine muscle control.

To an extent, movement counteracts muscular tension, which is why many athletes prefer to stay mobile just prior to the start of competition. In addition, several relaxation techniques can complement a warm-up routine or be used the night before competition to promote a good night's sleep. Relaxation is the basis of anxiety control. It can be defined as an absence of tension. If you can learn to induce relaxation at will, you will be able to manage some of the major negative symptoms of anxiety more effectively.

Because people are suited to different types of relaxation techniques, the only reliable strategy for discovering which is most effective is to try a variety of techniques. Three methods of relaxation are described in this chapter: progressive muscular relaxation, the relaxing place, and the five breath technique. We cannot emphasize enough that none of these techniques are likely to be effective immediately. Like any new skill, they require methodical practice and patience. You must remember that there is nothing inherently good about relaxation. It is an effective remedy for excess tension, but once you reach your ideal state of activation, further relaxation could leave you feeling too docile.

Progressive Muscular Relaxation

Dr. Edmund Jacobson developed the progressive muscular relaxation (PMR) technique in the 1930s. The technique involves progressing from one muscle group to the next, alternately creating and releasing tension. This increases your sensitivity to when and where tension is present in your body. In effect, PMR trains you to identify tension and release it automatically.

Becoming proficient in this technique takes time and requires effort, but the ability to induce deep relaxation has many benefits. While learning PMR, generate the tension artificially by voluntarily contracting specific muscle groups. This is how you begin to recognize where you are tense. At the same time, your body becomes used to relaxing the contraction, thereby releasing the tension. Initially, PMR is a long and thorough process, but once you become tuned in to the process of relaxing tense muscles, it becomes automatic and is a way of introducing a flowing quality back into your movements.

This exercise is quite long for you to memorize, so either ask a friend to read the instructions in a quiet, relaxed voice or record them yourself onto an MP3 file. At first, you should spend about 20 or 30 minutes on each PMR session, but gradually, as you become more proficient, you can reduce this time. *(Where you see ellipses [. . .], pause for a few seconds.)*

Sit comfortably or lie down with your eyes closed. Relax your arms by your sides and leave your legs uncrossed. As you follow the instructions, you will focus on the word *relax*. Try to ease into the relaxation; just let it happen. Do not concern yourself with how well you are doing; simply let the relaxation flow over you and let it deepen at its own pace.

Keep your breathing steady and shallow. Notice that when you breathe out, your body relaxes a little. Breathe in and out through your nose, and each time you breathe out, relax a little more.

Keep your breathing steady and regular, and concentrate on the word *relax* each time you breathe out. Now we will go through the muscle groups one by one so you can begin to feel the difference between tension and relaxation.

First, your *hands and forearms*. Tense these muscles by clenching your fists tightly. Feel the tension in your hands and forearms . . . hold . . . and relax. Relax your hands and forearms and notice the difference between tension and relaxation. Focus on the word *relax* while letting the muscles in your hands and forearms unwind. Concentrate on the feeling of letting go.

Now tense the muscles in the front of your upper arm—the *biceps*. Tense these by bending your arms at the elbow and trying to touch your shoulders with your wrists. Feel the tension in your biceps . . . and now relax. Let your arms fall back by your sides and notice the difference between tension and relaxation in your biceps. Focus on the word *relax* while letting your biceps loosen and unwind. Continue the feeling of letting go as the muscles unwind and relax.

Now tense the muscles in the back of your upper arm—the *triceps*. Tense these by straightening your arms as hard as you can so they feel like blocks of wood. Straighten your arms . . . feel the tension in your triceps . . . now relax. As you let go of the tension, concentrate on the word *relax*, and allow the feeling of relaxation to spread throughout your arms.

Now tense the muscles in your *shoulders*. Shrug your shoulders by drawing them up into your neck. Shrug them tightly. Feel the tension in your shoulders. Hold it . . . and relax. Let your shoulders drop and feel the tension ease away. As your muscles unwind, concentrate on the word *relax*.

Now tense the muscles in your *forehead*. Raise your eyebrows as high as you can and feel the tension in your forehead. Feel the tension . . . hold it . . . and relax. Let your eyebrows drop. Let the tension go from your forehead and focus on the word *relax*.

Now tense the muscles in your *eyebrows and eyelids*. Frown as hard as you can and squeeze your eyes tightly shut. Feel the tension . . . hold it . . . and relax. Smooth out your brow, relax your eyelids, keep your eyes still, and gaze straight ahead. Notice the difference between the feelings of tension and relaxation around your eyes and focus on the word *relax*.

Now tense the muscles in your *tongue and throat*. Press the tip of your tongue against the roof of your mouth. Press . . . feel the tension . . . and relax. Let your tongue drop to the bottom of your mouth and feel the tension ease away. Continue the feeling of letting go while you focus on the word *relax*.

Now tense the muscles in your *lips and face*. Press your lips together tightly. Press together . . . feel the tension . . . and relax. Relax your lips and allow your face to sag. Feel the muscles unwind. Let go of the tension as you focus on the word *relax*.

Now tense the muscles in your *chest*. Take a deep breath so your chest tenses like a bodybuilder. Feel the tension . . . hold it . . . and relax. Breathe out and feel the relief of letting go. Keep your breathing shallow. Every time you breathe out, notice how you relax a little more. Focus on the word *relax* as your chest unwinds more and more.

Now tense the muscles of your *abdomen*. Push down into your abdomen, making your muscles hard and rigid. Hold the tension . . . and now relax. Let the muscles loosen and unwind. Focus on the word *relax* as the feeling spreads.

Now tense the muscles in your *legs*. Pull your toes up tightly so that your thighs tense like tree trunks and your calf muscles become hard. Hold the tension . . . and relax. Notice the difference between tension and relaxation in your legs. Focus on the word *relax* as the muscles unwind.

Now let the feeling of relaxation spread right through your whole body. Keep your breathing regular and relaxed, and every time you breathe out, relax a little more. Let the relaxation flow over you. Feel as though you are sinking into an ever-deepening state of relaxation. You are calm and deeply relaxed, and there is no tension. Focus on the word *relax* and enjoy the feeling.

The Relaxing Place

The progressive muscular relaxation (PMR) technique works on the principle that relaxation in the muscles creates a sense of wellbeing in the mind. Several other techniques work in the opposite direction; that is, passive, relaxed thoughts spread relaxation throughout the body. One such technique is known as the relaxing place and involves visualizing a real or imaginary location that carries strong associations of relaxation. As with all relaxation techniques, do not force yourself to relax. This is counterproductive. Learn to just let it happen so there will be no distracting or unwanted thoughts.

The relaxing place is a visualization exercise designed to transport you from a stressful situation to a place that you associate with feelings of peace and quiet, where you can really take things easy. Practice this technique in a place where you will not be disturbed, either sitting or lying down. For maximum effect, you or a friend should record it onto an MP3 file. Before you start the exercise, close your eyes and take a few deep breaths, inhaling through your nose and exhaling very slowly through your mouth. If, at any time, for any reason, for example in case of emergency or any situation where full attention is required, by opening your eyes, you will be fully alert. *(Where you see ellipses [. . .], pause for a few seconds.)*

> First, to relax, put on some very relaxing music or sounds of nature and sit or lie down in a comfortable position in a place where you are unlikely to be disturbed.
>
> Look up at your eyebrows and begin to concentrate on the sounds around you . . . maybe the distant sound of traffic or the hustle and bustle going on outside. . . . Then concentrate on the sounds of the music, feel it washing over you as if it were the tide going in and out, in and out. . . . Now pay attention to the sound of your thoughts . . . concentrate on your breathing. Take deep breaths in and out . . . listen to your heart beat . . . become aware of your eyelids and feel them blinking quickly and notice that you have a strong desire to close your eyes. . . . Allow your eyes to relax. In a few seconds, you will imagine your favorite place of relaxation . . . maybe somewhere you have been before, a riverside, a deserted beach, a summer meadow, or somewhere you can imagine you would feel relaxed, . . . and now . . . just imagine that you are standing on a balcony . . . and there is a long set of stairs in front of you. . . . Leading down from this balcony . . . there are strong stairs . . . with wide steps . . . and a handrail on each side. . . . The stairs are well lit . . . and you can see them clearly. . . . Now begin to count down from 10 to 1 . . . and with each number . . . you take a single step down the stairs . . . and with each number you become more and more calm, more and more relaxed. . . . Each step down from the balcony takes you deeper and deeper . . . into *your* wonderful place of relaxation . . . and as you slowly descend these stairs . . . you experience a sense of ever-deepening relaxation . . . throughout your entire

body. . . . You feel the stairs under your feet . . . and when you eventually reach step 1, you pause and wonder where you might go next. . . . Again you feel very tranquil, and this tranquillity is accompanied by a sense of anticipation. . . . Now step off . . . and when you do so . . . you find yourself in your favorite place of relaxation . . . and enjoy . . . this beautiful place. . . .

(Allow the relaxing music or sounds of nature to play for as long as you wish the exercise to last.)

During your time in your relaxing place, take time to immerse yourself in the sights around you, the distinct smells and the gentle sound of your favorite music playing in the background. Feel yourself sinking into an ever-deepening state of relaxation.

While you are relaxed, give yourself some positive and beneficial suggestions relating, for example, to increasing your self-confidence, attaining peak performance, or mastering a specific sport skill that has proved elusive to you.

Now, without opening your eyes, bring your attention back to the room you are sitting in and very gently squeeze your left thumb with the fingers of your right hand. As you do, allow yourself to drift back to your relaxing place and immerse yourself in it once more. Notice all the little details of your relaxing place using each of your senses, and again feel totally relaxed and at ease.

Repeat the process of allowing the scene to fade and then squeezing your thumb to return to the relaxing place. Do this another two or three times before releasing your thumb and opening your eyes.

After sufficient practice, holding your thumb will act as a trigger that will take you to your peaceful little hideaway immediately when you feel the need to relax. It can become an effective way to stay calm before competition or during extended breaks in the action. Our experience has shown that when there is a great deal of background noise in a competitive environment, this exercise is not particularly effective. One way to counter potential distractions is to increase the volume of the soundtrack and to find a quiet corner well away from other competitors.

The Five Breath Technique

Another effective method of relaxing involves focusing attention exclusively on the rhythm of your breathing. The five breath technique, described in this section, is a breathing exercise that removes tension and clears the mind. Once mastered, this technique will help you relax very quickly indeed. It can be used anytime you feel yourself tensing up and can be effective even in highly charged situations.

First, though, you will need to spend time perfecting the technique. This is best done in quiet surroundings where you will not be disturbed. Just five minutes of practice a day should enable you to relax at will in a few weeks. Again, you will need to either ask a friend to read the instructions slowly and clearly or prerecord them onto an MP3 file. After some weeks of practice, you will most likely not require a recording of the instructions.

This exercise can be performed lying or sitting. Lie face up, arms by your side, palms down and legs uncrossed; or sit upright, head in a neutral position, hands in your lap, and feet flat on the floor. You should inhale slowly, deeply, and evenly through your nose, and exhale gently through your mouth as though flickering but not extinguishing the flame of a candle.

- Take a deep breath. Allow your face and neck to relax as you breathe out.
- Take a second deep breath. Allow your shoulders and arms to relax as you breathe out.
- Take a third deep breath. Allow your chest, abdomen, and back to relax as you breathe out.
- Take a fourth deep breath. Allow your legs and feet to relax as you breathe out.
- Take a fifth deep breath. Allow your whole body to relax as you breathe out.

Continue to breathe deeply, and each time you breathe out, say the word *relax*.

Enjoy this state of relaxation for as long as you like. When you wish to return to full alertness, count slowly from 1 to 5. Remind yourself that you will feel as relaxed and alert as you want to be for the task at hand. This sense of calm alertness will remain with you when you open your eyes. Count 1 . . . 2 . . . 3 . . . 4 . . . 5, eyes wide open. Notice how good you feel.

Learning to relax is a major factor in coping with competition stress. But there are many other things you can do that will deflect the pressure. We'll discuss two of these, keeping winning in perspective and controlling the controllables, to conclude this section.

Keeping Winning in Perspective

For a start, you need to keep winning in its proper perspective. Sport induces fear and tension because it is so important to its devotees. It arouses extremes of passion that few other activities can match. For some, sport seems to be as important as life and death itself, whereas for a few it is, as the late manager of Liverpool Football Club, Bill Shankly, famously said, "much more important than that." This, of course, is not true. The trick is to play the game as though your life depended on it but always to remember that it doesn't.

When England soccer player Gareth Southgate looked for a way to cope with the burden of his infamous missed penalty kick at the 1996 European Championship, he chose to visit a facility for terminally ill children. That experience soon put his weak shot at the goalkeeper into its proper perspective.

No matter how desperately you want to win, your self-esteem should not be on the line if you fail. If you believe you will be a lesser person if the result goes against you, you are condemning yourself to a career riddled with anxiety, a career that will never quite fulfill its true potential. By all means you should hate to lose, but you should not hate yourself when you do. This is fundamental to much of the psychology of personality: separating the person from the behavior.

A simple acknowledgment that your best is the most you can hope to give will, ironically, make winning that much easier. Even the greatest players suffer defeats, yet they are not defeated; they take something positive from the loss and treat it as a stepping-stone to future successes. The words of Rudyard Kipling, which greet tennis players at Wimbledon as they enter Centre Court, resonate with a powerful message: "If you can meet with triumph and disaster and treat those two impostors just the same."

You should learn to accept the occasional loss as the inevitable flip side to the winning coin, and as such, part of the game you have decided to play. Certainly, a philosophical approach to sport will help to create a more balanced and healthier view of successes and failures.

Coaches and parents should instill this balanced view in young athletes from a very early age. As we explained at length in chapter 1, an approach that emphasizes personal skill development and fun is best for children. When children get anxious in competition and stop enjoying their participation in sport as a result, there is a strong likelihood that they will drop out of sport before reaching adulthood.

Setting realistic goals is another way to measure success in a more objective manner (see chapter 2 for guidance). Your ultimate goal may revolve around becoming a winner, but your intermediate goals should relate to effort and long-term development. You may be surprised at how much less pressure you feel when you set effective day-to-day goals.

Controlling the Controllables

Many athletes are preoccupied with aspects over which they have absolutely no control: the weather, the decisions of officials, how other players perform, or the state of the playing surface. As we said earlier in this book, sport psychology is all about maximizing the probability of success. You and your coaches can do this by working on all the things that are within your control.

In our experience, the key to performing your best and controlling the negative effects of anxiety is to prepare very thoroughly. As the saying goes, "Failing to prepare is preparing to fail." You should taper down your training before major competitions, eat healthy and nutritious meals (see chapter 5), get to bed early so you get a restful night's sleep, check out the competitive environment in advance so you feel comfortable with it, compose a game plan that is flexible in case of changing circumstances, and arrive at the venue in plenty of time to complete your preevent routine (see chapter 6).

The weather conditions and playing surface are the same for everyone in the competition; the attitudes toward these factors, however, may be the telling factor. The circumstances you face may not be controllable, but your reactions to them most certainly are. An important part of the principle of controlling the controllables is dealing with the unexpected and adverse situations that sport so often presents. Learning to cope with adversity is a severe test of mental toughness.

Performance psychologist Dr. Jim Loehr advocates going one step beyond coping with adversity to learning to *love* adversity. Adversity is probably the norm in sport and comes in many forms, from difficult weather conditions, poor officiating, and equipment malfunctions, to facing the toughest opponent and sometimes just sheer bad luck. There are three reactions to adverse situations. Some people clearly hate adversity, shy away from it, and psychologically withdraw when things are not going their way. Others accept the reality of the situation and find a way to cope even though they may not truly relish the challenge. A few, usually the high achievers, actually welcome

The British Bobsled Team at the 1992 Winter Olympic Games

At the 1992 Olympic Winter Games in Albertville, the second author was psychologist to the British bobsled team. The two-man event, which featured driver Mark Tout and brakeman Lenny Paul, offered an outside chance of a medal for the team. An early draw on day 1 of the two-day race meant they would benefit from fast ice on the first run. A great start from Lenny and a precision drive from Mark saw them take an early lead. After the second run down the 19 bends of the 1500-meter ice track, they still led by a narrow margin overnight. This was a lead they really had no right to hold coming into the event ranked only 10th in the world.

That evening the team planned for the "what ifs" that could occur between then and the end of the competition. They covered every possible eventuality with meticulous attention to detail. Although sabotage of equipment was not unknown in the sport, it was perhaps with a hint of paranoia that the sled was locked away in a warm garage, a five-ton truck was parked tight against the garage door, and a member of the army parachute regiment was posted as sentry throughout the long sub-zero night.

Day 2 arrived with an air of expectancy; the fans keenly anticipated Britain's first Olympic bobsled medal in 28 years. Holding on to first place was going to be a monumental task, and everyone in the team knew it. The emotional melting pot of Olympic competition was boiling away, intensifying everyone's reactions. Staying calm was the challenge.

As Mark and Lenny stepped up to the line for run 3, a timing clock malfunctioned. Popular myth attributed this to a Swiss supporter pressing a snowball into the reflector that triggers the clock, but whatever the cause, it was a delay for which the team had planned. The starter announced, "One-minute delay." Stay in control, focus on the breathing, that's good. About 20 seconds later, the starter changed his decision to "Three-minute delay." Not a problem, coats on, back into the start hut as planned. A moment later, just as Mark and Lenny were entering the hut, the starter announced, "One-minute delay."

In that split second, the author thought, "Houston, we have a problem." Mark and Lenny turned on their heels back to the start, looking and doubtless feeling a bit rushed. As they reached the start line and stripped down to their race suits for a second time, the starter changed his mind yet again and declared, "Three-minute delay." Recollections are somewhat fuzzy at this point, but in the end the delay was seven minutes and coping strategies had been stretched to the limit.

The start, when it came, was average, but what happened then was extraordinary. Midway down the track Lenny, for the first and only time in his long career, raised his head (which should be tucked down aerodynamically between his knees) to get his bearings. He raised his head not once but twice. No one really knows how much time was lost, but in a sport in which medals are decided by hundredths of a second, the loss of aerodynamic efficiency was probably significant. The British team slipped from first to sixth place and stayed there. What caused Lenny's head to pop up? Again, no one really knows, not even Lenny himself. Perhaps it was the mind-numbing bang on the head suffered as the sled hit the exit from bend 8, or perhaps it was a product of the unbelievable tension generated during the start line fiasco. Either way, there were many tears that night from all involved.

Exercise 4.3
Coping With Adversity

British Bobsled Examples

	Dealing with the problem	Dealing with the emotions
Situation 1		
There is a riotous party in the Olympic village on the night before the final two runs.	Move to a teammate's room in a quieter part of the village.	Use the relaxing place technique to facilitate a restful night's sleep.
Situation 2		
There is a one-minute delay at the start.	Stay on the start line in your race suits.	Use centering to stay calm (see chapter 6).
Situation 3		
There is a three-minute delay at the start.	Put on warm clothes and return to the start hut.	Mentally rehearse the race to maintain an optimal mindset.

Threats to My Own Performance

	Dealing with the problem	Dealing with the emotions
Situation 1		
_____	_____	_____
_____	_____	_____
Situation 2		
_____	_____	_____
_____	_____	_____
Situation 3		
_____	_____	_____
_____	_____	_____

From C.I. Karageorghis and P.C. Terry, 2011, *Inside sport psychology* (Champaign, IL: Human Kinetics).

adversity either because it brings out the best in them, as in the case of facing a great opponent, or because they know that they will cope better than their opponents (e.g., in inclement weather). All athletes have to be prepared to face adversity. Those who can learn to love it have a distinct advantage over their competitors.

So what is the moral of the bobsledding tale on page 115? There is no substitute for planning responses to the unexpected and the adverse. Athletes and their support teams must develop well-rehearsed coping strategies to deal with potential problems and the emotions associated with them.

Exercise 4.3 includes some examples of problem-focused and emotion-focused coping strategies from the work of the second author with the British bobsled team. As you complete the exercise, ask yourself, "How's my preparation?"

SUMMARY

We hope that by now you have a better understanding of the processes that cause anxiety and have learned ways to keep it from disrupting your performance. It would be impossible to describe methods of coping with every eventuality in sport, so we have tried to use examples that will be recognizable to the majority of athletes and coaches. The challenge is to adapt the material in this chapter to your unique needs and circumstances. The skills required to stop anxiety from spoiling your performance can be summarized as follows:

- Recognize the level of activation associated with best performance.
- Learn to relax and facilitate optimal activation (for psych-up strategies, see chapter 7).
- Ensure that you do not measure self-esteem in terms of victories or defeats.
- Have realistic expectations of yourself.
- Control the controllables.
- Learn to love adversity.

The message we have tried to convey is that a major problem in competition is letting your mind work against you rather than for you. You must accept anxiety symptoms as part and parcel of the competition experience; only then will anxiety become a friend rather than a foe. Athletes should be given this message from a young age so they can channel the common anxiety symptoms into their performances and view them as a positive force.

The mental skills described in this chapter and throughout the book will help mind and body develop a far more effective partnership, but you will need to be patient. Learning to release your true potential takes time and much perseverance.

5

Mood and Emotion

If only I could tame the lion inside me without putting out the fire.

—John McEnroe, three-time Wimbledon champion

When athletes turn in a less-than-optimal performance, they sometimes attribute it to a mood-related factor: "You know, I just wasn't feeling quite up for it today." This is generally not considered an acceptable excuse for elite or professional athletes for whom there is a tacit rule that they should be in the right mood for every competition. However, our experience as practitioners and researchers has taught us that a bad mood or negative emotions can affect even those operating in the highest echelons of sport. Many athletes believe that mood is one of those random psychological factors over which they have no real control. In this chapter, we explain why this is a false notion and how, like self-confidence (see chapter 3), moods can be consciously manipulated.

Most athletes associate being in a good mood with a state that enables them to achieve their best performances. Athletes' moods and emotions help to determine how they perform and how motivated they feel across a wide range of circumstances and situations. Also, people interact with others based on their perceptions of their moods. All of us, at some point, have waited to catch a parent or guardian in the right mood before asking them for something expensive! The concept of mood and how it affects performance has received relatively little coverage in applied sport psychology texts despite the fact that it has been of considerable interest to sport researchers for many decades.

In this chapter, we explore the multifaceted nature of moods and emotions and the considerable impact they have in both facilitating and disrupting sport performance. We also provide a simple way to monitor mood on a daily or weekly basis, a method that we often employ with elite performers. Finally, we offer a variety of ways to manage, manipulate, and regulate mood that complement the interventions for competition anxiety detailed in chapter 4.

PERSPECTIVES ON MOOD AND EMOTION IN SPORT

Sport generates powerful emotional responses that influence both participants and spectators. The well-known American psychology professor Richard Lazarus suggested that emotion represents one third of the "trilogy of mind." The other two parts of this trilogy are thought processes and motivation, which, together with emotion, shape our behavior. In a nutshell, emotion is a response to the meaning we attach to our interactions with the world around us.

A mood can be described as a set of constantly changing feelings that vary in terms of strength and duration. Our moods usually involve more than one emotion. Therefore, a mood is an accumulation of emotional responses to daily events that combine to form a mindset. This mindset stays in place until altered by future events. As an example, a female athlete named Kate was having a terrible time with her partner, who could not understand why she spent so much time away at training camps with fellow athletes instead of spending time with him. The guilt associated with this situation caused Kate's mood to deteriorate, which had a disastrous effect on her performance. As a consequence, she was dropped from the squad and began spending more time at home. However, Kate became depressed and angry about being dropped and started to resent her partner. Only after relationship counseling in which Kate conceded that she had to devote more quality time with her partner, and her partner agreed to provide greater social support for Kate's athletic endeavors, did Kate's mood improve.

Moods are of longer duration than emotions and are also more general in nature. They provide an indication of psychological wellbeing at any given moment. That's why mood is sometimes referred to as a barometer of mental health. Athletes' moods can indicate the likelihood of success in both training and competition and play a critical role in mobilizing personal resources that enable them to cope with the demands of sport.

Emotions have some distinct signals that are universally recognized, such as the facial expressions associated with anger or hostility (frowning, intense focus, flared nostrils). We tend to infer a person's mood from emotional signals, although these inferences are not always accurate. For example, a man crossing his arms over his chest may be feeling oppositional or defensive (literally placing a barrier between himself and others), or he might simply be feeling cold!

People tend to intuitively monitor their own moods and emotions to gauge whether their feelings are pleasant or unpleasant and to maintain an awareness of how activated or energized they feel. There is a reciprocal, or two-way, relationship between moods and emotions, in that mood shapes the emotional reaction to a particular situation, and the emotional experience that follows contributes to mood.

Figure 5.1 shows a model of mood that reflects its two broad aspects (activation–deactivation and unpleasant–pleasant), along with some of the adjectives commonly associated with the feelings in each quadrant. This represents in a simple manner what is, in reality, a complex array of interrelations. On the vertical axis, *activation* refers to a state of readiness and high arousal, whereas *deactivation* is the converse (sluggishness and low arousal). On the horizontal axis, *unpleasant* is associated with negative feelings, which are generally undesirable, whereas *pleasant* is associated with the positive feelings that we often seek to create.

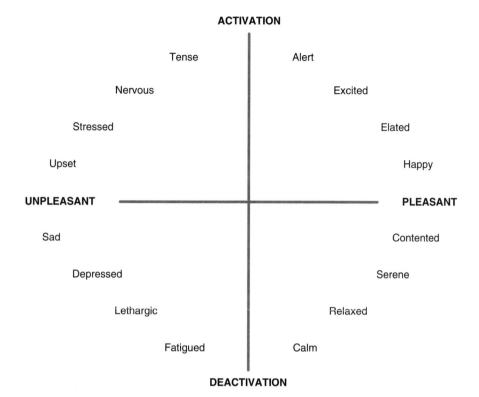

Figure 5.1   The circumplex model of mood and emotion.

As an alternative to this so-called circumplex model of mood, psychologists have often used a range of mood factors to describe the mood of a person. These include negative mood factors such as tension, depression, anger, fatigue, and confusion, and positive mood factors such as vigor and happiness. This latter approach lends itself very well to assessments of mood over time to gauge its effects on sport performance and has proven very popular among mood researchers.

MOOD STATES, SPORT PERFORMANCE, AND TRAINING

Many sport psychologists use the term *mood* rather than *emotion,* so, to keep things simple, we will also use this term to explain the relationship between our feelings and performance outcomes, and then provide some strategies to help you manipulate mood.

An understanding of the mood states associated with superior performance will help you use mood regulation strategies. The first thing we need to make clear is that there is no such thing as an ideal mood for superior performance; rather, athletes vary in terms of their optimal moods for a given challenge.

In the late 1970s, when mood research in sport was in its infancy, American psychologist William Morgan wrote that elite athletes typically reported what he called an iceberg profile. This profile is characterized by an above-average score for vigor and below-average scores for tension, depression, anger, fatigue, and confusion (see figure 5.2). Similarly, a disturbed mood is typified by an inverse iceberg profile, which has the opposite pattern of scores (see figure 5.3). This type of mood profile is associated with a poor state of physical and mental functioning. If an athlete repeatedly exhibits an inverse iceberg profile over a prolonged period (two or three months), a sport psychologist would normally refer the athlete to a clinical psychologist trained to deal with chronic mood disturbance.

The term *iceberg* is applied because the positive mood dimension of vigor is above the metaphorical water line (an average score of 50), whereas the negative dimensions are below the water line. Research led by the second author in the mid-1990s showed that athletes tend to report an iceberg profile most of the time—even recreational athletes! He proposed that what really indicated a superior mood was an "Everest profile" with scores above 60 percent for vigor and below 40 percent for tension, depression, anger, fatigue, and confusion (see figure 5.4).

The second author, along with research collaborators Professor Andrew Lane and Dr. Chris Beedie, subsequently conducted research using a technique known as meta-analysis, which provides a statistical summary of a large number of studies. They tested whether mood profiles could predict sport performance and also discriminate

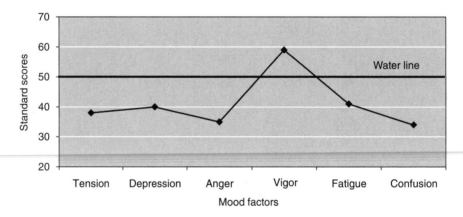

Figure 5.2   The iceberg mood profile.

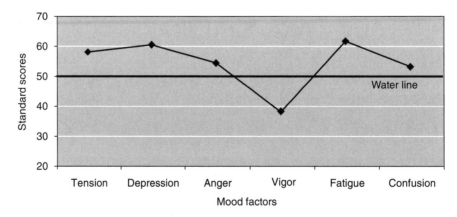

Figure 5.3   The inverse iceberg mood profile.

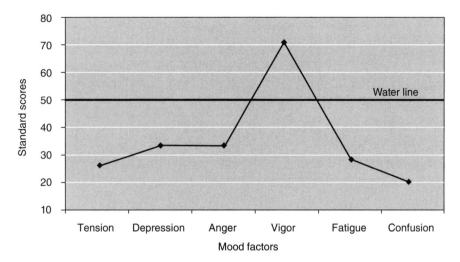

Figure 5.4 The Everest mood profile.

among groups of athletes at varying levels of achievement. Results from more than 3,400 athletes showed that mood profiles can help predict quality of performance. In particular, higher scores for vigor and lower scores for confusion and depression were associated with good performance. Mood profiles did not, however, differentiate among athletes at varying levels of competition. Elite athletes often reported the same moods as athletes at the club and recreational levels.

This research also showed that depressed mood plays a pivotal role in determining how the remaining mood factors affect performance. Even the mildest symptoms of depression in an athlete's mood profile act as a catalyst for other negative moods and can adversely affect performance. The major performance-related predictions of this model of mood, which is shown in figure 5.5 on page 124, are as follows:

- Athletes in a depressed mood tend to have increased anger, tension, confusion, and fatigue and decreased vigor.
- Vigor tends to facilitate (improve) performance, whereas confusion and fatigue tend to debilitate (reduce) performance regardless of the presence or absence of depressed mood.
- Anger and tension tend to debilitate (reduce) performance among athletes reporting symptoms of depression.
- Anger and tension tend to show an inverted-U relationship with performance among athletes reporting no symptoms of depression. (An inverted-U relationship means that as either anger or tension rise, performance improves up to an optimal point, after which further increases in either anger or tension lead to a downturn in performance.)

One of the key points to note is that as long as you are not experiencing symptoms of depression, even the supposedly negative mood factors of anger and tension can, to an extent, enhance performance. Anger can be channeled into determination and ultimately dissipated by the event, and tension indicates a readiness to perform and often disappears once competition starts. When performance outcome is important

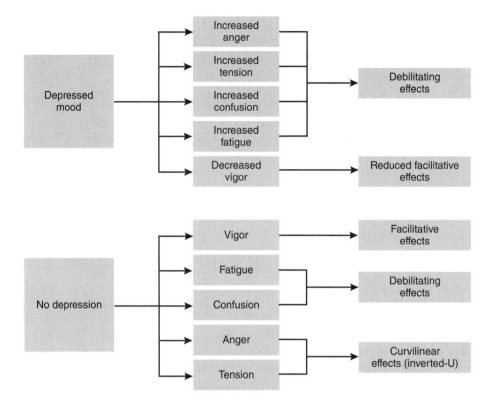

Figure 5.5 A model to predict sport performance from preperformance mood.

From A.M. Lane and P.C. Terry, 2000, "The nature of mood: Development of a conceptual model with a focus on depression," *Journal of Applied Sport Psychology* 12(1): 16-33. Reprinted by permission of Taylor & Francis Ltd.

to you, then a little tension can certainly have a motivating effect, as discussed in chapter 4. However, too much tension can inhibit muscular control and lead to movement patterns that lack fluidity.

MOOD PROFILING

In recent years, some sport psychologists have been monitoring their athletes' moods on a daily or weekly basis using of one of many self-report questionnaires. Frequently used questionnaires include the Profile of Mood States, the Positive and Negative Affect Schedule, the Multiple Affective Adjective Checklist, and the Activation-Deactivation Adjective Check List. Such questionnaires are used for a wide variety of purposes.

One of the most common uses of mood profiling is to determine the mood state associated with the superior performance levels of particular athletes. The information is used to try to recreate a similar mood state prior to future competitions. Another popular use of mood profiles is to monitor responses to training load. Such profiles are used to make recommendations to coaches or conditioning experts on appropriate volumes of training to help prevent overtraining. Profiles are also a good indicator of an athlete's general psychological state and thus serve as a useful starting point and stimulus for discussion.

How to Profile Mood

As mentioned earlier, various methods can be used to assess mood. The second author led the development of a mood questionnaire designed specifically for athletes known as the Brunel Mood Scale, or BRUMS, which was the measure used to monitor the mood profile of Richard Faulds (see Mood Profile of an Olympic Champion). The BRUMS is based on the much-used Profile of Mood States, which was developed in the USA in the early 1970s. We will explain how you can use the BRUMS to establish your optimal mood state and how to monitor your physical preparation so you can avoid staleness and overtraining. The BRUMS should be used for self-assessment only; it is not intended to be administered to others. Ideally, mood profiling should be overseen by a qualified psychologist who has been trained in its use.

Complete a mood profile (exercise 5.1 on page 126), but first, make a photocopy of it so you can reassess your mood in the future.

Mood Profile of an Olympic Champion

Figure 5.6 shows the mood profile of Sydney 2000 Olympic target-shooting gold medalist Richard Faulds. The second author began the profiling a day after Faulds arrived in Australia from Europe, and it continued until the morning of competition. The pattern reveals an early adjustment to the unsettling effects of intercontinental travel and the associated jet lag. This was followed by an extended period of mood stability, with a slight increase in tension as the competition day got closer. The optimal mood for this athlete had been identified at previous competitions, and the main challenge was to spot when optimal mood was achieved and to try to maintain it using appropriate strategies. Because Faulds had found the 1996 Atlanta Games emotionally overwhelming, he opted out of the Olympic Village environment in Sydney. He chose to stay in a house in the Sydney suburbs with a fellow athlete, the team coaches, and the team psychologist (the second author). Faulds used his own transport, shopped for the food he liked to eat, and generally created a "home away from home" environment.

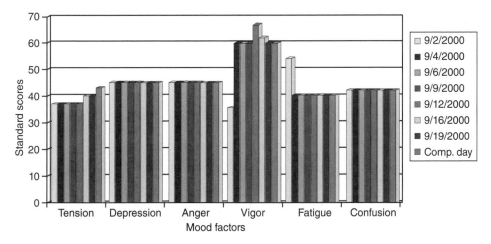

Figure 5.6   Mood profile of Sydney 2000 Olympic target-shooting champion Richard Faulds.

Exercise 5.1
Brunel Mood Scale (BRUMS)

Following is a list of words that describe feelings. Read each one carefully. Then check the answer that best describes *how you feel right now*. Make sure you respond to every word.

Mood items	Not at all	A little	Moderately	Quite a bit	Extremely
1. Panicky	0	1	2	3	4
2. Lively	0	1	2	3	4
3. Confused	0	1	2	3	4
4. Worn out	0	1	2	3	4
5. Depressed	0	1	2	3	4
6. Downhearted	0	1	2	3	4
7. Annoyed	0	1	2	3	4
8. Exhausted	0	1	2	3	4
9. Mixed up	0	1	2	3	4
10. Sleepy	0	1	2	3	4
11. Bitter	0	1	2	3	4
12. Unhappy	0	1	2	3	4
13. Anxious	0	1	2	3	4
14. Worried	0	1	2	3	4
15. Energetic	0	1	2	3	4
16. Miserable	0	1	2	3	4
17. Muddled	0	1	2	3	4
18. Nervous	0	1	2	3	4
19. Angry	0	1	2	3	4
20. Active	0	1	2	3	4
21. Tired	0	1	2	3	4
22. Bad tempered	0	1	2	3	4
23. Alert	0	1	2	3	4
24. Uncertain	0	1	2	3	4

Scoring the BRUMS:

Add items 1, 13, 14, and 18 for a Tension score.

Add items 5, 6, 12, and 16 for a Depression score.

Add items 7, 11, 19, and 22 for an Anger score.

Add items 2, 15, 20, and 23 for a Vigor score.

Add items 4, 8, 10, and 21 for a Fatigue score.

Add items 3, 9, 17, and 24 for a Confusion score.

From C.I. Karageorghis and P.C. Terry, 2011, *Inside sport psychology* (Champaign, IL: Human Kinetics). © 2003 Peter C. Terry and Andrew M. Lane.

How to Interpret a Mood Profile

The best way to interpret your score is to turn the raw scores you obtained in exercise 5.1 into what are known as standard scores, which have an average score of 50 and reflect how a large group of athletes responded to the BRUMS when asked, "How do you feel right now?" A standard score can be interpreted a bit like a percentage score. Read across from your raw score to the standard score. For example, a raw score of 5 for tension equates to a standard score of 50, a raw score of 4 for depression equates to a standard score of 62, and so on (see table 5.1).

Table 5.1 Brunel Mood Scale (BRUMS)—Standard Scores for Adult Athletes

	Tension	Depression	Anger	Vigor	Fatigue	Confusion
0	38	45	45	28	40	43
1	40	49	48	31	43	46
2	43	53	52	34	46	50
3	45	57	55	36	48	53
4	48	62	58	39	51	57
5	50	66	62	42	53	60
6	53	70	65	44	56	64
7	56	75	68	47	59	67
8	58	79	72	50	61	71
9	61	83	75	52	64	75
10	63	88	78	55	67	78
11	66	92	82	57	69	82
12	68	96	85	60	72	85
13	71	100	88	63	74	89
14	73	100	92	65	77	92
15	76	100	95	68	80	96
16	79	100	98	71	82	99

Write down your standard score for each mood factor here:

Tension	_____	Vigor	_____
Depression	_____	Fatigue	_____
Anger	_____	Confusion	_____

From these standard scores you can plot your mood profile on the graph in figure 5.7 on page 128 (remember to make photocopies so that you can use it over and over). If you recall, positive mood is associated with high vigor (standard score > 50) and low tension, depression, anger, fatigue, and confusion (standard score < 50). Of particular concern would be if your vigor score was low and your depression score was quite high. Remember that depressed mood plays a pivotal role in determining the effects of other negative mood factors on performance.

Whatever your profile looks like, the important thing is that you begin to monitor your mood on a regular basis—say, once a week—so that you can establish the profile

Mood profile of: _____ Date: _____ Time: _____

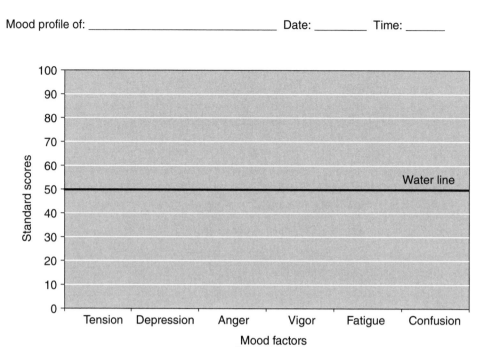

Figure 5.7 BRUMS profile sheet.

From C.I. Karageorghis and P.C. Terry, 2011, *Inside sport psychology* (Champaign, IL: Human Kinetics).

associated with your best performances in training and competition. Try to complete your profile at the same time of day on the same day of the week. This will control for some of the normal fluctuations in mood and should make comparisons from week to week more meaningful. To attain an optimal mindset, you will need to either maintain a preexisting mood or adjust your mood.

Gender Differences

Research has identified general differences between the moods and emotional responses of men and women. Women experience negative moods about twice as often as men and are more prone to experiencing prolonged bouts of negative mood. This is, of course, a broad generalization, and there are very many temperamental males! Furthermore, research has shown that these stereotypical gender differences are less evident in sport, where males and females tend to report similar moods.

Explanations given for the greater incidence of negative mood and emotions among women include socially acquired negative self-images (e.g., feeling fat as a result of media images of very thin women), the menstrual cycle, and a tendency for women to become submerged in negative thoughts and feelings. Some coping strategies that women use to regulate their mood include socializing, talking about or expressing their feelings, and engaging in self-nurturing activities (e.g., beauty treatments, grooming, shopping). By way of contrast, men tend to regulate their moods by isolating themselves socially and engaging in diversionary activities that require either concentration or skill (e.g., working on a car engine).

MOOD MANAGEMENT TECHNIQUES

Athletes usually have a general awareness of their moods and develop self-regulation strategies. Mostly this occurs intuitively, but we advocate a more systematic strategy. Quite often our role as sport psychology consultants has been to monitor and help direct this naturally occurring process to help promote superior performance. With a little bit of knowledge about how to change or maintain mood in a structured way, you can reach an optimal mindset with greater certainty. Consider the following:

- A profile comprising high vigor and low tension, depression, anger, fatigue, and confusion is most likely to be associated with superior performance.
- The presence of moderate tension and anger prior to competition coupled with high vigor and low depression, fatigue, and confusion can also aid performance. (This is particularly true in contact or combative sports such as American football and karate. Tension and anger are of less benefit in sports that require fine muscular control such as archery and snooker.)
- If you consistently exhibit a particular mood profile prior to your best performances, the reproduction of this profile is likely to result in superior performance.

Athletes use a wide array of mood-regulating strategies, some of which are very common and some of which border on the bizarre. Among the more bizarre is the public display of shadow boxing used by Jamaican sprinter Aleen Bailey prior to big races. Bailey does this because she associates punching the air with the aggression she wishes to channel into the race. Equally bizarre but just as effective is the hand clasp and quarter-squat position adopted by England rugby star Jonny Wilkinson prior to taking a place kick.

Effective Mood Regulation Strategies for Various Mood Dimensions on page 130 lists strategies relating to each mood dimension. Be sure to use the BRUMS to monitor your mood both before and after you try out these strategies so that you can assess just how effective they are.

Leo Mason/Actionplus/Icon SMI

England rugby star Jonny Wilkinson in his characteristic hand-clasp position prior to taking a place kick.

Effective Mood Regulation Strategies for Various Mood Dimensions

Management of Tension
- Use relaxation techniques.
- Use sport-related imagery.
- Engage in physical activity, such as stretching or jogging.
- Follow precompetition rituals or superstitions.

Management of Depression
- Deal with the cause of the feelings.
- Talk to someone about the feelings.
- Put the feelings into perspective.
- Seek physical affection.

Management of Anger
- Use relaxation techniques.
- Spend time alone.
- Put the feelings into perspective.
- Avoid the cause, or trigger, of the feelings.

Management of Vigor
- Engage in physical activity.
- Use sport-related imagery.
- Listen to fast, upbeat music.
- Focus on competition strategies.

Management of Fatigue
- Use relaxation techniques.
- Take a shower.
- Rest, take a nap, or sleep.
- Have a massage.

Management of Confusion
- Focus on competition strategies.
- Engage in positive thinking.
- Deal with the cause of the feelings.
- Talk to someone about the feelings.

Based on a study by the authors with a sample of 195 athletes. Data from P.C. Terry, S.L. Dinsdale, C.I. Karageorghis, and A.M. Lane, 2006. "Use and perceived effectiveness of pre-cometition mood regulation strategies among athletes." In M. Katsikitis (ed.), Psychology bridging the Tasman: Science, culture and practice—Proceedings of the 2006 Joint Conference of the Australian Psychological Society and the New Zealand Psychological Society (pp. 420-424). Melbourne, VIC: Australian Psychological Society.

Mood and Food

In recent years, a wealth of scientific evidence has emerged to support the long-held belief in a strong link between mood and food. For example, we now have a better idea of why people who are feeling low or depressed crave sweet carbohydrate- and fat-rich foods such as cakes and cookies. The reason is that the consumption of such foods has an almost immediate mood-enhancing effect, particularly among sufferers of seasonal affective disorder and women in the premenstrual phase of their cycle. Nonetheless, the consumption of such "comfort foods" among the general population is coming under fire from nutrition scientists, who suggest that although there is indeed a short-term gain, the long-term effects may be harmful.

In sport, the maxim "You are what you eat" is a central consideration in planning what to eat. The types of food you consume, the way these foods are prepared, and the timing of meals can have a profound effect on the quality of your training and how you feel generally.

As university lecturers, every year around late October or early November, we notice a wave of illness, absence, and general underperformance (mental and physical) among first-year undergraduate students (freshmen). The most likely cause is that, by this point in the academic year, the students have endured a sustained period of poor dietary habits, having been away from home for the first time and forced to fend for themselves. Typically, students skip meals during the day (often taking breakfast in a rush to get to morning classes) and binge on take-out meals and junk food late at night. They also drink excessive amounts of alcohol, often because of peer group influences, which leaves them feeling hungover and dehydrated the next day.

Our intention in this section is not to give sample diets or engage in a full discussion of sport nutrition (there are many texts on nutrition for athletes such as *Nancy Clark's Sports Nutrition Guidebook Fourth Edition,* which we often recommend to athletes); rather, we wish to provide some basic principles. When we give seminars for elite athletes and their coaches, participants often ask us about the relationship between what they eat and how they feel. Also, they want to know how to manage their food consumption most effectively.

First, you need to organize meals appropriately and plan well ahead so you are not forced to make bad choices owing to poor time management. The most important meal of the day is breakfast. A nutritious breakfast will set you up for the day and provide the sustenance you need for work, study, and training or competition.

Breakfast should include carbohydrates such as whole wheat toast with honey, cereal with skim or part-skim milk, fresh fruit (grapefruit, bananas, oranges, and strawberries are particularly good choices), fruit juice, and a cup of tea or coffee. Carbohydrates are the main energy source for the brain and working muscles and provide a sense of wellbeing. The fiber in cereal and fruit will help to regulate your digestive system and give you a sense of vitality. The caffeine in a cup of tea or coffee will stimulate your brain and make you feel more alert and awake. The protein requirement of breakfast can be met by options such as natural yogurt, tofu, oats, beans, or eggs.

Lunch should also be a relatively large meal. Evidence suggests that athletes should consume most of their protein at lunchtime rather than at supper, because the body will be able to use it more effectively. Foods such as steamed or poached fish, grilled chicken or turkey, grilled lean meat combined with legumes, beets, carrots, broccoli, and fresh salads are ideal. Among the so-called "superfoods" (in terms of mood regulation) is the avocado, which calms the nerves, reduces tension, and counteracts fatigue.

The first author conducted a small study for a BBC TV science program in which six sets of twins were divided into two groups, with one twin fed a "superfoods" diet and the other a regular healthy diet. The superfoods included blueberries, goji berries, salmon, spinach, walnuts, and spirulina. Mood was assessed at the beginning and end of the two-week study. Although there were no significant mood differences between the two groups, both diets resulted in lower scores for tension when compared with preintervention measurements.

A protein-rich meal, which many athletes prefer, also leads to the production of the brain chemicals dopamine and norepinephrine. These agents have been shown to guard against depressive symptoms and enhance alertness and vigor. Athletes—in particular, strength and power athletes such as discus throwers and weightlifters—have a tendency to overconsume protein. The most recent evidence suggests that athletes engaged in hard anaerobic training should consume between 1.2 and 1.5 grams of protein per kilogram of body weight per day.

Therefore, an athlete in serious training who weighs 176 pounds (80 kg) would need to eat the surprisingly large amount of five cans of tuna (7 oz, or 200 grams, each) or three medium-sized chicken breasts through the course of the day to satisfy his protein needs. It is best to spread protein consumption through the course of the day because there is a limit to the amount of protein that can be digested from a single serving. This approach also prevents *muscle catabolism,* which is when the muscle feeds on its own protein.

Evening meals should comprise primarily carbohydrates such as whole grain pasta, rice, potatoes, and other starchy foods. These carbohydrates should be combined with fresh vegetables, a salad, or both. Carbohydrates assist the release of the brain chemical serotonin, which helps in regulating sleep patterns and pain tolerance as well as enhancing mood.

Between meals there is often a temptation to snack on unhealthy foods such as sweets and chocolate. Part of good dietary organization involves carrying healthy snacks such as fresh or dried fruit, whole grain sandwiches, cereal bars, rice cakes, and energy bars. These give a mini energy boost and help you to remain focused on the task at hand. See page 133 for a list of "mood foods" and their effects.

Fat is a source of stored energy that is burned mostly during low-level activity (e.g., walking). Therefore, limit fat intake to no more than about 10 percent of your overall energy intake and attempt to consume only healthy fats (e.g., olive oil, oily fish, nuts). Excess fat intake can leave you feeling bloated and sluggish while also reducing your ability to concentrate. Approximately 65 percent of your energy intake should come from carbohydrate, and the remaining 25 percent should come from protein. However, if you are a strength or power athlete, you should derive closer to 30 percent of your required energy from protein owing to its role in the growth and repair of muscle tissue.

Research shows that a high-carbohydrate meal increases an amino acid called tryptophan. Amino acids are the building blocks of protein, and there are 20 of them. The increase in tryptophan results in more serotonin being produced, which makes

Mood Foods

Dark chocolate: Elation

Chamomile, bread, and pasta: Calmness and relaxation

Salmon, mackerel, tuna, sardines: Increased alertness and vigor

Leafy green vegetables, fortified cereals: Reduced depression

Oatmeal and low-GI (glycemic index) rice: Greater mood stability and more positive mood

Fish, chicken: Alertness

Coffee, ginseng tea: Stimulation

Bananas, leafy greens, and almonds: Increased vigor

All protein sources, grains, and nuts: Lowered anxiety and irritability

Dark, leafy greens, avocados, yogurt, tuna, and milk: Improved positive mood

you feel sleepy. A high-protein meal has directly the opposite effect: it decreases levels of tryptophan so less serotonin is produced. Therefore, if you want to feel alert in the afternoon, you should eat a high-protein meal for lunch. If you want to feel sleepy in the evening, you should eat a high-carbohydrate meal.

We suggest that you avoid eating too many spicy foods (e.g., containing onion, garlic, high salt content) because these can cause restlessness and mild tension. The same holds for caffeinated tea, coffee, and soft drinks. Eat at regular times and slowly, taking care to chew your food thoroughly; this will prevent you from overeating and then feeling bloated or lethargic. Also, do not eat more than five different foods in one meal because complex mixtures hinder digestion. Finally, if you want to change your diet to make it healthier, do so gradually over a period of a few weeks.

Mood Music

Chapter 8 is devoted to the use of music in sport and exercise. In this section we focus briefly on ways you can use music specifically to change or maintain your mood. Research we've conducted shows that music is one of the most popular and effective mood regulation strategies used by athletes. One reason it is so popular for mood regulation is that it is easy to use. Playlists can be personalized using MP3 technology, and we are conditioned from a young age to respond to music in certain ways. Such conditioning occurs through popular media such as radio, film, the Internet, and television.

To use music effectively, first decide the precise mood you want to achieve, either individually or as a team. We see mood-regulating music as falling into three general categories. If you want to increase vigor, loud, upbeat music with inspirational lyrics tends to work best. If you want to increase aggression also, then play music associated with a heroic character or a violent film. For example, Australian tennis player Lleyton Hewitt gets pumped up for big matches by listening to the boxing anthem "Eye Of The Tiger" from the Rocky film series. He is known to have watched all five Rocky films hundreds of times and claims that the Rocky music gives him a huge adrenaline rush.

The second type of music for regulating mood is soft, slow music, which is calming and can keep you from expending too much psychological energy. A music tempo below 100 beats per minute is ideal for this purpose, as are the sounds of nature (e.g., a running stream, birdsong, waves breaking). Ballads generally have a calming effect, as does slow classical music such as Samuel Barber's *Adagio for Strings*, the second movement (Andante) of Mozart's "Eine Kleine Nachtmusik," and Brahms' Lullaby. The 2000 Olympic super-heavyweight boxing champion Audley Harrison famously used Japanese classical music to keep himself from bubbling over prior to his fights as he progressed through the qualification rounds.

The third type of music for regulating mood has a slow tempo and either inspirational lyrics (e.g., Whitney Houston's "One Moment In Time") or motivational associations (e.g., Vangelis' "Chariots Of Fire"). The slow tempo will keep your body relaxed and relieve muscular tension, while the inspirational lyrics or extramusical associations will keep your mind focused on the task at hand and promote feelings of optimism and wellbeing.

If you have a tendency to suffer from excessive tension, anger, or frustration prior to competition, slow but inspirational music may be very helpful. Such music is a particularly good choice when traveling to a competition or to conserve energy between rounds. Some athletes make very unusual choices for their preevent routines, but these can be very effective owing to the associations the music conjures (see England Rugby Team Takes a Gamble With Music).

Music is one of the best ways to change or maintain mood because a particular piece can really encapsulate a specific mood. A piece of music can also encapsulate a particular mindset, as was the case for the England rugby team at the 2007 World Cup. The guiding principles are that the music should match your personal preferences, the characteristics of the music should match your target mood or emotion, and the associations that the music carries should inspire superior performance.

Musical Choices of Two British Double Olympic Gold Medalists

Double Olympic rowing gold medalist James Cracknell used an album by the Red Hot Chili Peppers titled *Blood Sugar Sex Magik* to optimize the arousal and aggression components of mood while at the same time shutting out potential distractions. Fellow double Olympic gold medalist Kelly Holmes, who competed in middle-distance events on the track, used Alicia Keys' music as the backdrop to her preparation for the 2004 Athens Olympic Games. The music soothed the anxiety she had relating to injuries that had dogged her for much of her career. It also gave her energy and drive that she was able to channel into her training. Holmes claimed that the soulful lyrics of Keys' music had a particularly potent effect on her emotional state.

England Rugby Team Takes a Gamble With Music

During the 2007 Rugby World Cup in France, England's rugby players sang Kenny Rogers' song "The Gambler" to boost team morale after prop Matt Stevens began strumming it on his guitar in their hotel lounge. The song became a staple part of the squad's social gatherings and their prematch buildup as they made their unexpected progress through the tournament into the final. Martin Corry, the England captain, told reporters: "Given where we are as a team, the lyrics seem to have struck a chord with us." He highlighted the chorus: "You've got to know when to hold 'em, know when to fold 'em, know when to walk away and know when to run." Centre Mike Catt revealed that the song had become the squad's lucky charm. The players clearly identified with its underlying message: It's not the hand you have, but the way you play it.

Exercise Type

The use of exercise to regulate mood has generated a great deal of scientific research. The findings suggest that exercise can bring about positive short-term changes in mood. These changes are most often attributed to mood-enhancing agents such as endorphins and anandamide that are released into the bloodstream. You may think it slightly strange to include exercise as a mood regulation strategy, given the high volume of exercise or training that athletes engage in almost daily. However, brief adjustments in the type and intensity of exercise can bring about positive changes in mood that may filter through to improve performance. Changes made to exercise or training regimes can have a particularly potent effect in the days leading up to competition.

Among the general population it is widely accepted that regular physical activity helps to promote mental health and positive mood states. Among athletic populations, particularly endurance athletes, the sheer volume of physical activity can routinely cause high fatigue and low vigor. A prolonged experience of this combination can also bring about symptoms of depressed mood with an associated negative impact on performance.

We often use mood profiles to monitor the impact of training load on athletes' mental health. During heavy periods of training, we fully expect to see some disruption in mood. Sometimes the disruption is evident a week or even a few days prior to a major championship. In such cases, we might intervene by suggesting that an athlete's training load be reduced slightly. On occasion the change is as subtle as a change of running surface—say, from tarmac to grass. We continue to monitor mood to ensure that the reduction in training load brings about the desired effect.

You can monitor your mood in the same way using the BRUMS to help you taper off for important competitions. Psychological peaking should occur in parallel with physical peaking as part of the periodization process. Quite often athletes and coaches overlook psychological peaking: The body is primed to perform optimally, but the athlete's mood is subdued by the volume of training leading up to the event. This results in an ineffective partnership between mind and body. For an effective union to exist, you should feel energized and entirely free of other distractions that might interfere with your mental preparation.

Research suggests that the best type of exercise for mood enhancement involves rhythmic and abdominal breathing. Good examples include Pilates, tai chi, and yoga as well as a whole range of aerobic activities such as jogging, swimming, cycling, and rowing. As a result of their highly repetitive nature, aerobic activities promote self-reflection and creative thinking, which in turn can lift mood. Ideally, the exercise should not have a competitive element. Further, low- to moderate-intensity exercise has greater mood-enhancing properties than high-intensity exercise. Athletes who train at very high intensities, such as weightlifters, sprinters, and throwers, should include some gentler bouts of exercise in their weekly routines. Such lighter work also helps the process of building up to a peak in intensity or recovering effectively from such a peak.

Rest and Recuperation

One of most common mood interventions that we prescribe in our work with athletes is a period of rest or abstinence from a particular activity. Athletes sometimes report disturbed mood over a prolonged period. This can result from conditions such as glandular fever, overtraining, or unexplained underperformance syndrome. A radical approach is required in dealing with such cases. Often we prescribe a period of complete rest followed by very low-intensity training accompanied by daily mood monitoring until the athlete begins to display positive mood for at least two weeks. At this point, we increase the training volume gradually, day by day, until the athlete reaches normal training intensity and continues to report positive mood.

At the end of a competitive season, athletes often experience disturbed moods. This is caused by fatigue, prolonged competitive stress, and staleness. The prescription in such cases is usually a one- to two-week complete break followed by a three- to five-week period of active recovery. This involves participating in sports or activities that do not inflict the same physical demands as the regular discipline.

For example, during recuperation, track and field athletes may enjoy playing basketball, Australian Rules footballers such as Geelong's Cameron Ling might try their hand at surfing, and tennis players may like to dip into the pool. This approach maintains basic fitness while at the same time recharging the batteries and lifting mood in preparation for the period of off-season heavy training that lies ahead. The change works because of the distraction of trying out a new, enjoyable activity or one that is not part of the normal daily routine. Research shows that as long as people enjoy exercise or training, it is likely to produce a positive mood profile.

> *Surfing is a good escape from footy where you can have your mind on something else and it's a good recovery from footy as well. I always like to keep busy outside of footy and have something else to do.*
>
> —Cameron Ling, Australian Football League player

Finally, to overcome the day-to-day rigors of hard training and competition, you might want to try an alternative therapy on your rest day. Particularly effective therapies for mood enhancement include sports massage, aromatherapy, and reflexology. In addition, the occasional use of a spa, sauna, or steam room can leave you (or your coach) feeling zestful.

Pep Talks and Team Banter

Psychologists have taken increasing interest in what coaches and team managers say to their athletes just before competition and during breaks in the action (e.g., timeouts) to enhance player mood or team morale. They are also interested in the effects of interactions between coaches and athletes or among athletes—so-called banter—after the game in the changing room or in the bar.

The speech that coaches, team managers, or captains deliver pregame is known as a *pep talk*. It is usually designed to unite the team, spell out the exact nature of the task at hand, recognize individual and collective strengths, and raise spirits. Having given and witnessed many pep talks, we believe that leaders should prepare thoroughly for them.

At worst, we have seen coaches scream expletives at the players and denigrate them without providing any real sense of direction. At best, we have observed coaches use fluid and passionate oratory to articulate a clear vision of what was required. In such cases, the players hang on the coach's every word; they are inspired to give their all and enthused by the impending challenge. The pep talk has been portrayed many times by Hollywood; one of the most noteworthy examples was delivered by Al Pacino as hard-line coach Tony D'Amato in the gridiron movie *Any Given Sunday* (see page 138 for a brief extract of this classic speech).

The pep talk is also an important element in defining the motivational climate that exists within a team. In chapter 2 you learned that a performance climate is one in which winning and social comparison are emphasized, whereas a mastery climate is one in which self-referenced goals and feelings of competence are emphasized. Research shows that positive mood is generally associated with a mastery climate. This is particularly so in youth sports where too much competition too early can lead to disillusionment and burnout. In professional or elite sports, however, a strong emphasis on both performance and mastery is required.

The discussions that take place after the match are also important in determining athletes' moods and the motivation they have for subsequent competitions. Coaches and team managers should emphasize the things players did well and the individual contributions they made in the collective endeavor. The period immediately after a match is not the time for recriminations and tongue-lashings. Reflections can be made on the lessons learned at this time; however, these need to be positive.

Corrective feedback is best given a few days later, after the emotion of the game has dissipated; even then it should be sandwiched between positive comments. This approach makes it easy for athletes to internalize the feedback, because it doesn't threaten their self-esteem or cause undue mood disturbance. For example, "Jack, you defended brilliantly on Saturday. Just make sure that you remember to support Leighton when he makes those breaks through the center, and keep those crosses flying in—you showed some pinpoint accuracy!"

Self-Talk

Many athletes create or change their moods by controlling their thoughts through self-talk. This is subtly distinct from the positive self-talk discussed in chapter 3. The internal dialogue involved in self-talk can take place silently or out loud. You can use it to give yourself encouragement and instructions as well as to interpret what you

Extract of Inspirational Speech
From *Any Given Sunday*

We are in hell right now,

. . . . we can fight our way back into the light.

We can climb out of hell.

One inch at a time.

. . . . You know when you get old in life

things get taken from you.

That's, that's part of life.

But, you only learn that when you start losing stuff.

You find out that life is just a game of inches.

So is football.

Because in either game, life or football,

the margin for error is so small.

I mean, one half step too late or too early,

you don't quite make it.

One half second too slow or too fast,

and you don't quite catch it.

The inches we need are everywhere around us.

They are in every break of the game,

every minute, every second.

. . . when we add up all those inches

that's going to make the difference

between WINNING and LOSING

between LIVING and DYING.

I'll tell you this, in any fight

it is the guy who is willing to die

who is going to win that inch.

And I know, if I am going to have any life anymore,

it is because I am still willing to fight and die for that inch

because that is what LIVING is.

The six inches in front of your face.

are feeling or perceiving. A big advantage of using self-talk is that it helps you remain focused on the present and not to drift (this is also explained in chapter 6; see Cue Words on page 162).

To use self-talk to create a mood, you need to come up with words and phrases that capture the very essence of the mindset you seek. For example, golfers often use swing words such as *fluid* and *smooth* that embody the desired feeling during their swing. Tennis players like to use power words such as *smash* and *blast* or short phrases such as *Hit through the ball* and *Keep your feet moving* to help them maintain correct form.

Sometimes self-talk has to change during the event. For instance, in the initial stages of a marathon, you will want to use self-talk that encourages consistent pace and conservation of energy: *Hold the tempo* and *Bide your time.* In the middle stages, phrases that promote persistence and tuning in to the body are required: *Stay focused* and *Keep breathing smoothly.* Toward the end of the marathon, particularly in a tight finish, speed and pain dissociation become important: *Drive the elbows back* and *Feel the crowd urging you on.*

To use self-talk to change your mood, you need to appraise your current mood and then find an appropriate word or phrase to take you into your optimal mood. Often this is done either to calm yourself if you are feeling tense or aggressive or to overcome sluggishness and raise your energy level. Table 5.2 provides some phrases we have used to bring about such changes in mood. Each word or phrase you use should have an emotional quality that is closely associated with the desired change in mindset. Use self-talk repeatedly in training so that it becomes automatic in competition.

Table 5.2   Examples of Self-Talk Used by Athletes to Change Mood

Reduce tension	Control aggression	Reduce sluggishness	Increase energy levels
Stay calm	Channel the force	Lift yourself up	Let's get revved
Cool as a cucumber	Keep your head	Wake up now	Pump it up
Breathe deeply	Use it, don't lose it	Move and groove	Come on now
Take a chill pill	Take control	Eyes wide open	Take it to them
Loose as a goose	Let *them* make the mistakes	Full of pep	Ready for it

Socializing

The human species depends on interaction for its survival. We all have a basic psychological need for affiliation, communication, and recognition. If you are immersed in the sport world, the majority of your friends, contacts, and acquaintances are likely in the sporting environment. Moreover, your social activities likely revolve around your sporting life.

Socializing in the sport world is fine, but only to a point. Fellow athletes obviously share your interest in sport, enjoy discussing common experiences, and can show empathy, which means they can see things from your perspective. They are also useful sounding boards when you want to talk through sport-specific problems that may be having a negative impact on your mood. However, there is also a distinct downside to restricting your social activities to the sport world.

Some sports have a culture of "lifestyle negative behaviors" (stereotypically, contact team sports). These may take the form of heavy alcohol consumption and drinking games, overt aggression toward other groups, excessive consumption of junk food, and in some instances drug abuse and unsociable antics. Such behaviors are particularly common during away trips and tours. Clearly, many of these aspects of the social side of sport have a harmful impact on mood and performance. Arguably the most prevalent lifestyle negative behavior in sport is the excessive consumption of alcohol, which is particularly harmful during the period leading up to competition.

Socializing with teammates can have a positive impact on mood by allowing you to dissociate from the stresses and strains of your busy training and competition schedules. It recharges your batteries. A social event also gives you a chance to share concerns and talk through them. As the old adage goes, "A problem shared is a problem halved." We explained earlier that this mood regulation strategy is particularly favored by women. When teams socialize, the cohesion within the team is often strengthened, which later reflects in performance on the field. Furthermore, if tensions exist between individual players, these can be smoothed over in a social context, particularly with some skillful mediation from a team coach or manager.

We suggest that you pursue a social life both within and outside of the sport world. Sporting pals will certainly understand what makes you tick and be able to share common experiences and anecdotes, but you also need friends outside of sport who can give you objective opinions and keep you in touch with other aspects of life. In

Roberto: American Football Player Forced to Drink

Roberto is a defensive lineman playing for a small college in South Carolina, USA. He was seriously considering quitting football because the social activities that followed games were entirely at odds with his moral and religious views. The team tradition entails drinking to a state of oblivion. The team actively espouses a philosophy of "Win or lose on the booze," and team management chooses to turn a blind eye. The social activities usually culminate in drinking games in which players force beer down their gullets until they projectile vomit. At that point, there are great guffaws of laughter and everybody cheers.

When Roberto refused to continue to take part in these games, he felt alienated by his teammates. Not knowing how to cope with this, he paid a visit to the college counselor to talk the problem through. She teased out that Roberto still had a passion for football but simply could not cope with some of the social aspects of the game. Together they devised a strategy whereby the local bar staff were informed that whenever Roberto ordered a beer or someone ordered for him, they would serve him the nonalcoholic variety. Further, to avoid the drinking games, Roberto decided to speak to the head coach to explain that they caused him nausea, which prevented him from attending classes or practice the next day. An effective compromise was reached, and Roberto's enthusiasm for the sport was rekindled.

years to come, when you retire from competition, unless you have friends outside the domain of sport, you may find the transition very difficult. A careful balance is required in using social activities to regulate mood.

Variety in Preparation

Variety is the spice of a good physical and mental preparation program. Highly repetitive routines often result in boredom, staleness, and performance plateaus. There are many sound psychological and physiological reasons for maintaining variety in a training program. Most notably, variety refreshes the mind and provides new stimuli that challenge both mind and body. Variety is also a safeguard against burnout, which occurs when the sustained pursuit of sporting success causes chronic mental fatigue and reduced interest in the sport. The coach has an integral part to play in preventing burnout through effective scheduling and monitoring of athletes.

New challenges and alternative training venues will force you to make slight adjustments that promote development. For example, you might, on occasion, try altering the time of day at which you train. Research shows that mood is most positive in the early afternoon (although not immediately after lunch) and most negative early in the morning. So you could try training just after you wake up as a way to enhance mood, which might pose a considerable challenge if it's not something you do regularly.

Because a future competition may well be scheduled very early in the day, training in the morning would help you prepare for such a scenario. Similarly, you might conduct the occasional session quite late in the day when your mood begins to dip and you are forced to overcome the onset of mental fatigue. Learning to perform consistently through the daily peaks and troughs in mood will increase your mental toughness (see page 25 for a description of mental toughness).

Another good strategy is to have at least one training session a week away from your regular training venue. For track athletes, this might involve hill sprints in a local park or running over sand dunes. For basketball players, this could involve going downtown to play some outdoor three-on-three or joining in the plyometric training of a long jumper or triple jumper at the local track. For swimmers, this might entail having a circuit training session in the local high school gym. Also, attendance at training camps in warmer climes or at altitude often has an extremely beneficial effect. A change is, as they say, as good as a rest.

The benefits of training in different climates and at different altitudes go beyond acclimating to extreme atmospheric conditions or high temperatures; rather, training camps remove you from the everyday hassles of life allowing you to focus exclusively on your preparation. When we accompany athletes to such camps, we tend to monitor mood on a daily basis. Any mood disturbance that we observe at the beginning of the camp has often disappeared by the end. Training camps prime you both mentally and physically and are best attended just before the start of a competitive season.

Finally, within sessions, change the order of the drills you perform fairly regularly (see also chapter 1), and vary the people you train with so you get used to regulating your mood in response to different personalities. Practice starting after both long and short warm-ups to emulate competition scenarios (see also the "what if" scenarios in chapter 7), and practice mood regulation strategies that you intend to employ in competition.

SUMMARY

This chapter described the nature of moods and emotions in sport using current approaches and a range of examples. Emotions merge to form a mood that can shape the way you respond to the world around you. The Brunel Mood Scale (BRUMS) provides a quick and convenient method of assessing and interpreting mood responses on a regular basis. There is a well-established relationship between mood and performance in sport: high vigor scores coupled with low negative mood factors are a good indication of a positive mindset.

An absence of symptoms of depressed mood coupled with moderate tension and anger can aid performance particularly in contact or combative sports such as rugby and karate. In such circumstances, the tension and anger are directed outwardly and geared toward the execution of skills. Symptoms of depressed mood, such as feeling unhappy, miserable, or downhearted, direct tension and anger inwardly and risk dramatically hindering performance.

Coaches and parents and guardians should bear in mind the significant gender differences in mood responses. Female athletes experiencing a negative mood may benefit from social support and the opportunity to express their thoughts and feelings, whereas male athletes often require more space and less intervention.

This chapter provides a range of mood regulation strategies, including consuming certain foods and food groups; exploiting the emotional qualities of music; reducing the frequency, intensity, or duration of training; resting and recuperating; engaging in self-talk to create specific mindsets; socializing; and maintaining variety in training to avoid staleness.

You now have practical strategies and psychological techniques to use to tune in to a mindset that is likely to bring about better and more consistent performance. This mindset will enable you to constantly push the boundaries of what you previously thought possible.

Concentration

If you can keep playing tennis when somebody is shooting a gun down the street, that's concentration.

—Serena Williams, highest career prize money winner of any female athlete in history

Concentration has been called the executive psychological skill because to some degree it controls all others. With appropriate levels of concentration, some of the negative reactions to competition described in chapter 4 can be prevented, dealt with effectively, or temporarily sidelined. Also, an athlete with unflinching concentration can sometimes wear down an opponent who has superior physical characteristics. Sportspeople who consistently display rock-solid concentration, such as 16-time grand slam winner Roger Federer and swimming superstar Michael Phelps, are much admired by the public.

Once in a while we hear a coach scream at a player, "Hold your composure" or "Stay focused." What exactly does this mean? Athletes often attribute a poor performance to a momentary lapse in concentration. In such cases, the entire sporting community listens sympathetically and gives a nod of recognition. Everybody has suffered a lapse of concentration at one time or other. This chapter is of equal use to athletes and coaches—some of the techniques included involve athletes helping themselves, while others can be initiated or directed by the coach.

Because we use the closely related terms *attention, concentration,* and *focus* repeatedly in this chapter, we begin by identifying the main distinctions among them. We use the term *attention* to refer to the withdrawal from some things to deal effectively with others. This is extracted from a longer definition dating back to 1890 and credited to William James. *Concentration* involves directing attention toward a specific goal, such as the intense gaze of the archer on the target before releasing the arrow. The term *focus* refers to a point on which attention is concentrated.

CONCENTRATION UNRAVELED

To explore the nature of concentration, consider a time at school when the teacher banged a hand loudly on the front desk while your classmates were chatting or fooling around. Most probably, the entire class immediately sat bolt upright with their eyes locked on the teacher. This demonstrates that we have the ability to change where we direct our concentration.

This example highlights more of a reflex, or involuntary focus, which comes from the unexpected stimulus of the sound of the bang on the desk. Good students can consciously manipulate their concentration toward a range of important tasks that will enhance their learning. Good athletes strive to do the same.

In sport, concentration occurs when thoughts and senses are focused totally on an object, player, activity, or set of circumstances to the exclusion of everything else. Concentration is dynamic, which means that it is constantly shifting from one set of stimuli to another. To concentrate effectively requires that attention remain fixed on the right thing at the right time.

Successful athletes are often said to have a great eye or superior vision, which helps them anticipate what is going to happen on the field of play and gives them more time to react appropriately. A loss of concentration occurs when the focus of attention becomes divided or when it shifts to something that is irrelevant or peripheral to the task at hand.

Appropriate concentration cannot be forced. *Trying* to concentrate is a paradox, because it is not actually concentrating at all. Concentration involves passive avoidance of distraction by the irrelevant to focus on the relevant. This is a skill that can be learned in the same way as learning to kick a ball through the uprights or perform a backflip. Concentration skills are improved by either decreasing attention to irrelevant stimuli such as crowd noise or taunting from an opponent or by increasing attention to relevant stimuli. The learning process results in what psychologists call selective awareness, which involves a task-appropriate focus (focusing exclusively on the execution of the skills involved).

When working with athletes—and in particular, young athletes—we often teach them about the three dimensions of attention: selectivity, direction, and width. To become a master of concentration, you must understand how it works and how it applies specifically to your sport.

Selectivity

The first dimension of attention, selectivity, involves what you choose to focus on. The central nervous system is bombarded with an enormous quantity of sensory information—people's voices, environmental conditions, smells, sights, internal feelings, and so on—so much so that you cannot process it all. You have become quite adept at filtering out most of this information so that your concentration capacity is devoted to the most relevant sensory information. Of course, this is not always a conscious process. For example, when daydreaming, your entire concentration capacity may be filled with internal thoughts so that you notice almost nothing of what is going on around you.

Tiger Woods at the U.S. Masters

At the 2005 U.S. Masters in Augusta, Georgia, Tiger Woods was in a state of emotional turmoil. His father Earl, the rock on which Woods' career was built, was desperately ill. He had just overcome heart surgery and was concurrently battling an aggressive cancer. Owing to a run of lackluster performances, Tiger had not won a major title in two and a half years. The golf pundits thought he had no chance of regaining the Masters' title that he had claimed during the peak of his powers in 1997, 2001, and 2002. They put this down to Tiger's firing of coach Butch Harmon in 2002 and hiring of Hank Haney, who forced him to play in an "unnatural way." Tiger battled on regardless and played some truly outstanding golf. However, the unflinching concentration that Tiger showed early in the tournament evaded him in the closing stages when he hit three consecutive bogies and squandered a four-shot advantage. Perhaps all the problems had finally begun to play on his mind. Nevertheless, his father had long since prepared him for any eventuality. Said Earl:

> I pulled every nasty, dirty, obnoxious trick on my son every week. I dropped a bag of bricks at the impact of his swing, I imitated a crow while he was stroking a putt. When he was ready to hit a shot, I'd toss a ball in front of him; I would stand in front of him and move as he was about to hit the ball. I played with his mind, and sometimes he got so angry he would stop his club on the downward swing and glare at me. Then, one day, instead of glaring, he smiled. I knew then he had learned and he would be a great, mentally strong golfer.

So when Chris DiMarco pulled the championship level at the final hole and Tiger was forced into a dramatic play-off, he was able to concentrate entirely on the task at hand to clinch a memorable victory.

Perhaps even more remarkable was the feat of concentration that Tiger demonstrated at the 2008 U.S. Open. He was battling a severe knee injury in the aftermath of a two-month layoff due to an arthroscopy and simultaneously incurred a double stress fracture of his left tibia. Tiger limped and grimaced his way around the course, with former U.S. Open champion Retief Goosen accusing him of "putting it on." Subsequently, Tiger needed almost a year off to get over the injury, but when it mattered, he produced a winning performance in a tightly fought play-off.

A slip in concentration is often caused by unconsciously focusing on the wrong things. The competing sensory input sometimes forces a sort of bottleneck effect so that the brain is unable to process information quickly enough. This is very often when breakdowns in performance take place. This bottleneck effect is made even more acute when you are highly fatigued or your physiological arousal is high.

Although our sensory systems function in very complex ways, the underlying principle of selective awareness, which some performers have mastered and others struggle with, is a very simple one. Figure 6.1 on page 146 shows how sensory input competes for attention and outlines the process by which skills are then produced.

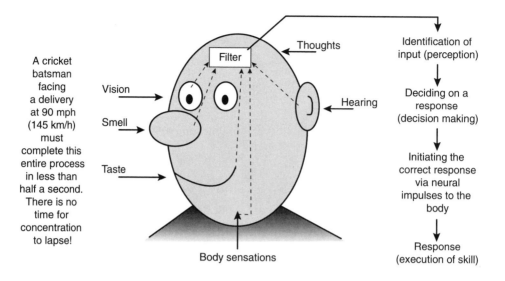

A cricket batsman facing a delivery at 90 mph (145 km/h) must complete this entire process in less than half a second. There is no time for concentration to lapse!

Vision

Smell

Taste

Filter

Thoughts

Hearing

Body sensations

Identification of input (perception)

↓

Deciding on a response (decision making)

↓

Initiating the correct response via neural impulses to the body

↓

Response (execution of skill)

Figure 6.1 How sensory input competes for attention.

If Ricky Ponting wasted his valuable concentration capacity attending to the noise or movement of the crowd, he would become less aware of the important details that aid successful batting. In a sport in which facing a 90 mph (145 km/h) delivery leaves less than half a second to identify sensory input, decide on which stroke to play, and

Superstar Batsman Ricky Ponting

Some sportspeople are very adept at homing in on the key elements of successful performance in their sport. For instance, when a star batsman such as Australian captain Ricky Ponting is at the crease, his concentration processes play a prime role. The blistering centuries he regularly produces are only possible through the effective synergy of several sensory systems: vision to perceive the telltale idiosyncrasies of the bowler; the speed, position, and swing of the ball; hearing any subtle changes of spin; and an acute sense of timing, which permits accurate positioning of the bat and body in unison.

AP Photo/Jon Super

Ricky Ponting's success as a batsman has much to do with his superior powers of concentration.

initiate the necessary bodily movements to produce the stroke, any inefficiency in concentration would prove disastrous. The actual skill of swinging the bat is relatively easy; it's the timing, which is largely perceptual, that separates cricket legends from also-rans.

During any sporting contest, an almost infinite variety of things compete for attention. Experience eventually teaches how to distinguish what is central to performance and what is best ignored, but this may take years. Athletes and their coaches can short-cut this learning process by spending a little time identifying those things that are indispensable to performance and those that are potential distractions. Coaches responsible for young athletes need to teach concentration drills while the athletes are in a state of physical fatigue and under time constraints, as a form of simulation training. We have designed exercise 6.1 (on page 148) to assist you in better directing your attention to the task at hand.

The following list includes the key details and distractions of a driver we helped prepare for the World Rally Championship. What key details and common distractions do you face in your sport?

Name: Marcus Pink

Key Details

1. Sound of the engine
2. The road ahead
3. Instructions from codriver
4. Line in and out of bends
5. Timing gear changes
6. Hand position on steering wheel
7. Maintaining speed
8. Staying in the here and now
9. Regulating my breathing
10. Minimal use of brakes

Sport: Rally Driver

Distractions

1. Cars behind me
2. On-course spectators
3. Surrounding landscape
4. Reporters between stages
5. What the sponsors are thinking
6. Past errors
7. Mind drifting to private life
8. What I will do with my winnings
9. Feeling hot and sweaty
10. Fear of taking a risk

Many things can happen to drag your attention from the relevant to the irrelevant. Excitement, frustration, anxiety, self-doubt, conflict, anger, and a host of other emotions can all cause attention to wander no matter how hard you try to guard against them. Inevitably, when attention is diverted away from the action, performance suffers. This is why learning how to overcome distractions is crucial.

Exercise 6.1
Importance of Task-Focused Attention

Imagine that you have been asked to walk the length of a wooden plank that is 5 inches wide (12.7 cm) and 20 feet long (6 m). The plank is positioned just 10 inches (25 cm) off the ground. You could probably do this quite comfortably again and again without ever falling off—even with your hands tied behind your back! Try this in your mind's eye.

Now, imagine completing the same task hands free but with the plank raised 50 feet (15 m) off the ground and positioned as a bridge between two buildings. There is no wind.

This may well paralyze you with fear, but the task is the same as before. There is absolutely no difference in the physical skill required, but the additional psychological skill required is considerable. To negotiate the 50-foot-high plank, you would need to block out thoughts of the height involved and the risk of falling, while controlling your emotions and focusing exclusively on the task at hand. In sport, the risks involved are usually far less severe than a 50-foot drop; however, your psychological reaction to even the most minor threat can be quite inhibiting. By focusing on mastering the task, you can overcome such inhibitions and perform with flair.

Direction and Width

In addition to selectivity, concentration has the dimensions of direction and width. At any given moment, attention can be directed either externally toward objects outside your body, such as this book, or internally on thoughts and feelings. Also, attention can have either a narrow focus (on a specific object or thought) or a broad focus (taking in the panoramic view from the top of a skyscraper).

The dimensions of direction and width are independent of each other, which means that there are four distinct concentration styles: broad-external, narrow-external, broad-internal, and narrow-internal. The easiest way to gain an understanding of these forms of concentration is to experience them. Exercise 6.2 will help you explore the various dimensions of attention. The switching of concentration that you will experience is explained in figure 6.2.

What you should notice from doing exercise 6.2 is that although your visual field did not change at all, the objects and thoughts to which you were giving your attention varied enormously. As figure 6.2 shows, you were initially concentrating on the picture in front of you, with your attention directed externally and narrowed to a specific object. Next you became aware of specific internal feelings in your upper back and shoulders. This was not a loss of concentration but rather a voluntary switch of concentration from a narrow-external focus to a narrow-internal focus.

As you began recalling a sporting victory, your attention was still fixed internally (this time on your thoughts rather than on your bodily feelings) but had broadened to consider many factors at once. In other words, you had switched to a broad-internal focus. You then returned your attention to external objects and tried to observe many things simultaneously. Here you had switched to a broad-external focus. Eventually,

Exercise 6.2
Exploring the Dimensions of Attention

Find a picture on a wall of a sport star or a sporting scene and position a chair a few yards away facing it. Sit comfortably in the chair and relax. Feel it absorbing your weight. Ask a friend to read these instructions to you slowly and clearly:

1. Study the picture closely. Notice the size, shape, color, and texture of all the objects in the picture. While staring at the picture, mentally list all the features you can see. Try to keep them all in your head at once. Now select a specific object that grabs your attention and stare intently at it. Spend some time studying this object.

2. Now, while you are still looking at the picture, shift your attention to the feeling in your upper back where it is in contact with the chair. Feel the pressure your back is exerting against the chair and any tension in your shoulders. Drop your shoulders and try to feel relaxed. Now sit more upright in the chair and relieve the pressure between your upper back and the chair.

3. Now, while still looking at the picture, imagine yourself in sporting action achieving a glorious victory. Decide which tactics brought you success, and spend some time reviewing yourself in action as if watching the entire scene on a large screen.

4. Now return your attention to what you can see in front of you. Keep your eyes on the picture, but try to notice everything around you in the whole of your visual field. Try to be aware of everything at once.

5. Now focus on the picture once more and look closely at the object that held your attention earlier. Notice every detail about that object until it is the only thing you can see and everything else has faded.

6. Now let that object fade from your attention too and slowly return to full awareness of your surroundings.

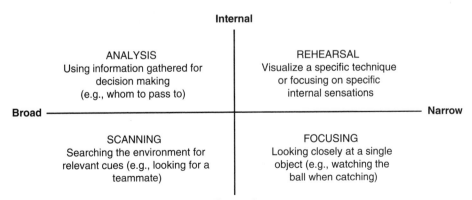

Figure 6.2 The direction and breadth dimensions of concentration.

Adapted, by permission of the American Psychological Association, from R.M. Nideffer, 1976, "Test of attentional and interpersonal style," *Journal of Personality and Social Psychology* 34(3): 394-404.

you narrowed your focus once more to a single external object, thereby returning to your original narrow-external focus.

As you can see, concentration processes are quite complex; it is not helpful to view concentration as something that simply comes and goes. The process of controlling the direction, width, and selectivity of attention lies at the very heart of all skilled action and is particularly vital to sport performance. If you find it difficult to concentrate for long periods of time, exercise 6.3 will help you develop the sort of discipline over concentration that will greatly benefit your sporting performance.

Exercise 6.3
Focusing and Refocusing: The Irresistible Flow

Look either at one of your favorite sport action photos or an object from your sport. If you choose a photo, pick out one of the most relevant details such as a particular player or a playing implement. Focus intently either on the object in the picture or the object in front of you. If any distracting thoughts enter your mind, patiently refocus your concentration by gently bringing your thoughts back to the relevant object. Try to imagine your thought processes as a wide, powerful, irresistible river where unwanted or random thoughts come floating along from time to time. Rather than fighting against the flow, which serves only to fix the unwanted thought in consciousness, go with the flow by refocusing on the object of interest while the unwanted thoughts drift away.

You should practice this for five minutes a day while charting your progress by timing how long you can retain the required focus. This exercise will prevent concentration-breaking thoughts from adversely affecting your performance. For the exercise to work at critical moments in which you suffer from lapses in concentration, you will need to practice it regularly.

CONCENTRATION ERRORS IN SPORT

Every sport skill has one type of concentration focus that aids performance and others that hinder it. For instance, if a basketball player taking a free throw is thinking about previously missed efforts instead of focusing on the ring of the basket, he will significantly increase his chance of missing again. This is because to swish the ball into the basket requires predominantly a narrow-external focus rather than a broad-internal one. Table 6.1 lists examples of the four types of concentration focus highlighted in figure 6.2 and problems associated with them. It also identifies the errors that cause them.

Table 6.1 Types of Concentration Focus and Typical Errors in Sport

Dimension and types of concentration	Common problems	Concentration error
Broad-external • Reading situations • Finding teammate to pass to • Noticing opponents' positions • Anticipating the action	• Failing to notice tactical ploys of opponents • Failing to notice a teammate in a good position • Ignoring environmental conditions when initiating a play • Missing opportunities • Hogging the ball	External focus is too narrow
Narrow-external • Focusing on a specific object • Focusing on a target when taking aim • Anticipating a sound (e.g., starter's gun)	• Mis-hitting, mis-shooting, mis-cueing, and simple errors • Failure to focus on the ball or target • Wasting time by focusing on things peripheral to performance • Getting distracted by sounds irrelevant to performance (e.g., taunts from a hostile crowd)	External focus is too broad
Broad-internal • Planning tactics or plays • Analyzing how the competition is going • Recalling set plays • Increasing or decreasing bodily anxiety	• Overanalyzing situations • Indecision in pressure situations • Considering consequences of an action • Thinking about the past or the future (i.e., not immersed in the here and now)	Inappropriate broad-internal focus
Narrow-internal • Noticing fine aspects of technique • Using cue words • Recognizing bodily tension • Controlling heart rate	• Recurring negative thoughts • Fixating on a particular thought or feeling and missing important things going on • Getting caught up in a mistake • Focusing on fatigue or a pain that could be ignored	Inappropriate narrow-internal focus

INDIVIDUAL DIFFERENCES IN CONCENTRATION

People differ greatly in the ways they process sensory information. Some innately focus on their own thoughts and feelings, whereas others are constantly distracted by the colors, images, and sounds around them. Some like to focus intently on the finest of details, and others are interested only in establishing the bigger picture. Some are able to focus on one specific stimulus like a hawk homing in on its prey, whereas for others attention flits from one point of interest to another, almost like channel surfing on a TV. Sport embraces all of these concentration styles in one way or other.

Some researchers believe that sportspeople have dominant concentration styles. For example, people involved in sports that involve aiming an implement at a target, such as shooting and archery, have a tendency to focus their attention narrowly and externally. At the same time, they are able to maintain total control over their bodies so that they can regulate their muscles and breathing appropriately. Contrastingly, people who play team sports such as rugby, soccer, and basketball are able to switch attentional focus from narrow to broad very effectively. They also have temporal and spatial awareness, which means that they can time their movements well and anticipate particular patterns of play.

© Icon Sports Media

Basketball players such as the Miami Heat shooting guard Dwayne Wade are able to switch attentional focus from narrow to broad very effectively.

Researchers have discovered some minor gender-related differences in concentration that warrant a brief mention. Women are generally better at multitasking, which may relate to the fact that they have a wider breadth of responsibilities in their everyday lives. Also, girls appear to be more adept at planning and articulating strategy than boys are, although these differences are not discernable during adulthood. Research on collegiate athletes revealed that males were more analytic and self-critical than females were. They were also more likely to express their anger and criticize other athletes. Overall, gender differences in concentration are relatively few and can be negated with appropriate training.

Although earlier we noted differences in concentration styles across sports, individuals differ markedly even within the same sport. One of the most fascinating contrasts in sporting history occurred between former Wimbledon tennis champions Björn Borg and John McEnroe. These giants of lawn tennis reigned supreme in the 1970s and 1980s. However, their personalities and concentration styles could not have been more different. Borg was cool, calm, collected, intense, and solitary. He rarely showed any emotion and was famous for grinding down opponents with his unflinching concentration and tenacious brand of tennis. Conversely, McEnroe was hot-tempered, frantic, passionate, and volatile and reveled in the interplay with his audience. Never has a player shown so much emotion on court before or since.

McEnroe's irreverent on-court antics earned him the epithet "Superbrat" from the British press. His fans tuned in avidly to feast on a spectacle of umpire abuse and self-degradation coupled with breathtaking tennis. Despite the

Colorsport/Imago/Icon SMI

John McEnroe during an outburst at Wimbledon in 1981.

tantrums, McEnroe was able to focus effectively at key times in a match. His pattern of concentration was very different from that of Borg. Whereas Borg appeared to be focused the whole time, McEnroe would almost tune in and tune out. It was a style that certainly worked well for him. His ability to concentrate for certain periods and then use delays and gamesmanship was a constant source of frustration for his opponents.

Because differences in concentration styles are attributed largely to personality, you need to find a style that works for you. The important point that comes from the distinction we have drawn between Borg and McEnroe is that despite stark differences in their styles of concentration and the ways they interacted with the crowd, they were both able to focus totally on the relevant, the whole relevant, and nothing but the relevant.

Our advice is to develop the ability to refocus your concentration at will, rather than attempt to harness it for the duration of a contest. Innately, some athletes have a long concentration "battery life"; they can remain totally focused for long periods. Others experience a deficit in concentration at key moments because they have spent too much of their mental energy early on. To counteract such deficits, consider the analogy of a dimmer switch that can be used to increase or decrease the level of concentration at key points. The brain actually burns more glucose when concentrating hard; therefore, it is important to focus intensely only when required. Ultimately, the ability to banish distractions and produce a clear, uncluttered view of all the relevant details lies at the heart of effective concentration.

Although exercise 6.4 doesn't work for everyone, what this simple task demonstrates is that, even in a relatively controlled environment (the pages of a book), there can be numerous interpretations of the same visual stimulus. Imagine how complex this process can be on a sport field or a race track where the environment is a great deal less stable, all of the senses are involved, and decisions need to be made in a split second.

Exercise 6.4
Beware: Your Eyes Can Deceive You

As well as having a dominant concentration style, you can be deceived by your own eyes. Try this exercise: Focus on the dot in the middle of this square and nothing else for about one minute. What happens?

You will notice that one or a number of the following phenomena occurred:

- The haze around the dot appeared to shrink.
- The dot disappeared.
- The dot and the haze disappeared.
- The haze went a lighter shade of gray.
- The picture split in two with the same design on each side in a near symmetrical pattern.
- The haze seemed to shrink and then expand.
- The haze appeared to swivel around the dot.

The important thing is to establish the key concentration processes in your sport and then set about developing the skills necessary to maintain an appropriate focus in whatever situation the sport presents.

INCREASING POWERS OF CONCENTRATION

Researchers and sport psychologists agree that a key to gaining control over concentration is to be able to recognize the level of arousal associated with the optimal processing of information. You may have observed that when you get overaroused, you tend to execute skills in either a jerky or reckless manner. This disrupts your flow and usually prevents you from achieving peak performance. Often you make the wrong decision at a critical moment in a game. Psychologists refer to this as reverting to the *dominant response*, which is the one associated with the early stages of learning a skill. This dominant response is more often than not the wrong response, which can lead to a sharp downturn in performance.

It is important to restrain the thinker within and to just let things happen. Thinking too much about the skills involved can result in the psychological phenomenon known as choking, which is a skill breakdown resulting from devoting too much thought to executing key skills (see also chapter 4). This happens because actions that are autonomous or ingrained are broken down into constituent parts, which is similar to what happens during the early stages of learning a skill (see chapter 1 for details on skill development). As an example, consider a fielder in cricket who, in an effort to throw the ball at the stumps accurately, tries to guide the throw rather than complete the action instinctively. The guiding, or conscious, effort not only results in a less accurate throw, which is "pushed" out to the right, but also slows down the movement, which allows the batsman sufficient time to make it to the popping crease.

The years of training and conditioning you have completed should kick in and skills should come naturally without a huge amount of conscious effort. As a simple demonstration of just how superior the performer is over the thinker when it comes to physical action, lie down on the floor, flat on your back, and try to explain to yourself the procedure for standing up. Analyze the required movements, and only move your limbs when instructed to do so by the logical left hemisphere of your brain—*Bend the right leg at the knee until your right foot is flat on the ground. Lift your right arm and move it across your body. Place it palm down on the floor by your left elbow,* and so on. If frustration does not get the better of you, eventually you will figure out how to do it. Your performance will, however, be a poor imitation of the highly efficient way you would normally get up when you allow the creative right hemisphere of your brain to run things on autopilot.

Simulation Training

The hullabaloo of match day or race day can wreak havoc on concentration processes. Just as good coaches implement the specificity principle in physical training, we advocate giving it priority during mental training. Doing things in practice in exactly the same way as they will do them in competition, while also anticipating potential mishaps, is a hallmark of champion athletes.

How Overarousal Affects Decision Making

Rudi was a prodigious track athlete at a U.S. high school. He won the state 400-meter title a record three times in succession and was ranked in the top 10 in the country for his age group. His sights were set on going to an Ivy League college and eventually winning the NCAA championships. Although Rudi was gifted athletically, he sometimes suffered from lapses in concentration when he felt anxious. This would often manifest in simple absentmindedness such as forgetting to take his spikes to a meet or pinning the front and back of his vest together when attaching numbers.

Rudi grew up in Mobile, Alabama, where there was no indoor track. In his freshman year at university, Rudi was selected to compete over the unusual distance of 300 meters in a warm-up meet. The head track coach explained to Rudi that unlike the outdoor 400 meters, which is always run in lanes, he would need to break into the inside lane after the first 200 meters. Rudi felt a little nervous. This was his first opportunity to represent his university, and he was eager to impress the coaching staff and his teammates. He went out in a characteristically aggressive manner, and by the 100-meter mark was 5 meters ahead of the rest of the field. Rudi relaxed his shoulders and began to drive hard into the second bend.

At the breaking point, the other athletes immediately shuffled into lane 1, but Rudi continued to storm down lane 4. At first, Rudi's teammates assumed this was a tactical ploy that would keep him well clear of the inevitable jostle for position. But when Rudi hit the third and final bend and was still running in the same lane, his teammates began to scream, "Break, Rudi, BREAK!" By this point Rudi was like a headless chicken and didn't know how to respond.

Rudi did what he knew best from outdoor 400-meter running, which was to stick rigidly to his lane. He could hear his teammates but couldn't translate their screams into any meaningful instruction to direct his leg movements. The five runners in lane 1 eased past Rudi, and he trailed in last to the amusement of rival supporters. Although Rudi had previously played the coach's instructions through his mind over and over again, when the race was in progress, he reverted to his dominant response of staying in his lane. That was entirely the wrong decision for an indoor 300-meter race.

We once worked with a concert pianist who was always unnerved by performing in public. One of the most effective strategies that we came up with was to have him don his recital tuxedo and play in front of a powerful spotlight that he had installed in his lounge. He would imagine playing with style and panache to a packed venue. After just a few weeks of this dress rehearsal, his fears of performing in public had vanished. The unknown element of public performance had been allayed by devoting many hours to recreating a similar sensory experience while practicing at home.

Athletes rarely practice in their competition uniforms, which are usually reserved for the big day. With the difference between winning and losing often being so small, this can put them at a disadvantage. If the team uniform is blue and white but players practice in odd colors, they will be less well conditioned to reacting to the subtle moves of their teammates. Being accustomed to the moves of teammates in uniform may result in reaction times that are fractionally shorter because the central nervous system will have less information to process. In essence, they will be able to anticipate slightly more effectively.

Even in individual sports, practicing in uniform is important given that the material will have its own distinct feel and texture, which may not be entirely comfortable. Dress rehearsal is particularly important for fast-paced technical sports such as gymnastics, figure skating, and jumping events (e.g., pole vault and high jump). Such rehearsals are best done after skills have been mastered and then scheduled at regular monthly intervals, like fire alarm drills, which effectively serve the same purpose.

In some cases, we have recommended that athletes throw out their uniforms and purchase entirely new uniforms as part of a strategy to overcome a slump in form. This symbolizes a disconnection from poor form and often leads to a kind of renaissance, or rebirth, that signals an upturn in performance.

Another kind of simulation that we often employ is to recreate the competition environment in training. To facilitate this, we produce MP3 files or CDs of crowd noise (hostile and friendly), booming announcers, officials, and background music. We train athletes first to concentrate on these noises and then to completely dissociate from them so that they just melt into the background. We recommend that you produce a recording of your competition environment and practice over the sounds at regular intervals. Combining this with a dress rehearsal is all the better.

You might even persuade a stadium attendant to put the competition floodlights on for an hour or so to help you get accustomed to their glare. If you are really

Gary Bowen at the World Snooker Championships

Gary Bowen is a snooker player who worked with us in preparation for the 2010 World Championships. Unusually, he didn't cite any specific problem in an initial consultation; rather, he wanted to look at how sport psychology might be used to give his entire approach a lift. He was the type of person who left absolutely no stone unturned.

We spent considerable time exploring the kind of distractions that might present themselves in the intense environment of the Crucible, the traditional venue for this premier event. As part of our strategy, we recorded a stereo CD that contained loud clapping and cheering as well as gasps and crowd taunts that alternated on stereo channels to emulate the multitable matchplay environment of the Sheffield Crucible Theatre (UK). We had discovered that having multiple games in progress with the presence of large crowds was a particularly severe distraction. We also included intermittent coughs on the CD, the click of balls being struck, and calls from referees at neighboring tables to make it really lifelike.

While having the CD played in the practice room of Gary's local club, we employed a couple of our students to act as camera operators. One of the cameras covered the action on the table while the other was focused on Gary's face. He later used the footage, played simultaneously on a split screen, to rate his composure on a scale of 1 to 5 each time a major distraction occurred on the soundtrack. The cameras added a further distraction that was part and parcel of the World Championship experience. After a month of simulation training, Gary went on to play the best snooker of his life.

persuasive, you might even convince the attendant to play crowd noise through the public address system.

Simulation is a technique that has long been used to great effect by astronauts and pilots but seldom employed to the same degree by athletes and coaches. In addition to outfits, noises, and bright lights, we suggest that you simulate the use of wet implements if your sport is played outdoors: balls, sticks, batons—whatever you use. If your sport is played on grass, from time to time ask the groundsperson to switch the sprinklers on before practice to emulate wet conditions. If you are going to compete at high altitude, in very humid conditions, or at an unusually early hour, then reproduce this again and again in practice to condition both your mind and body for the task ahead. Finally, practice occasionally in a strong or swirling wind. This is particularly useful for track and field athletes, whose performance is, to some extent, dependent on wind conditions. Simulation is one of the most powerful weapons in the armory of sport psychology techniques.

Preevent Routines

Sport fans sometimes question why athletes perform idiosyncratic routines prior to important competitions. A soccer player may always wait to put his shirt on until just as he is walking onto the pitch, a sprinter may try to be the last to settle into her blocks, or a bald player may have several teammates kiss his head before a match. Such rituals are a key part of the preevent routine, which is sometimes based on sound logic and other times on pure superstition.

A preevent routine is the same as a prematch ritual or prerace action plan. It involves a standardized series of behaviors that help to ease anxiety and focus attention prior to competition. The routine often starts on the night before competition and continues right through until the start of play. Of particular importance are the three minutes before the competition begins, because your mindset at that point will determine how well you start. Clearly, performance in events of very short duration such as sprinting and ski jumping relies heavily on the athlete's mindset in the few minutes beforehand.

Common to all sport participants is the need to enter the competitive arena in a state of mind that will enable them to perform at their best. Although routines on the day of competition will vary greatly from sport to sport, getting well rested the night before is a universal requirement. Athletes are well advised to take the right nutrition (see pages 131-133) and get ample sleep (8 to 10 hours). Some athletes require even more than 10 hours. For example, world marathon record holder Paula Radcliffe sleeps 11 hours at night and then two more in the afternoon! Like a big cat, she needs to conserve energy, so she spends most of her time relaxing.

Because of the effects of precompetition anxiety, you may have difficulty sleeping on the eve of competition. Although competition-related insomnia is common, much can be done about it (see Strategies to Help You Sleep). We also recommend that you take a day off training on the eve of competition so you feel mentally refreshed.

What happens on the morning of competition varies greatly from sport to sport. Some teams engage in a regular ritual such as breakfast at a set time, a team talk, or a rubdown, whereas other teams simply meet in the changing room. In individual sports, there is even greater variation in how people prepare. Some of the guiding principles include eating a hearty breakfast of complex carbohydrates, fiber, fruit, and fruit juices, provided competition is not scheduled early in the morning (see Mood Foods on page 133 in chapter 5). For early-morning competitions, a lighter snack is advisable, but you should eat it at least an hour before the start. Always check your bag to ensure that you have everything required for the competition. We recommend having a checklist of equipment and packing your bag the night before. It's also a good idea to watch an inspirational video such as one of your peak performances or a top sportsperson that you really admire.

Leave plenty of time for your journey to the competition venue, and anticipate delays so you do not arrive in a flustered state. On a long journey, it is a good idea to take regular breaks to stretch and have a drink of water or fruit juice. If you are flying, take regular walks along the aisle and do not be at all embarrassed about stretching in public—people *will* understand! On arrival at the venue, find out where all the relevant officials and sport medics are sited. Then deal with any administrative procedures such as registration or getting accreditation right away so you can prepare without distraction.

A standardized warm-up or preparation routine of flexible duration is a good idea in case of changes to the published program. One of the problems we've encountered with preevent routines is that athletes are sometimes too rigid in their approach. For the routine to be really effective, you must have some flexibility and an understanding of things that might go wrong (see the section on "what if" scenarios in chapter 7).

Strategies to Help You Sleep

- Read a fictional book or a comic that draws you in and captures your imagination.
- Avoid using your computer or viewing a bright screen for 45 minutes before going to bed because such screens mimic the effect of sunlight on the brain.
- Listen to soft, relaxing music or a CD containing the sounds of nature.
- Use progressive muscular relaxation (see chapter 4).
- Have a milk-based hot drink such as hot chocolate (avoid caffeinated drinks).
- Avoid cheese, spicy food, and caffeine in the lead-up to bedtime.
- Use a self-hypnosis CD or MP3 file.
- Meditate by focusing intently on one thought or feeling.
- Visualize successful performance in your upcoming competition (see chapter 7).
- Soak in a hot bath containing six to eight drops of lavender oil.
- Use any dual-processing task such as trying to run the nine times table backward and forward at the same time.
- Watch your favorite comedy or a "feel-good" movie.
- Keep your room warm but not too hot; 64-68 °F (18-22 °C) is the optimum temperature range to promote sleep without risking dehydration.
- Sleep alone if the activity of your partner (e.g., snoring, turning over, talking in his or her sleep) disturbs you.

Preevent Routine of Austin, A College Quarterback

Morning of competition: I like to sleep in on match days and to take breakfast late—usually at around 10:00 a.m. Actually, it's more of a brunch that I have. If we are playing out of state, we usually leave our hotel straight after breakfast; otherwise, I watch old footage of Dan Marino in his Miami Dolphins heyday. I always check my uniform bag before leaving—I'm kind of neurotic about that.

On arrival: Because I'm team captain, when we're playing away, I try to find us the best changing room available. I put on my pads and team uniform—always in the same order—then tape up my fingers to protect an old injury. I spend a few quiet minutes just visualizing the plays that I will be initiating during the game.

Warm-up routine: I get my teammates to complete their individual warm-ups; then I bring them together into a tight huddle in the changing room. I give each player verbal affirmations and confirm their strategic role in the game. Coach Johnson gives the pep talk and hypes people up before we run confidently onto the field.

Three minutes before: We converge into a huddle once again, and I talk people through the opening offensive plays. I take note of the prevailing weather conditions and the nature of the opposition. Everybody assumes his starting position in accordance with whether we are taking an offensive or defensive formation. I take a last glance to register each player's position and make adjustments if necessary.

You may benefit from doing what many athletes do, which is to keep verbal communication with opponents to a minimum, maintain strong body language at all times, and look opponents directly in the eyes. Also, keep a check on whether events are running on schedule so you can make adjustments if necessary. It is especially important not to warm-up too much or too little. Performing your routine with near military precision in the minutes prior to the start of competition will give you a feeling of confidence and control. Preevent Routine of Austin, A College Quarterback outlines the preevent routine of an athlete with whom we have worked.

Race Plans

In sports such as swimming, rowing, and kayaking, in which people compete against one another in lanes, it is very common for athletes to develop detailed race plans to optimize tactics and aid concentration. Race plans usually cover strategies for things such as pacing, as exemplified in the verbal cue *Start fast, lengthen, and hold on;* motivation, as in *Dig deep; you can do this*; and concentration, as in *Focus on back rotation.* It is critical that you adopt the tactics that are likely to bring about the best results for you. If a particular competitor goes off very fast, it may be tempting to follow her; however, optimal results often come through following an individualized strategy that might involve maintaining an even pace and leaving something in the tank for the closing stages.

Centering

A technique that is particularly useful for controlling physiological arousal and for ignoring negative and task-irrelevant stimuli is referred to as centering. This was popularized by the American sport psychologist Robert Nideffer in the late 1970s. Dr. Nideffer had a great deal of success with centering, particularly in sports that have frequent breaks in the action such as tennis and baseball.

The technique is known as centering because it involves focusing attention on the center of your body, the area just behind your navel. According to Dr. Nideffer, you are centered when your body weight is distributed about the center of your body in a way that feels comfortable—in other words, so that your body seems to communicate that it is primed and ready to perform.

Centering has a calming and controlling effect, providing a simple but effective way to counteract the negative effects of overarousal. It is best to practice centering in a standing rather than a sitting position because seats are often not available during a contest. You will need to commit the procedure to memory (see exercise 6.5). The technique works in competition only if it is first practiced thoroughly during stressful situations in training.

Exercise 6.5
Centering Instructions

1. Stand with your feet flat on the ground, shoulder-width apart, arms hanging loosely by your sides.

2. Close your eyes and breathe evenly, in through the nose and out gently through the mouth. Notice that when you breathe in, tension in your upper body increases, but as you breathe out, there is a calmer, sinking feeling.

3. Inhale deeply from your abdomen, and as you do, be aware of the tension in your face, your neck, your shoulders, and your chest. As you exhale, let the tension fall away and focus on the feeling of heaviness in your abdomen.

4. Continue to breathe evenly, focusing all your attention internally on the area immediately behind your navel.

5. Maintain your attention on that spot and breathe normally, feeling very controlled and heavy and calm.

6. On each out-breath use a word that encapsulates the physical feelings and mental focus that you want; for example, *loose, calm, focused, sharp,* or *strong.*

During moments of extreme emotion, this simple technique allows you to recapture a feeling of relaxation and control very quickly. With sufficient practice, you will be able to achieve this in only a few seconds or three to five deep breaths. Where precisely you center your attention will depend on the feelings you want to create. If you need to be deeply relaxed, heavy, and like an immovable object, then your attention should be focused just below your navel. Likewise, if you want to be alert and aggressive, you should aim to center just above your navel. Make these fine adjustments during practice to find out what suits you best.

It is useful to quantify your ideal focus level by using the number 5 to represent your optimal level on a scale of 1 to 9 and then breathing yourself either up or down to this level depending on how aroused you are to start with (see figure 6.3). For example, let's say that you are about to take a kick for goal in Australian Rules football, but you feel quite anxious because your team needs 6 points to win and only five seconds remain on the clock. You might rate your arousal at 8 (very high). So, to take yourself to an optimal level, you can center using three deep breaths, each of which takes you 1 point down the scale toward your optimal level of 5.

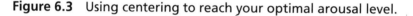

Extremely underaroused		Moderately underaroused		Optimally aroused		Moderately overaroused		Extremely overaroused
1	2	3	4	5	6	7	8	9

Figure 6.3 Using centering to reach your optimal arousal level.

The technique of centering will enable you to prevent changes in physiological arousal from interfering with concentration, but you will need to recognize when you are under- or overaroused. During practice, get into the habit of identifying situations that tend to make you tense and others in which you are sometimes a little too relaxed. You might also do this by recalling your previous competitions and jotting down these details. By doing this, you will be able to predict the times when centering will help the most. Exercise 6.6 provides coaches with a centering exercise they can use to demonstrate the technique to their athletes.

Cue Words

One of the easiest ways to improve concentration is to verbalize the important cues of particular situations. Verbal anchors can direct your attention to critical performance-related information. For example, if you are a swimmer, you will be keen to obtain a fast start; a way to verbalize the appropriate focus is to use a cue such as *B of the buzzer* to reinforce starting with the electronic starting mechanism. If you are a discus thrower, you will want to use the powerful muscles in your legs and trunk to maximize momentum prior to whipping through the throwing arm to deliver the discus. A useful cue would be *Arm fast and last* to achieve good form. Be creative in the use of cue words and find them for situations in which a high level of concentration is necessary. Using your own personalized cue words will help you embrace them more easily into your competition routine.

Exercise 6.6
A Test of Centering Effectiveness

If you are a coach, here's an exercise you can use to demonstrate the effectiveness of centering to your athletes:

Arrange athletes of similar build and stature into groups of three. Ask one of the athletes to stand between the other two. This athlete should bend his arms until his hands are level with his shoulders and his elbows are tucked into his sides (see figure 6.4). Ask the athlete to brace himself so that he feels immovable. The pair on either side should now be asked to lift the athlete pushing up underneath one elbow each. This will prove to be quite easy. Then ask the athlete in the middle to center using the deep form of centering (i.e., focusing just below the navel). Now have the athletes on each side repeat the lift; this time it should prove much harder.

Figure 6.4 The athletes to the left and right find it difficult to lift their teammate off the ground after he has centered.

Photo courtesy of Sally Trussler, Brunel University photographer

Triggers

A trigger is any action, phrase, or stimulus that reminds you of the need to focus. For example, fielders in baseball can lose concentration owing to the long duration and repetitive nature of the game. Being unable to maintain intense concentration for the entire duration of an inning, they tend to use behavioral cues to focus before each pitch. This behavioral cue, or trigger, may involve walking in toward the batter, conducting a shoulder stretch, or even spitting at the ground.

Such triggers focus attention on the cues the fielder has learned will offer the best chance of anticipating where the ball will go. Wiggling the bat prior to a pitch serves the same function for batters. The trigger should not interfere with technical or tactical aspects of performance. For example, if the wiggling of the bat is excessive, the batter can easily be wrong-footed by the pitcher, who is responsible for determining the rhythm of play.

Triggers are particularly helpful in long-duration sports because there is a greater likelihood for attention to drift. They should always be positive and related to the process of competition rather than to the final outcome or current score. Another good example is the "waggle" of the club in golf as a kind of preinitiation of the swing; indeed as the old Scottish saying goes, "As ye waggle, so shall ye swing."

Responding to Errors

All sportspeople make errors during performance. This is unavoidable because sport places relentless demands that cannot be met the whole time. Some sporting events force a huge number of errors because of the very short time athletes have to make complex decisions. Consider the quarterback in American football or the fly-half in rugby union. Massive concentration demands are placed on such key playmakers, and inevitably, every now and again, they slip up. The important point is not to dwell on errors.

All mistakes are followed by an initial emotional reaction, usually a mixture of dejection and anger, which is very often accompanied by internal name calling, in which one half of you chastises the other half for its sloppiness. The self-recrimination usually continues silently as you replay and analyze the mistake, planting the seeds of self-doubt. As the action proceeds, the inner conversation often continues in ever-decreasing circles:

> *You missed the last penalty kick but don't miss this one.*
> *Don't you dare miss this one.*
> *You simply cannot miss this penalty.*
> *Oh God, you missed this one as well.*

The original error magnifies and reproduces itself because your attention becomes internally focused, locked on your own thoughts and feelings, when in fact the skill demands an external focus. It is important to avoid such negative self-dialogue and to focus on the specific demands of the next play. Also, it is advantageous to reflect on what you can learn from an error to prevent its recurrence.

Forced or unforced errors in sport can lead to dramatic lapses in concentration that in turn upset performance. Most often, clashes with opposing players or disputes with officials prompt adverse responses. Consider the case of England soccer hero David Beckham playing in a hotly contested match against old adversaries Argentina at the 1998 World Cup Finals in France. Having been hacked down from behind by Argentinean striker Diego Simeone, rather than just accepting the free kick in his team's favor, Beckham lashed out at Simeone with his heel. This resulted in a red card (sending off) and an early departure for his team from the championships.

When an error causes great frustration, rather than getting caught up with it so that it debilitates your performance, you can try to "park it." This is a way of symbolically ridding yourself of the error. You do this by wiping it away on your shorts or on a playing implement (racket, bat, club). Some sportspeople like to spit the mistake away, although this is clearly only possible outdoors! Parking an error is a way to quickly forget it so you can remain focused on the here and now.

Angela Onissi: Aspiring International Diver

Diving is a technically challenging sport that requires deep concentration for successful execution of the skills involved. Angela Onissi was aspiring to be selected for her national team for the first time, and a good result at upcoming national championships would be sure to impress the selectors. Angela often became distracted while standing at the back of the board preparing to initiate a dive. Typically, thoughts of what could go wrong would enter her mind, such as hitting the board after the launch, performing sloppy somersaults, or failing to nail the entry. Sometimes she also felt slightly flat and lethargic, particularly in very important competitions.

To prevent such negative thoughts and feelings from debilitating her performance, Angela's coach suggested she use a behavioral and verbal trigger just prior to launching into each dive. She taught her to feel a rush of energy rising through her feet and ankles into her knees, thighs, and then her entire body. The energy rush would occur with eyes closed while Angela simultaneously visualized the successful execution of the dive. When she was fully energized and had seen and felt the successful execution of the dive, she would open her eyes. Angela followed with the verbal trigger *Spring and fling,* which reinforced the kinetic energy she would generate off the board and the uninhibited way she would throw her body into the dive. The use of the trigger helped Angela tremendously in gaining her first selection for the national team.

As an extension to error parking, some teams employ a no blame policy, which means that if any player messes up, the team takes collective responsibility. This ensures that the concentration of individuals is not compromised when they make a mistake. Further, it binds the team together because players are not singled out for errors of concentration. Teams such as the 2003 World Cup–winning England rugby union team dismissed errors with a pat on the back for the offending player or a reassuring statement such as: "Just let it go" or "Forget about it." This prevented players from feeling guilty that they had let their teammates down and from ruminating over the error.

The point underlying error parking and the no blame policy is that the past is gone and you cannot do anything to change it. The future is uncertain, but it depends on what you do at the present moment. When you review past events or get ahead of yourself, you just do not attend as well to your current situation resulting in further errors of concentration. If you direct attention totally toward the here and now, past mistakes will not influence your performance and the result will take care of itself.

Letting your thoughts drift away from the here and now can prove disastrous to performance. This was exemplified by international rugby union player Matt Giteau during a 2010 test match in which Australia lost 20-21 to England. Fly-half Giteau, who until his concentration lapse had been the dominant player on the field, went from hero to zero by inexplicably missing a simple match-winning kick in the final moments of the game. Afterwards he told reporters "I was already thinking of the next play—receiving the kick-off and playing field position. That's the only thing I can probably learn from that—to stay in the moment."

Anything that pulls attention away to another time or to irrelevant details threatens the success of the outcome. Sport performance, like life, is composed of an endless series of present moments. The more of them you are able to control, the better you will play, the more consistently you will perform, and the less frustrated you will become when setbacks occur. Work on your "bouncebackability" so that when things go wrong, you can take immediate remedial action.

FUTURE DEVELOPMENTS IN CONCENTRATION TRAINING

We are at the crest of tremendous advancement in the training of concentration skills using new technologies. Because the scope of this book is to provide athletes and coaches with mental training techniques they can use without going to any great expense, we do not intend to provide detailed coverage of these new technologies. Following are some of the methods currently in vogue that you may want to explore. We also provide relevant Web site addresses where applicable.

Video games: 3-D games have been developed that emulate some of the perceptual and concentration demands of sport. Such games are particularly effective in shortening reaction times and improving hand–eye coordination. A very wide variety is available. See:

- www.easports.com
- www.2ksports.com
- www.dot3dgames.com
- www.shockwave3d.com

Virtual reality: There are developments afoot to create virtual reality software for a number of sports (visit the first of the following Web sites for a good example from American football). In a virtual environment, you are placed into a situation that looks, feels, smells, and sounds to a large extent like the real sport setting. Trainee pilots and surgeons have used such software for a number of years. Virtual reality technology offers the potential for more sophisticated use of simulation training, allowing you to "practice" in venues you have not yet visited, in environmental conditions you have not yet experienced, and against competitors you have not yet faced. There is the added advantage of being able to isolate the development of a specific sport skill such as the backhand smash in tennis. See:

- www-VRL.umich.edu/project/football/
- www.vresources.org
- www.pycfitness.com/Fitness_news/112908.htm
- www.sega.com/virtuatennis2009/

Portable electrodermal feedback devices: These devices measure and feed back skin conductance, which reflects tiny changes in perspiration on the palmar surface of the hand. Hence, they assess arousal levels and have been used to illustrate how thoughts influence the body, monitor relaxation, and identify stressful aspects of sport performance during mental rehearsal. See:

- www.bfe.org
- www.mindmedia.nl/english/index.php
- www.mindmodulations.com/products.html

Eye training equipment: Companies are now manufacturing sporting equipment that behaves in unpredictable ways to make the task of completing a skill more challenging. For example, a zigzag ball, also known as an odd bouncer, is a tennis ball surrounded by rubber rings that cause it to bounce erratically. Another example is the bat-rac, a wooden or plastic bat with a hole in the sweet spot. The idea of this piece of equipment is for the batter to make contact with the ball using the edge of the bat or to make the ball pass through the hole. It helps to enhance eye–hand coordination. See:

- www.sporteyes.com/vtp.htm
- www.sports-training-aids.com/visionp.html
- www.program-for-better-vision.com
- www.visualtraining.com

Eye scanners: Scanners are currently in use in some universities to track eye movement in response to a variety of sport scenarios such as tennis serves and penalty kicks. The scanners indicate the precise pattern of the athlete's visual focus using a head monitor and are used to identify strengths and weaknesses as well as to train people to focus on relevant cues. See:

- www.peakachievement.com
- www.eyetracking.com
- www.s-oliver-associates.com

Eye training and concentration software: "Eye coaches" are becoming increasingly popular in the highest echelons of sport. They use specialized software to train athletes to recognize relevant advanced cues in their sport to improve their anticipation times in a variety of situations. This method was brought to public awareness by Sir Clive Woodward, the England rugby supremo who employed South African eye coach Dr. Sheryl Calder to help his team prepare for the 2003 World Cup, which they won in emphatic style against hosts Australia. See:

- www.racingsecrets.com/drag_racing_eye.shtml
- www.eyeperformance.com
- www.transparentcorp.com

Visual occlusion: A body of research is currently in progress to assess the cues that athletes focus on when executing complex skills. New computer technology allows athletes to be trained to react to sporting situations with key details from the action missing or visually occluded. For example, a soccer goalkeeper could be shown footage of a striker in a penalty shootout with various body parts of the striker removed such as the head, kicking foot, or right arm. This forces the goalkeeper to anticipate where the ball will be placed with less visual information than she would normally have. This enables her to identify the most important aspects of the kick and any idiosyncrasies that a striker may have, which give a clue as to which part of the goal the ball will be aimed at. See:

- www.visualfitness.com
- www.transparentcorp.com

SUMMARY

The executive psychological skill of concentration can be enhanced just like a dribbling or batting skill. We have highlighted the pitfalls associated with dividing attention between the task at hand and irrelevant thoughts or distractions. Hopefully, you have a better understanding of what good concentration entails and how you can achieve it. You need to work hard at these control skills, which will likely reap rewards in the competitive arena. Here are five key points to remember:

- Think about the demands your sport places on concentration and decide where and when your attention should be focused.
- Learn to restrict self-analysis during performance and allow your instincts to take over. Superior performance, as we learned in chapter 1, is associated with automaticity.
- Learn how to narrow your attention effectively and how to fix your attention on specific objects—the "information rich" aspects of your performance domain.
- Control arousal appropriately so that it does not inhibit your ability to concentrate effectively.
- Practice concentration drills in training so you can execute the relevant skills automatically in competition.

Although concentration training is often the final frontier for sport performers, it should be one of the first ports of call. There is no point in missing opportunities and becoming frustrated when there is so much you can do to become a master of concentration. Use your creativity to develop concentration drills that will take your performance to a new level.

Visualization and Self-Hypnosis

Before the [Olympic] trials I was doing a lot of visualization. And I think that helped me to get a feel of what it was gonna be like when I got there.

—Michael Phelps,
14-time Olympic gold medalist swimmer

Athletes and coaches often become so immersed in the process of physical conditioning and practicing skills that they overlook other ways to enhance sporting performance. Psychological techniques can be used to enhance performance without the need for any physical movement. By recreating images from information stored in long-term memory, you can rehearse set plays, bust out of performance slumps, and get the better of old rivals. Sometimes sporting excellence requires that you create in your mind what you have yet to achieve physically.

Through years of formal education many of us are conditioned to use predominantly the left side of the brain, which deals with logic, reason, and structure. The right side, which deals with imagery, creativity, and abstract concepts, is widely underused by most people. A bright and active imagination facilitates progress in sport just as it does in other aspects of life. Athletes routinely engage the right side of the brain in pursuit of sporting ambitions, and, as we will show, imagination and creativity play a vital role in unlocking sporting potential.

However modest or mighty your sporting ambitions might be, you need to create future moments of glory repeatedly in your imagination. After all, if you cannot imagine them, how can you hope to achieve them? To fulfill your true potential, you need to take control of your imagination and use it to help facilitate your performance. Two popular techniques that can be used in parallel with each other—visualization and self-hypnosis—will help you harness the power of imagination.

MENTAL IMAGES AND SPORT PERFORMANCE

Visualization is the process by which we recreate experiences in our minds using information stored in memory. Effective visualization is promoted by a vivid imagination. The true force of imagination is revealed in dreams and nightmares, where images are often so vivid they cause us to wake up in a cold sweat. But imagination has an equally real effect on our conscious lives. It has the power to release hidden strengths or to inhibit performance. Therefore, the more you can control your imagination, the more you can expect to control your performance. Remember that if you can see it, you can create it; if you can feel it, you can perform it; if you can imagine it, you can achieve it.

Our ability to use visualization varies greatly. Some people can evoke only visual images, whereas others can more readily imagine how actions feel. The fortunate ones are able to recreate experiences using all five senses. People also vary in the vividness of their imagery and the degree to which they can control action during visualization. Some cannot hold a clear picture in their mind for any length of time, nor can they create moving images effectively. Similarly, whereas some people can visualize in brilliant color, others are restricted to dreary monochrome images. Whatever your current level of ability, you can develop effective imagery with sufficient practice.

It was previously thought that a lack of eidetic visualization ability (the ability to recall images, sounds, or objects accurately and abundantly) would reduce the benefits derived from visualization techniques. Many athletes we have worked with have initially believed that their efforts would be wasted because they could not visualize with clarity and vividness. Recent research has shown, however, that a lack of visualization ability does not necessarily diminish the potential benefit of engaging in the visualization process.

As you attempt to develop your visualization skills, aim for maximum vividness and controllability. The more clearly you can experience mental images and the more accurately you can control imagined movements, the more likely you will be to translate these images into improved performance.

How Visualization Works

Using imagination constructively involves much more than idle daydreaming. Only when you can use it skillfully and systematically to help create or revive the ultimate performance will you benefit. Imagination channeled in this disciplined way is referred to as visualization or imagery. Although it may sound a bit complicated, in reality, imagery is a simple concept with very basic applications. Most of us use imagery every day but in an unstructured or sporadic way.

You may be fairly confident that you can distinguish between events that happen in reality and those that you imagine. This distinction, however, is actually much less obvious than you might think. The messages sent in the form of neural impulses to and from the brain during imagined action closely resemble those sent during physical action. Visualization establishes a mental blueprint for sport skills and tactical ploys. Thus, WYSIWYG (i.e., *What You See Is What You Get*) is a popular acronym used by sport psychologists.

Harry the Fly-Half

Harry is a second-year undergraduate on a sport scholarship at the University of Bath. From his secondary school days, Harry's coach encouraged him to use the power of his imagination to run offensive moves in his mind just prior to their execution. Harry honed these skills during his sixth-form years and has now become very proficient at using visualization to rehearse moves. He mentally rehearses an attacking sequence through his own eyes, creating a mental blueprint of how he will receive the ball from his scrum-half. He feels the ball land in his hands as though a strong magnetic attraction were drawing it in. Harry then imagines accelerating, sidestepping, and advancing beyond the gain line. His visualization includes how he will evade the opposition players, counter their defensive moves, and then move the ball to his outside backs. This brief mental process, conducted just after he calls each move, allows him to anticipate effectively and gain a split-second advantage that often proves decisive.

Visualizing yourself performing any skill causes electromyographical (EMG) activity in the relevant muscle groups, similar to what would occur during the physical performance of the imagined movement. For example, if you were to visualize yourself flexing your arm from the elbow joint, it would be possible to monitor electrical activity in the biceps muscles even though no physical movement occurs. Recent research has shown that the pattern of such activation during imagery does not match precisely the pattern of EMG recorded during actual movement. However, neural impulses that are passed from the brain to the muscular system during imagery can be retained in memory almost as if the movement had actually occurred.

Imagery therefore has the effect of "priming" the appropriate muscles for subsequent physical action, and this clearly has potential benefits for the performance of many sport skills. Physical skills may be improved even when they are only practiced in the mind.

The ways visualization can be used to benefit sport performance and skill development are limited only by your imagination. This chapter outlines several tried and tested imagery strategies as well as a few state-of-the-art applications of visualization techniques. With practice and a little ingenuity, however, you should be able quite easily to devise your own.

Perspectives on Visualization

Visualization involves freeing the creative right side of the brain so that you can think without the need for words. Although this usually means creating pictures in the mind, or "seeing with your mind's eye," there are several perspectives you might use to create or recreate sporting experiences.

- The **visual-internal** form of imagery involves viewing what is going on as though you were actually there performing. (It is also known as associative imagery.) A downhill skier, for instance, using this form of first-person visualization would view each bump and turn approaching in her imagined run down the mountain and would see the scenery flashing by as though her eyes were a video camera.

- In contrast to visual-internal, **visual-external** imagery is like watching yourself through a camera. (It is also known as dissociative imagery.) It is third-person visualization in which you step outside your own body momentarily to watch yourself perform. Here the downhill skier would picture herself hurtling down the mountain crouched in the tuck position, carving turns or jumping, as though seeing herself on a TV sport show. This is the most common imagery perspective used by athletes.

- The **kinesthetic** form of imagery involves recreating the physical feeling of performance. The downhill skier would imagine the feeling of pushing her heels back and shins forward in the ski boot, notice the sensation in her knees as she hit bumps, and her thigh muscles starting to burn toward the end of a long run.

- **Visual-internal kinesthetic** is a combination of visual-internal and kinesthetic imagery. It involves experiencing a performance through your own eyes while at the same time recreating the bodily sensations.

- **Visual-external kinesthetic** combines visual-external and kinesthetic imagery. You see your performance from the outside while at the same time recreating the physical sensations. Later in this chapter, we explain how this perspective is often employed as a useful stepping-stone to visual-internal kinesthetic imagery.

Most people have a natural inclination toward one of the first three visualization perspectives, but because each one relies heavily on a single sensory mechanism (either sight or feel), none fully exploits the true potential of imagery. The best uses of imagery involve a complete sensory experience that engages the senses of taste, smell, and hearing, as well as those of sight and feel. That is why the fourth and fifth perspectives are generally most effective.

For example, a volleyball player using imagery to recreate the experience of serving should imagine the feeling of stretching up and priming his dominant arm, the sound of the ball as he strikes it, the smells in the air, and the taste of sweat, in addition to seeing himself perform the action.

Choosing the Right Perspective

Some clear trends are beginning to emerge in imagery research. It has been suggested that visual-internal imagery comes fairly naturally to us because it represents how we normally experience the world. This means that external imagery often has the potential to add something new. For example, researchers have shown that a visual-external kinesthetic perspective is superior for learning and retaining new sport skills, especially those that are technically challenging such as martial arts moves or sequences in diving and gymnastics.

Another trend identified in recent research is that visual-internal imagery tends to aid the kinesthetic sensations to a greater degree than visual-external imagery does. The implication is that an internal perspective is superior when you want to psych up or prime yourself for superior sporting performance. Both internal and external perspectives have their merits, and you should aim to combine all of the senses for maximum effect. The acid test for any form of visualization is whether it works well for you.

A Theory of Imagery

Allan Paivio, a prominent Canadian psychologist, developed a model of imagery that is widely used among researchers and practitioners in sport psychology. Professor Paivio proposed that imagery plays two central functions: a *cognitive,* or thought-related, function and a *motivational,* or energizing, function. The cognitive function entails using imagery to experience sport skills and strategize in advance of competition, whereas the motivational function involves using imagery to attain goals, to cope effectively with the demands of sport, and to manage arousal levels. Paivio also explained that imagery use can be either situation-specific or general in nature (see figure 7.1).

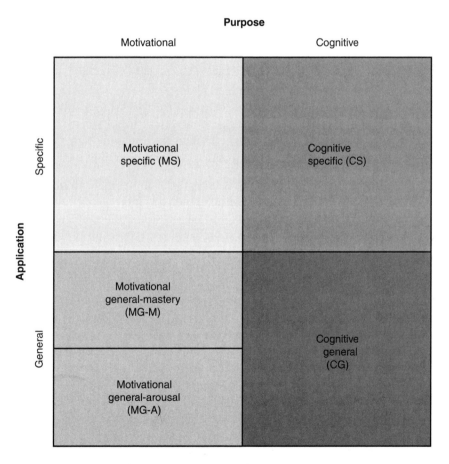

Figure 7.1   Paivio's two-dimensional model for imagery use.

Adapted from A. Paivio, 1985, "Cognitive and motivational functions of imagery in human performance," *Canadian Journal of Applied Sport Sciences* 10(4): 22S-28S.

Accordingly, there are four main types of imagery, although Paivio and his colleagues subsequently split the motivational general dimension into arousal and mastery components. The five types of imagery use noted in figure 7.1 are described as follows:

1. **Motivational specific.** This involves an athlete imagining herself in a specific setting that is highly motivational. For example, a bowler in cricket might imagine herself taking the final wicket of the opposing team in a limited-overs match.

2. **Motivational general-mastery.** The athlete would imagine himself in a typical scenario in his sport exhibiting the ability to remain correctly focused. For example, a goalkeeper in soccer might envisage readying himself and checking his angles each time the ball comes into his half of the field.

3. **Motivational general-arousal.** In this scenario, the athlete imagines herself controlling her anxiety in a situation that is typical of her sport. For example, a golfer might envisage how she would generate calmness before attempting a short putt.

4. **Cognitive specific.** This type of imagery requires that the athlete imagine himself correctly executing a specific skill. For example, a rugby goal kicker might visualize himself kicking a penalty from close to the right-hand touchline and propelling the ball between the uprights.

5. **Cognitive general.** In this type of imagery, the athlete imagines herself reviewing and considering strategies that affect tactics or overall strategy. For example, the captain of a hockey team might imagine herself revising her team's formation in response to a particular passage of play.

Research shows that some gender differences exist in imagery ability. With reference to cognitive specific imagery, for example, men are more proficient than women in visualizing technical aspects of sports—in particular, skills that involve a spatial element such as kicking a ball or "selling a dummy," as a rugby player might attempt to do. This difference is partly due to upbringing and the types of activities in which boys and girls typically engage. Accordingly, both males and females should improve their visualization skills by using the exercises described in the remainder of this chapter, but females may have slightly greater potential for improvement!

USING VISUALIZATION TECHNIQUES

Exercise 7.1 is a simple introduction to visualization skills that will help you understand how you visualize situations. It will identify those senses you are best at imagining, those that are most realistic, and those you can control best. You may need to repeat this exercise several times before you become proficient at creating and controlling vivid images in your mind, but do persevere.

Before you start, sit in a comfortable chair and relax by closing your eyes, breathing slowly and deeply, and allowing the tension to leave your muscles each time you exhale. Spend a few minutes doing this until you feel really relaxed.

Now you are going to imagine a series of sounds, feels, smells, tastes, and sights. Take time to explore each image, and enjoy the experience.

Exercise 7.1
Introduction to Visualization Skills

Sounds

The crunch as you bite a crisp apple

The crash as a dinner plate hits the ground and smashes

The plop of a pebble dropped into a stream

The sound of a tennis ball as it contacts the sweet spot of a racket

Feels

The dimpled skin of an orange

The cold metal surface of a weight disk in the gym

The scaly skin of a frozen fish

The slippery smoothness of a wet bar of soap

Smells

The aroma of freshly ground coffee

The fragrance of your favorite perfume or after shave

The pungent smell of chlorine as you enter an indoor swimming pool

The smell of newly mown grass on a hot summer's day

Tastes

The sweetness of honey

The bitterness of dark chocolate

The sharpness of a lemon

The taste of pepper on the tip of your tongue

Sights

A long, sandy beach that stretches to a point where it merges with the horizon

All the colors of the rainbow, one after another: red, orange, yellow, green, blue, indigo, violet

Your favorite sport video game

Riding a bicycle on a rough path

Try to identify which senses are really vivid and which are difficult to evoke. Can you see movement in your images? Are you able to visualize in color? Make brief notes in answer to these questions, and write down anything else that seems important about your images. This will be useful information in subsequent imagery exercises.

Now try using all five senses to create images. Start with something simple like making and then eating a toasted sandwich. Then try to recreate the experience of performing sit-ups or push-ups. It may help to physically perform the action and then recreate it in your mind immediately afterward. Repeat the exercise once a day until your visualization becomes vivid and easily controllable.

As we outlined in chapter 2, the loss of self-consciousness is an essential part of reaching a flow state and performing really well. Excessively focusing on how people perceive you and what they might be saying can cause you to choke at a critical moment. Thus, you should try to lose yourself in your competitive environment in the same way you might get lost in music while dancing at a club. Exercise 7.2 is a good way to deal with excessive self-consciousness and will help you feel at ease with yourself in challenging situations when it might feel as though all eyes are on you.

Exercise 7.2
Center of Attention

- Before the start of a sporting contest, mentally rehearse being the total center of attention and really enjoy every moment. Notice how people make a fuss of you, how they stare at you admiringly and hang on your every word.

- Initially, do this in a dissociated state, seeing yourself from the outside, so that you can change anything that doesn't look good or sound, feel, smell, or taste right.

- Then step inside and become fully associated, seeing events through your own eyes. Try to be aware of every piece of feedback your senses are providing.

If you have a personality trait of high self-consciousness, you might find it quite challenging to conduct visualization exercises in the presence of others. If you are acutely aware of how you present yourself to the outside world, any unusual practice—such as visualization—may heighten your presentational concerns. If this is the case, find somewhere to practice imagery where you will not be observed by spectators, officials, or fellow competitors. Many athletes we have known conduct their imagery in the bathroom.

Skill Development

When learning a new skill, visualization has two very specific uses. First, when you observe a demonstration of the skill to be learned, it pays to run through your own slow-motion replay of the movement, placing yourself in the role of performer (i.e., a cognitive specific type of imagery with a visual-internal perspective). This can help to fix the basic movement pattern in your memory before even attempting the movement physically. It is, however, vital that the demonstration you observe—perhaps by your coach or another performer—is a good one because mentally practicing a poorly executed skill will do more harm than good. A particularly effective way to develop your skills is by visualizing an expert in your sport. Exercise 7.3 gives you an opportunity to do just this.

Exercise 7.3
Visualizing an Expert in Your Sport

This exercise will help you to use the perfect form of a leading exponent of your sport to enhance your own performance.

1. Obtain a DVD or find a YouTube clip of one of the leading experts in your sport; go for one of the very best, a Lionel Messi, Jaques Kallis, Rebecca Adlington, or Kim Clijsters. Perhaps choose someone with whom you share some physical or playing characteristic.

2. Watch the expert perform a particular skill that you wish to master repeatedly, about 10 to 15 times.

3. Now switch off the video or computer, sit in a relaxed position, and gently close your eyes.

4. In a dissociative state, looking at the expert from the outside, watch him or her execute the skill perfectly five or six times.

5. Then merge with the expert by stepping into his or her body and seeing through his or her eyes so that you fully associate with the person (visual-internal kinesthetic perspective). Repeat this five or six times. Your imagined movements will gradually become more fluid and efficient and eventually show expert form.

In addition to helping you learn the skill, visualization can also be used to remember important details about the skill. For instance, when first learning to swim the breaststroke, think of kicking through the water like a frog. A simple image like this always conveys so much more about the technique than an elaborate explanation ever could. The same applies to the "back scratch" position in the tennis serve, which captures the correct movement pattern with great economy of detail.

Frequently Used Images in Reinforcing Sport Skills

Free-throw in basketball	Shooting out of a telephone booth
Front crawl in swimming	Hold on to as much water as possible
Long-distance running	Float like a gazelle
Pitching in baseball	Whip arm
Pulling in archery	Draw your shoulder blades together to hold an apple
Shot in netball	Make the arm into a gooseneck on follow-through
Power clean in weightlifting	Scrape your belly with the bar
Batting in cricket	Watch the ball onto the bat like a hawk

The more images replace explanation in learning, the more simply and effectively techniques will be mastered and the faster learning will progress. This approach is particularly potent when young athletes are being taught new skills; they often don't have the attentional capacity or the patience to absorb detailed instructions, and therefore a simple image can accelerate learning. Whether you are in the position of teacher or learner, visualization has a big part to play in communicating and understanding skills. If the heart of a skill can be captured in a simple image, practice is less arduous.

Skill Refinement

As mentioned earlier, research has shown that when you visualize performing an action, the muscles used to perform the action are physically activated. This means that even in the absence of physical movement, movement patterns can be practiced and retained in memory. When you practice mentally, your muscles are to some extent rehearsing the movement. You can literally think with your body as well as with your mind.

Consider the potential advantages of developing physical skills through mental practice. Practice has long since been established as the most important factor in skill development, and mental practice can be performed anywhere, at any time. It requires no equipment and can take place even when you are ill or injured. This does not mean, of course, that mental practice is as beneficial as physical practice, but it is certainly better than no practice at all. Importantly, research shows consistently that a combination of mental and physical practice is better than physical practice alone.

It would be wrong to think of mental practice as easier than physical practice; many athletes say that they actually find mental practice harder to do. Also, visualizing is not the same as daydreaming. Visualization is a skill in itself that needs considerable practice before it becomes effective. But with planning and effort, mental practice has been shown to contribute significantly to skill development, and, because it causes no bodily fatigue, it sometimes allows athletes to progress more rapidly than with physical practice alone.

Individual sports such as figure skating, archery, target shooting, and gymnastics lend themselves particularly well to mental practice. This is because they involve no direct interaction with opponents, and so the actual competition environment can be reproduced in the mind with a high degree of accuracy. However, many other less predictable sports have also been shown to benefit from mental practice. Basketball players, for instance, have demonstrated significant improvements in their free throw success rates after supplementing physical practice with mental practice, and swimmers and track athletes perfect their pacing strategy by running through races in their minds several times.

Joseph Rengatu: Big Race Pacemaker

Joseph Rengatu is often called on to set the pace at big athletics meetings. He gives the stars of distance running a helping hand in their record attempts. Joseph spends a lot of time practicing his races mentally to ensure that the pace he sets is on a tight schedule. He talks about his preparation as "a mental exercise, in which I shut my eyes, start my watch, then imagine seeing the first lap unfold and stop the watch at 400 meters. I am rarely more than half a second out."

Tactical Rehearsal

Additionally, in sports in which the skills required appear to remain unchanged from competition to competition, the vagaries of sun, wind, and rain can dramatically alter circumstances of play. Sports that can be adversely affected by the elements include golf, downhill skiing, motor racing, and triathlon. The use of visualization to adapt tactics in such circumstances can be highly beneficial.

Skills in which the emphasis is on thought processes rather than physical movement tend to benefit most from mental practice. For instance, repeating a cell phone number over and over to yourself is much more likely to embed it in your memory than physically dialing the number several times. In chess the essence of the contest is to outfox your opponent by playing the game in your head many moves in advance; the physical movements of the pieces on the board simply confirm the outcome of the mental visualization. Therefore, the control of images, rather than the physical action of moving the pieces, determines skill level in chess.

Team games such as American football, rugby, soccer, and hockey, with their intricacies and strategies, are a bit like giant games of chess. If you are responsible for deciding tactics, visualization is an important means of exploring the potential effectiveness of various moves and countermoves. We described this type of imagery earlier as cognitive general.

Anthony J. Causi/Icon SMI

Record-breaking quarterback Peyton Manning of the Indianapolis Colts has developed the skill of visually rehearsing the execution of a play so that he can optimize its effectiveness.

Exercise 7.4
Tactical Rehearsal

This exercise can be used either during a quiet moment at home or in the throes of competition to help you create a mental blueprint for a particular play or tactical ploy.

1. Take a deep breath and focus on controlling your breathing. Repeat twice, and on the third out-breath, allow your mind to clear.

2. Close your eyes and visualize your field of play in an associative state (visual-internal). Feel yourself in that environment (kinesthetic perspective), and engage all your other senses to make the experience more lifelike.

3. Mentally rehearse a play or tactic through your own eyes, first in slow motion and then gradually faster until you reach full speed. Execute it successfully, and fully anticipate what your opponent(s) might do to counter your moves. If your sport takes you into battle against the elements, then practice under various conditions and circumstances to ensure that you can adapt appropriately.

4. Focus on making sure your movements are fluid and efficient and that each time you mentally rehearse, you bring about the desired outcome. If at first you do not obtain the desired outcome, rerun the play until you do.

Mental practice can also be useful for team members to rehearse their roles in each play and to practice reacting to every eventuality until it becomes second nature. If you use visualization to increase your familiarity with a wide range of tactical situations, when they occur in reality, your reactions will be considerably faster. This is because you will have less information to process before recognizing the situation for what it is. As a result, you can initiate the appropriate response more rapidly.

For players in individual sports, tactical rehearsal is useful in creating a mental blueprint of strategy in various playing conditions: in extreme heat or cold, in high humidity, on a blustery day, and in driving rain. Many athletes make the mistake of not preparing thoroughly for performance in extreme weather conditions. In our experience this is one of the most common factors to adversely affect athletes' performances and therefore requires due consideration. We have designed exercise 7.4 to give you some experience of tactical rehearsal.

Precompetition Preparation

In many achievement-related situations, the unknown is often perceived as a threat. This holds for actors, musicians, public speakers, and sportspeople alike. The more unknown elements present in a sporting situation, the more likely the adrenaline will be to flow. In general, this increases blood supply to the muscles and reduces the sensation of pain, but it can very easy result in becoming overexcited or anxious, either of which can lead to poorer performance (see chapter 4). Exercises 7.5, 7.6, and 7.7 cover visualizations that will help with three aspects of your precompetitive routine:

Exercise 7.5
Getting to Know Your Sporting Environment

This exercise will create an expanded sense of awareness in your sporting domain. It is particularly valuable if you perform your sport within physical confines (e.g., squash, table tennis, weightlifting). You can also use this exercise to feel more comfortable in an unfamiliar environment such as an away game, or an iconic venue like Centre Court at Wimbledon or an Olympic stadium.

1. Stand at one end of the pitch, court, gym, room, or hall and focus on a specific object or point at the far end just above your eye line. Give this object or point your complete attention and notice every detail about it.

2. Now expand your focus to take in the two far opposite corners and notice every detail in your vision. Do this without moving your head.

3. Now expand your awareness even further along the walls, banks of seats, and so on, and around toward yourself. Do this very slowly and notice every detail.

4. Without moving your head, take your expanded awareness behind you. Use all of your senses to immerse yourself in the environment and get used to how you feel. Repeat four or five times as necessary.

Exercise 7.6
Getting Psyched Up for Competition

1. Think back to the start of a previous performance during which you were optimally psyched up. Recall the precise state you were in before the competition commenced (e.g., focused, in control, poised, full of self-belief).

2. Step into that state of readiness, experiencing it in the first person (i.e., through your own eyes). Notice exactly how it feels, both mentally and physically.

3. Now try to encapsulate that sensation in a single word, image, or feeling.

4. In the future, use that word, image, or feeling whenever you need to feel fully psyched up.

getting to know your sporting environment, getting psyched up for competition, and increasing arousal for practice.

Visualization can be used to reduce the unknown from an upcoming contest, thereby deflecting this sense of threat. You can achieve this by creating in your mind the complete competition experience from the moment you enter the changing room before the contest to the time you return there after victory. We have often taken this process one step further by asking athletes to write a newspaper report of their

---

Exercise 7.7
Increasing Arousal for Practice

1. Sit down in a comfortable position, gently close your eyes, and focus on your breathing pattern.
2. Imagine a situation in which you are underaroused using all of your senses; perhaps you feel flat or lethargic.
3. While imagining feeling like this, your arousal level may be only 5 or 6 on a scale of 10.
4. Inhale deeply, and as you do so, say the word *focus* and feel the energy coming in.
5. Your arousal scale will begin to approach 10.
6. As you exhale, the energy will quickly spread through your entire body.
7. After a few more breaths, your arousal level will top out at 10.
8. You are now optimally aroused to embark on your practice session.

---

performance in advance of the competition, particularly emphasizing their thoughts, feelings, and exactly how they performed. This approach relates most closely to the motivational general-mastery category of imagery.

Sometimes athletes find it difficult to get optimally aroused for an upcoming competition. This can happen toward the end of a crowded competitive schedule, following a long journey to an away venue, or against seemingly weak opposition. Often it is difficult to get excited about a certain type of training session. For example, we have noted over the years that young tennis players are far from enthusiastic about performing tough sprint intervals as part of their speed training routine.

Underarousal is just as much a limiting factor to peak performance as overexcitement and anxiety are. Thankfully, the power of your imagination can also be used to get you feeling up for a competition or practice session. You may only rarely require these exercises, which relate to the motivational general-arousal imagery category, but they will be a valuable part of your repertoire of mental skills.

"What If" Scenarios

From our experience of working with teams at the highest levels, one of the most useful applications of visualization is to use a team's collective imagination to come up with things that might go wrong—what we call "what if" scenarios. We then systematically devise strategies for each possible "what if." Strategies are discussed in detail and mentally rehearsed. The benefit is that when something does go wrong, there is a clear blueprint for dealing with it.

Typical "what ifs" include *What if we encounter a seemingly biased or incompetent official? What if our star player is sent off in the first half? What if we get stuck in traffic and arrive at the competition venue an hour late?* and *What if the playing surface gets waterlogged?* In individual sports we conduct this exercise with athletes accompanied by their entire support team—coach, manager, agent,

Exercise 7.8
Dealing With "What If" Scenarios

Spend 10 to 15 minutes thinking about some of the eventualities that you some-times have to deal with in your sport. Stretching your imagination now may really pay dividends sometime in the future if something really unusual happens:

	What I should do	What others should do	Additional information I need
Scenario 1:			
Scenario 2:			
Scenario 3:			
Scenario 4:			

From C.I. Karageorghis and P.C. Terry, 2011, *Inside sport psychology* (Champaign, IL: Human Kinetics).

physiotherapist, and so on. This is an example of cognitive imagery, of both general and specific varieties, depending on the circumstances.

Principles underlying the use of "what ifs" include staying calm when something unexpected happens and immediately accepting the situation. You will need to quickly plan a detailed response to the new reality and to implement the revised plan. If the plan doesn't quite work, then you need to remain flexible to find a plan that does. A limitation of "what ifs" is that, on occasion, things that are totally unpredictable can crop up. For example, we have had to deal with athletes on the same team fighting with each other during competition! When players are overcome by emotion, bringing things back onto an even keel can prove very challenging. Exercise 7.8 is focused on your own "What If" scenarios.

Within-Competition Uses

When you visualize yourself performing a skill just prior to performing it physically, this is known as mental rehearsal and relates to the cognitive specific category of imagery. It is a very simple and effective application of visualization. Running through a successful attempt in the mind immediately before performing helps to remove doubt at crucial moments and also fine-tunes the body for action by priming the relevant muscle groups.

When preparing for competition, avoid indulging in unrealistic fantasies. Imagery should be kept in line with what you can realistically expect, based on what you already know about your opponent, the situation, and yourself. Included in the visualization should be the inevitable mistakes you are bound to make, along with strategies for coping with them. You should also envision moments when the contest appears to be slipping away from you so you can analyze how to regain control.

You will benefit from anticipating every eventuality and deciding in advance the best way to handle it. Not only does this help remove any fear of the unknown, but it also prepares you to respond in the most effective manner to the changes in momentum that are an inevitable part of any sport contest.

Like most pole-vaulters, Russian world record holder Yelena Isinbayeva, the only woman to have exceeded 5 meters, is a devotee of mental rehearsal. Before every attempt, she runs through the complete vault in her mind several times, seeing in great detail each stride of her run-up, the upward drive of her left knee, locking her arms at take-off, and most important, a successful clearance. Only when she has beaten the bar mentally does she attempt the jump physically.

The order of events described in the sidebar on page 185 is important because the last thing Iain visualizes just prior to playing a shot is the swing itself. This keeps the movement pattern fresh in his memory. Other golfers attempt to capture the essence of the required swing by visualizing an arc of light as the path that the club head will follow. When actually playing the shot, the player can concentrate solely on taking the club head back along this illuminated line. This visualization technique can be adapted quite easily to a wide variety of skills (e.g., any place kick in team sports such as rugby and soccer).

When using mental rehearsal, try to develop the conviction that if you can visualize it happening, it will happen. Naturally, mental rehearsal does not guarantee a successful outcome, but it does increase the chance of producing your best effort. If something disturbs your rehearsal or your visualized attempt is unsuccessful, start the process again until you visualize a successful execution of the skill. Our experience has shown that excessive background noise is a threat, so visualization in a relatively quiet environment works best.

AP Photo/David J. Phillip

Yelena Isinbayeva is a devotee of mental rehearsal.

Iain, the Semi-Pro Golfer

A while back Iain Palmer suffered a downturn in his golf form that he attributed to a lack of consistency in his driving. To get out of the rut, he undertook a program of mental skills training. At the initial consultation we realized that Iain practiced the physical skills of golf religiously but devoted hardly any time to mental training. We encouraged him to spend a little extra time thinking about each drive and to slow down his game to enable shots of greater accuracy and consistency. We used Jack Nicklaus—one of Iain's great idols—as a role model. Nicklaus was famed for his diligent use of visualization. Specifically, Iain learned to visualize exactly where he wanted the ball to end up, the flight that it would take to get there, and the type of shot it would take to achieve this flight. As well as seeing all of this in perfect detail, he was trained to feel the stroke during his preparatory swings. Only once Iain had seen and felt the swing that would bring the desired outcome did he strike the ball. This attention to detail eventually led Iain to give up a part-time job as an accounts clerk to join the European tour.

Although mental rehearsal is usually considered in the context of self-paced skills in which the performer has time to prepare before each movement, many famous players in very spontaneous sports report using imagery even during fast-moving action. British tennis player Alex Bogdanovic, for example, said: "The ball whizzes towards me and I see, in my mind's eye, precisely where I want to place it—I hit the shot sweetly, it goes exactly where I had intended and it gives me an inner glow."

Nonetheless, it is probably during endurance events that imagery can do most to sustain a high level of performance from the body when the mind starts to feel like giving up. During most endurance events, there comes a point at which the battle between the body and mind begins to rage. When the body starts to complain, the mind can either cope with the discomfort or succumb to the body's demands to ease off the gas.

Visualization can play a part in the coping process in two ways. First, it can help you dissociate yourself from the situation causing discomfort. For instance, controlled experiments have shown that athletes performing endurance tasks while visualizing themselves lying on a beach or strolling along a riverbank actually believe they are working less hard than when they perform the same task and focus on their bodily signals of discomfort.

You can also use visualization to sustain effort all the way to the finish line in less protracted but equally discomforting events. Visualizing a huge hand helping you along can make the effort seem just that little bit easier. Picturing yourself being spurred on by a huge crowd can also help you cope with the strain.

Many athletes use heroic imagery to sustain effort in the face of adversity. Images of Olympic glory, or of getting dispatches through to HQ, or any personal image that conveys the notion that "When the going gets tough, the tough get going" will help to tap into reserves of willpower and determination.

The body will only cease trying when the mind allows it to; there is an endless list of people who have overcome seemingly impossible odds through sheer doggedness. As the legendary American football coach Vince Lombardi put it: "The spirit, the will

Tara, the Marathon Runner

The marathon is an event that requires as much mental strength as it does physical endurance. Tara Byrd runs the major European marathons every year—Seville, London, and Berlin. Her mental ruggedness is complemented by a dissociation strategy that helps distract her from the aches in her legs and the burning sensation in her lungs. Tara was a creative writing student at university, so when she wants to switch off from the pain, she composes poems in her mind. For the most part, these are quite banal, but at time the poems are so good she writes them down immediately after her run. Either way, they make the long, lonely hours of training far more bearable, and time appears to whisk by.

to win, and the will to excel are the things that endure. These qualities are so much more important than the events that occur."

Postperformance Review

Smart athletes realize that every performance, good, bad, or indifferent, is an opportunity to learn something. Even the most disappointing effort can be transformed into a valuable experience if something positive can be extracted from it. Using visualization to create a replay of performance is often one of the simplest and most effective ways to analyze it.

At a conscious level, it is sometimes very difficult to recall precise details of a performance. The more you master the skills of your sport, the less you require conscious thought to perform those skills and consequently the more attention you can devote to tactical considerations. As highlighted in chapter 1, high-level performers perform skills almost automatically, and because this gives them more time to gather information about situations, they are able to make correct decisions earlier and to anticipate the movements of opponents better. Nonetheless, this mastery of skills can, on occasion, be a double-edged sword.

Performing skills unconsciously results in a reduced awareness of the mechanisms by which skills are generated, which can lead to difficulties in identifying faults in technique. Basically, because the highly skilled devote less thought to how the skills are produced, they are also less aware of the small changes in technique that creep in over time. This can leave even champion athletes despondent and bewildered after a poor performance.

Admittedly, this is a relatively small price to pay for the advantages that these skills provide. Nonetheless, athletes find it very frustrating when a technical fault arises and they are unable to identify its exact cause. The trained eye of an experienced coach is usually required to identify faults among such athletes, but this may prove difficult or costly to arrange. Video analysis is another way of reviewing the finer points of performance, but again, this requires some expert analysis.

Visualization is often the most effective compromise. Conducting your own detailed replays of poor performance may provide the clue to technical faults about which you would otherwise remain oblivious. Using imagery in this way will also help to identify patterns of behavior or methods of preparation that contribute to good or bad performances. The tactical rehearsal procedure described earlier in exercise 7.4 can easily be modified for performance analysis.

To facilitate a review, plan and start the session in the same way you would for mental practice, but while visualizing yourself performing, slow the movement down and go through a mental checklist of all the important technical aspects of the skill in question. For example, double Olympic javelin champion from Norway, Andreas Thorkildsen, might visualize himself running up, withdrawing the javelin, lengthening his stride, getting his legs ahead of his body, and driving and twisting his hips as his arm comes through long and fast. In slow motion, his visualization might reveal that the snap with his hips was too labored to unleash the javelin with full power, and therefore that is where he should concentrate his efforts on the next attempt.

When analyzing performance during imagery, it is a good idea to capture the key elements of technique with labels that act as vivid reference points during subsequent performances (see exercise 7.9). For example, just prior to take-off, long jumpers prepare to transfer forward momentum into upward momentum by lowering their center of gravity and then generating an upward surge of the leading leg. They often capture the essence of this two-part maneuver with the labels *sink* and *drive,* which neatly sum up the required process.

Increasing your awareness of critical aspects of technique in this way improves your chances of accurately identifying performance errors. Moreover, these action replays will prove just as useful in isolating reasons for outstanding performance as they are for analyzing poor performance.

When you are really in top form, try to "capture in a bottle" all of the mental components of your performance (see also exercise 3.8, The Winning Feeling, in chapter 3). This will help you recreate that winning mindset in the future. This relates to both the motivational general-mastery and motivational general-arousal facets of imagery.

Use a notepad immediately following a successful performance to jot down everything you sensed. If you are injured or currently experiencing below-par form, try to complete the exercise retrospectively, with reference to your last peak performance. Hopefully, this will still be fairly clear in your mind.

Exercise 7.9
Holding on to a Peak Performance

- After a successful performance analyze through each of your five senses what you saw, heard, smelled, tasted, or felt at the time of peak performance.

- Take particular note of any self-talk that was taking place inside your head and the impact it had on your performance. Perhaps there was no self-dialogue whatsoever.

- Practice recreating the key signals of success in your mental warm-ups and mental rehearsal.

APPLYING HYPNOSIS IN SPORT

For more than 20 years, hypnosis has been popular among athletes in their ever more sophisticated attempts to make legal performance gains. Hypnosis has been used to make boxers think they are invincible, bolster the confidence of professional cricketers, and even help Olympic wrestlers enhance the quality of their mental skills training. It is a psychological state that is quite similar to that experienced during visualization, although the level of relaxation involved is usually somewhat deeper.

You may well have experienced something similar to a hypnotic state when driving a car. When you are entirely familiar with a route, let's say driving to work or college, the driving becomes automatic. In such a state, when you're not thinking about the action of driving, it is easy to miss your turning or completely forget the bread and milk that you should have collected en route. This phenomenon is known as highway hypnosis.

A common misconception about hypnosis is that it involves a deep trance, in which you are unaware of what is going on around you and have no control over your actions. In reality, all hypnosis is self-hypnosis and involves a state of heightened awareness and pleasurable relaxation rather than a state that allows somebody else to pull the strings. The theory that we espouse, based on the writings of Milton H. Erickson, is that hypnosis is essentially an altered state of consciousness.

You may have witnessed a hypnotic stage show in which an expert hypnotist embarrassed volunteers from the audience. The techniques described in this chapter relate to self-hypnosis rather than heterohypnosis, which entails being hypnotized by another person. In stage shows, volunteers are aware of what they are doing and are usually complicit with the hypnotist. In other words, they are being cooperative. The relaxation techniques, or hypnotic induction, they experience in the early part of the show makes them lose their inhibitions and be more susceptible to the hypnotist's suggestions.

The main benefit of self-hypnosis is that, following a brief period of relaxation, you can give yourself positive suggestions that will help you enhance your performance and adopt more positive attitudes toward training and competition. You can also use the visualization skills described in the first part of this chapter while in a state of hypnosis. This state is not the same as sleep, nor is it related to sleep (although people often come out of a hypnotic state feeling refreshed and reenergized).

Self-hypnosis can be an empowering technique that complements visualization and accelerates many aspects of mental training. The visualization exercises relating to skill development (7.3), tactical rehearsal (7.4), and postperformance review (7.9) presented earlier can easily be conducted in a hypnotic state. This section focuses on hypnosis-related exercises for precompetition and within-competition applications.

A Script for Self-Hypnosis

The following script is intended to take you into a state of deep relaxation.* The purpose is to help you calm your mind and allow you to focus on the moment, enjoying the here and now. The script can be used as a lead-in for many of the visualization exercises presented earlier in this chapter. The first couple of times you try it, we advise that

---

*The script should not be used prior to or while driving a vehicle or operating machinery. The authors and Human Kinetics accept no responsibility for any inappropriate use of the script or for any consequences associated with its use.

you ask a friend or relative to read the instructions. The script is also written to enable you to use it yourself, by recording it as an MP3 file or onto a CD. Be sure to read it through carefully before attempting to make an audio recording. In time, you should try to memorize the script so that you can use it anywhere. When you do memorize it, change *you* to *I* and *your* to *my*; in other words, put it into the first person. This will make the exercise even more powerful. *(Where you see ellipses [. . .], pause for a few seconds.)*

Find a comfortable chair or lie down in a place where you are unlikely to be disturbed. . . . Make yourself comfortable, leaving your arms by your sides or in your lap. . . . Allow the chair or mat to absorb your entire body weight. Over the next few minutes, your body may feel as though it's sinking . . . while at the same time, it may feel as though your mind is drifting. . . . That's perfectly OK. . . . Now, keeping your eyes wide open, look right up toward your forehead. Look upward really intently and all the time notice how your eyelids are feeling heavier and heavier. . . . As you look up, become aware of just how tired your eyes are becoming . . . but you must keep them wide open, wide open. You would really like to close your eyes . . . but hold out for just a little bit longer. . . . Close your eyelids now. Begin to go deeply relaxed, deeply, deeply relaxed and slow your breathing right down. . . . Take long, slow, deep, controlled breaths . . . long, slow, deep, controlled breaths. . . . Now, become aware of the ambient noise around you . . . notice every detail about it . . . tune in to it . . . the hum of the heating or ventilation system, a conversation going on in another room that perhaps reminds you of a pleasant conversation you once had . . . a vehicle passing by outside . . . and so on. Now, focus on the pattern and regularity of your breathing. . . . Regulate your breathing in such a way that you breathe in for a slow count of 4, hold the breath for a slow count of 4, and release it for a slow count of 4. . . . Get a steady rhythm going . . . 1, 2, 3, 4 . . . each time . . . 1, 2, 3, 4 . . . and enjoy the sensation as you relax your entire musculature. . . . Now, notice a warm feeling of relaxation starting in your toes and feet and spreading slowly through your entire body . . . through your ankles . . . through your calves and shins . . . through your knees . . . through your thighs . . . and up into your abdomen and lower back. . . . Allow that warm sensation of relaxation to spread up into your chest and from there to the remainder of your body . . . to your fingertips and to the top of your head. . . . Enjoy this warm, relaxing sensation and notice what a calming effect it has on your entire being. . . . Now, count down from 1 to 10. Each time you count down a number, you will go 10 percent, one tenth, more relaxed than you are now . . . one tenth, 10 percent more relaxed than you are now. . . . Here we go . . . very slowly . . . 10 . . . 9 . . . 8 . . . deeper and deeper relaxed . . . 7 . . . 6 . . . 5 . . . deeper and deeper still . . . 4 . . . 3 . . . really deep, 2 . . . 1 . . . all the way, deep down relaxed. . . . Now, you feel completely relaxed. . . . Enjoy this wonderful sensation. . . .

Give yourself positive and beneficial suggestions relating, for example, to increasing your self-confidence, attaining peak performances or mastering a specific sport skill that has perhaps proved elusive to you. (See Examples of Positive Suggestions That

Can Be Used in a State of Self-Hypnosis for some examples of positive suggestions that we have used in the past.) If at any time you need to return to full alertness, for any reason, such as in the case of emergency or any situation for which full attention is required, by opening your eyes you will be fully alert.

To take yourself out of the trance state, count up slowly from 1 to 10. On reaching the number 8, open your eyes, and at the number 10 you will be fully awake and alert. You will be as awake and as alert as you need to be for everything that lies ahead in the day. As you stand up, notice how good you feel.

Our experience has shown that athletes need to be very motivated and fully accepting of the potential benefits to practice techniques such as self-hypnosis. Athletes who are openly skeptical or show a negative attitude toward such approaches should never be forced to adopt them. Moreover, a hypnotic susceptibility trait documented in the literature suggests that some people have a greater predisposition toward entering a trance and experiencing hypnotic phenomena. We reemphasize that not all of the exercises presented in this text are appropriate for all athletes. Thus, take an eclectic approach and select what works best for you.

Creating Positive Suggestions

Positive self-suggestions, either long or short, can be reinforced through hypnosis. You can deliver positive suggestions to yourself once you have reached a reasonably deep level of relaxation. The self-hypnosis script presented in the preceding subsection is an ideal way to facilitate this. The affirmations can of course be played in your mind or recorded onto an MP3 file or CD as you prefer.

Examples of Positive Suggestions That Can Be Used in a State of Self-Hypnosis

- You will be able to exhibit complete self-control in any competitive situation.
- You will have all the time you need to make your movements technically correct.
- You will be able to channel any nervous energy into your performance.
- You will become more focused in training, and this will increase your rate of improvement.
- You will focus only on what's relevant to your performance and not be distracted by irrelevant details.
- You will be able to obtain an optimal state of mind to compete.
- You will be able to immerse yourself entirely in competitive situations and really enjoy the challenge.
- You will be able to rely on instinct to make the right movements and decisions.

The relaxation response makes the right brain far more accessible to positive suggestions that will affect how you feel about yourself. In framing such suggestions, avoid negativity; suggestions should always be worded positively.

For example, a soccer striker may come up against a larger and stronger defender. An auto-suggestion such as *I will be alert and agile* would be better than *I will run rings around him every time,* because clearly the latter is highly unlikely. Similarly, using suggestions such as *I won't be nervous* draws attention to nerves and makes competition anxiety likely. A better auto-suggestion would be *I will remain calm and in control* (see also chapter 3).

Exercise 7.10 on page 192 is intended to improve your attitude toward competition and allow you to perform with less psychological inhibition. Before engaging in the exercise, use the self-hypnosis script on page 189. This ego-strengthening routine should be inserted immediately after you have descended from 10 to 1, and followed immediately by a return to full wakefulness by counting up from 1 to 10. While in a state of light trance, you are more disposed to the positive messages this exercise carries.

Precompetition Preparation

The beauty of self-hypnosis is that it can be used to accelerate all aspects of mental training. It can also help you harness more of your muscular power. It does this in two ways: first, by increasing the amount of energy during a muscular contraction, and second, by incorporating all of the relevant muscles (prime movers and stabilizers) during that contraction. Accordingly, hypnotic-type techniques can be used to increase the energy produced in muscular contractions as detailed in exercise 7.11.

Generally speaking, hypnosis will relax you, whereas general arousal techniques such as those described in the first part of this chapter (e.g., exercises 7.6 and 7.7) are best for enhancing muscular power and endurance. Nonetheless, the judicious use of exercises 7.11 and 7.12 on page 193 will help you narrow your attention and harness a greater proportion of your physical resources. A light trance is advantageous for both of these exercises.

Achieving a deeply relaxed state for an impending competition is not always the most appropriate course of action. Sportspeople require a certain degree of tension and arousal to function at their best. The appropriate level of tension varies greatly from athlete to athlete and from sport to sport. The mental preparation profile (exercise 4.1 in chapter 4) will certainly help you identify your optimal mental state for competition.

Exercise 7.10
Ego Strengthening for Athletes

(Where you see ellipses [. . .], pause for a few seconds.)

Before you return to a state of full wakefulness, I want you to know that as the next few days and weeks and months go by, you will feel stronger in every way. You will feel physically and mentally stronger . . . more alert, more attentive to detail, more responsive to the demands placed upon you . . . less easily fatigued or bored. . . . You will become completely immersed in the things that are most important to you. When demands are placed on you . . . whether these be in your sport, in your social life, at work, or at school, you will have abundant energy, not only to cope with what is asked of you, but to go that extra mile . . . to give a little bit more . . . even to exceed other people's expectations of you. And because this will happen, precisely as I say it will happen, so your confidence and zest for life will grow considerably. . . . You will ooze self-confidence . . . not in a way that borders on arrogance or self-importance, but an inner confidence that will radiate and draw people toward you and inspire those around you. . . . It may be that you hear a reassuring voice, maybe in your mind's ear or from deep within you, saying the things you most need to hear, giving you positive suggestions that you need to receive right now. . . . You can internalize these positive suggestions . . . hold them deep within your subconscious mind, safe in the knowledge that as the next few days and weeks and months go by, you will be able to put the suggestions into action. I want you to see yourself improving . . . and imagine how it will feel to accomplish some of your main goals. . . . If you can create a clear picture of what you want, it will be much easier for you to attain it. . . . Enjoy these positive images for a few seconds . . . make them entirely lifelike. . . . Very soon, you will come back to a state of full wakefulness . . . and when you do, you will feel as though a load has been lifted from your shoulders, allowing you to lead your life in a way that is so much more satisfying and rewarding. . . . Above all else, you will have a deep sense of inner confidence that you will exude to all around you.

The wake-up instructions follow as described at the end of the self-hypnosis script (page 190).

For a detailed explanation on how to write ego-strengthening scripts, see *Sport Hypnosis* by Donald R. Liggett, 2000, Human Kinetics, pp. 107-111. Some of the exercises presented in this chapter have been adapted from exercises presented in the Liggett text.

Exercise 7.11
Increase Energy in Muscular Contractions

- As you inhale, feel energy entering your body.
- Exhale after a deep breath; then inhale again.
- Perform the movement specific to your sport after exhaling the second time.
- The timing of your breaths will vary from sport to sport. A long jumper will inhale and exhale at the end of the runway, then breathe deeply on the approach run while exhaling on the takeoff board. Similarly, a weightlifter with a barbell across the top of her chest will breathe in and then exhale vigorously to "jerk" the heavy weight above her head.
- Practice this technique thoroughly in training before applying it to a competitive situation.
- Reinforce the technique by practicing it during self-hypnosis.

Exercise 7.12
Getting All Your Muscles to Work for You

- Once you have reached a relaxed state, visualize through your own eyes walking around your competitive environment in a confident manner just before the start of your event.
- Use all of your senses together to make the experience vivid and real.
- Now, while continuing to look through your own eyes, feel each muscle move in the correct sequence for the activity that you're engaged in. In particular, focus on the role of the muscles involved in the early part of the movement such as the rotation of the upper torso in the "moveaway" of a golf swing or planting the feet when playing a tennis forehand.
- Spend a few minutes feeling the entire kinetic chain of muscular contractions that brings about superior performance.
- Use task-related self-statements to reinforce the action, such as *Arm fast and last* if you're a javelin thrower or *Eye on the ball* if you're a batsman in cricket.

Within-Competition Uses

Light hypnotic states can sometimes be used during competition, although a key consideration is the structure of the sport. If your sport takes place in segments or rounds throughout the course of a day or weekend, there is no need to remain psyched up for the duration of the competition; rather, you need to stay relaxed between rounds so as not to expend mental and physical energy unnecessarily. A really good way to stay relaxed in such circumstances is through use of the well-known Benson's relaxation response (exercise 7.13).

Posthypnotic suggestions can also have an important part to play during competition. For example, British double-trap shooter Richard Faulds used the image of himself as the Iceman to stay cool, calm, and collected at successive Olympic Games including the Sydney Games, where he won the gold medal. The suggestions he was given prior to competition by the second author were initially triggered during competition by the sight of a circular blue sticker on his wristwatch. Many great shooters, including 2008 Olympic trap shooting champion David Kostelcký of the Czech Republic, enter a mild trancelike stage to stay relaxed and focused between shots. Now try exercise 7.14, which allows you to build up your own posthypnotic suggestions.

David Kostelcký during the 2008 Olympic final.

Photo courtesy of Max Naldoni

Exercise 7.13
Benson's Relaxation Response

Benson's technique comprises seven easy steps:

1. Sit in a comfortable position and adopt a relaxed posture.
2. Pick a short focus word that has significant meaning for you and that you associate with relaxation (e.g., *relax, smooth, calm, easy, float*).
3. Slowly close your eyes.
4. Relax all the muscles in your body.
5. Breathe smoothly and naturally repeating the focus word.
6. Be passive so that if other thoughts enter your mind, dismiss them with, "Oh well" and calmly return to the focus word. Don't concern yourself with how the process is going.
7. Continue this for 10 to 15 minutes.

Exercise 7.14
Using a Posthypnotic Suggestion

- Use the self-hypnosis script on page 189.
- When you have reached a deep level of relaxation, think of an image that encapsulates how you want to feel in competition—perhaps a legendary athlete, a powerful creature such as a tiger, or a mythical character. It doesn't matter what the image is as long as it's potent and meaningful for you.
- Think of a way you might trigger this image during competition, perhaps by looking at a sticker on your watch, wiping your brow with an armband, or focusing on a particular part of your body.
- Tell yourself that whenever you use this trigger in competition, the positive image of yourself will ensue and characterize the way you perform.
- Spend a few minutes visualizing yourself in the first person with all the normal competition-related senses in your body, while embodying your special image, whatever it may be.
- Tell yourself once more that whenever you use this trigger in competition, the positive image of yourself will ensue.
- Bring yourself back to a state of full wakefulness by counting slowly from 1 to 10. On reaching the number 8, open your eyes, and at the number 10 you will be fully awake and alert. You will be as awake and as alert as you need to be for everything that lies ahead in the day. As you stand up, notice how positive you feel.

SUMMARY

Imagination and the subconscious mind can be used to develop skills that will improve performance. Two mental skills that can be used in parallel are visualization and self-hypnosis. Naturally, there are many other ways to profit from visualization techniques, and several of these are dealt with in other chapters. Chapter 3 showed how to use visualization skills to develop a winning attitude and improve confidence, chapter 4 included a section on how to use visualization to control anxiety, and chapter 5 explained further the part visualization plays in psyching up for competition.

The five visualization perspectives are visual-internal, visual-external, kinesthetic, visual-internal kinesthetic, and visual-external kinesthetic. Combining all the senses during visualization will bring about the best results. If your goal is to learn and retain new skills, the visual-external kinesthetic perspective is possibly the most effective. The well known acronym WYSIWYG (*What You See Is What You Get*) applies equally to visualization and self-hypnosis techniques that involve imagery (e.g., exercises 7.10 and 7.12).

Paivio's imagery model is a theoretical backdrop for many of the exercises in this chapter. This model has two main dimensions, or elements: the *purpose* of imagery, which can be motivational or cognitive (thought related), and the *application* of imagery, which can be general or specific. Although the model promotes the use of imagery, in a number of instances visualization or imagery techniques may not work so well (e.g., when athletes who are high in self-consciousness are being observed or when there is excessive background noise).

Most of us have already had lots of informal visualization practice in our dreams. Indeed, if we can't dream success, it's unlikely that we'll ever be able to achieve it. The important thing is to try to follow formal mental practice with physical practice of the same skill as soon as possible. This approach has been shown to be the most effective method of developing superior sport skills. Similarly, the positive suggestions detailed in the self-hypnosis section should precede physical practice or competition.

The vast but often unexplored powers of the human imagination can be viewed as your ultimate energy, the gateway to superior performance. To leave such a resource unexploited is to limit yourself to a level of achievement well below your full potential. Although nothing in this book will transform your performance overnight, investing time in developing psychological skills such as visualization and self-hypnosis will add a new dimension to your training program that will certainly pay dividends in the long run. Remember that the mind is much like a parachute—it works best when open.

The Power of Sound

In training build-ups for major races, I put together a playlist and listen to it during the run-in. It helps me psych up and reminds me of times in the build-up when I've worked really hard, or felt good. With the right music, I do a much harder workout.

—Paula Radcliffe, marathon world record holder

The use of music to enhance sport performance has been of deep interest to us for two decades, and many of the interventions in this book stem either from scientific studies we have conducted using music or from our experiences working with athletes. The exercises will benefit individual athletes as well as anyone responsible for a group of athletes, such as team coaches and managers.

Music is essentially the organization of five primary elements: melody, harmony, tempo, rhythm, and dynamics. *Melody* is the tune of a piece of music, the part to which you might hum or whistle along. *Harmony* acts to shape the mood of the music to make you feel happy, sad, soulful, or romantic through the meshing of sounds. *Tempo* is the speed at which music is played and is measured in beats per minute (bpm). *Rhythm* refers to the way music is accented and combines with tempo to make people instinctively move in time with it. *Dynamics* have to do with the energy transmitted by musicians through touch or breath to influence the volume of their instruments.

History books reveal that from the dawn of civilization, ancient cultures combined sounds in ways that affected the human psyche. As time progressed, primitive forms of music evolved into ever more structured and artistically pleasing arrangements. Music became common in many types of activity: worship, education, entertainment, healing, and not least, athletic performance.

Music was incorporated into the ancient Olympic Games where rhythmic clapping and drumming accompanied some of the events. The modern Olympic Games have continued to formalize the association between music and athletic endeavor. Music is an integral part of some Olympic events such as rhythmic gymnastics and synchronized swimming. Live music also features prominently at the opening and closing ceremonies of the Games. One of the most spectacular examples of this was during the opening ceremony of the 2004 Athens Games, at which large drums beat the sound

---

Football's Coming Home

An abiding memory of the European Soccer Championships in 1996 was that of the England fans singing "Three Lions" as the England team entered Wembley Stadium to play Germany in the quarterfinals of the competition. The lyrics of the chorus, "It's coming home, it's coming home, football's coming home" alluded to the fact that England, the spiritual home of soccer, had not hosted or won a major championship since the 1966 World Cup (when they beat West Germany) and that the time had come for another famous victory. The music lent a certain aura to the championships, which bridged the gap between a mere soccer tournament and a stage for the nation's hopes and dreams. Although it was not to be for England on this particular occasion, it was a defining moment in reinforcing the link between music and sporting endeavor.

---

of the human heart while 180 bouzouki players strummed traditional Greek music in unison as an accompaniment to scores of dancers (a bouzouki is a traditional string instrument common to the eastern Mediterranean region; it looks like a mandolin and can be either plucked or strummed). Finally, the national anthem of the winning athlete for each event is played at the medal ceremony, often reducing seasoned competitors to tears as the emotion of the occasion becomes completely overwhelming.

The ancient tradition, inherent in the Olympic movement, of combining art with athletic competitions eventually led to musical accompaniment becoming popular in many sports. It is rare not to hear music blaring out of soccer and baseball stadiums and basketball courts around the globe, and indeed, most teams have their own anthems or signature tunes. For example, at West Ham United FC it's the classic "I'm Forever Blowing Bubbles," and the University of Kansas football stadium reverberates to the 125-year-old "Rock Chalk Chant."

During the last two decades, music has become ubiquitous in training venues. It is played in gymnasiums, athletic stadiums, and even swimming pools. Is such music played to promote an ergogenic (work-enhancing) effect, or does it simply make the environment a little more pleasurable? If music does increase our work output or enjoyment of an activity, how can we best maximize such benefits? In this chapter we attempt to provide some answers from our own research and applied practice and from the work of others. We also offer guidelines in how to use music to maximize its beneficial effects with a scattering of examples from the world of sport.

MUSIC AND SPORT PERFORMANCE

The effects of music can be quite startling; indeed, they are the stuff of legends. The Pied Piper of Hamelin reputedly entranced children with his beautiful music and led them away, never to be seen again. Odysseus told of the songs of Sirens that cast a spell on sailors whose ships were subsequently dashed against the rocks. David's harp playing enabled King Saul to overcome his deepest depression. In recent history, the blues emerged from the dark shadows of slavery and oppression to lift the spirits of African Americans and give them hope for a brighter future.

Scientific studies into the effects of music in sport and exercise contexts have reported slightly more modest reactions than these. Nonetheless, music has been shown to have the potential to make a significant difference in performance in the hotbed of competition in which skills and abilities are often closely matched. Research has supported at least five ways music can benefit sporting performance and preparation (see the boxes on the right side of figure 8.1).

A basic premise is that some aspects of music selection have to do with how music is composed and performed, whereas others have to do with how it is interpreted by the listener through the prism of their cultural background. Rhythmic response and melody and harmony, which shape the mood of the music, are internal factors. This means that they have to do with the way the music has been put together—the composition, tempo, instrumentation, and so on. In our research papers, we have termed the elements of melody and harmony *musicality*.

The cultural impact of the music and extramusical associations are external factors, meaning that they are associated with listeners' interpretations of the music and their musical experiences. Our research shows that the internal factors are more important in predicting how a person will respond to a piece of music. Hence, even when selecting for a group with different musical experiences, it is still possible to select music with motivational properties. The relationship between internal and external factors, the motivational qualities of music, and potential benefits are represented in figure 8.1.

Music can help you dissociate, or turn off mentally, from feelings of pain or fatigue, lift or regulate your mood (see also chapter 5), and alter your arousal level. Generally speaking, loud, upbeat music functions as a stimulant (increasing arousal), whereas

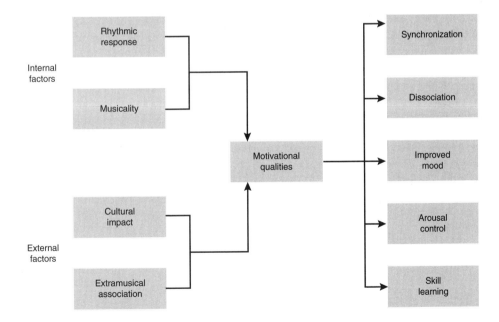

Figure 8.1   Motivational music in sport and exercise.

From C.I. Karageorghis, P.C. Terry, and A.M. Lane, 1999, "Development and initial validation of an instrument to assess the motivational qualities of music in exercise and sport: The Brunel Music Rating Inventory," *Journal of Sports Sciences* 17(9): 713-724. Adapted by permission of Taylor & Francis Ltd.

soft, slow music functions as a sedative (reducing arousal). You can synchronize your work rate to a musical tempo, which is particularly useful if you participate in a sport that requires repetitive actions, such as long-distance running or cycling. For safety reasons, any activity that takes place on the roads should not be accompanied by music. Finally, music can help you learn motor skills more easily, such as ball control or complex movement patterns.

Synchronization

People have a strong tendency to respond to the rhythmic qualities of music. Indeed, Elvis Presley once said, "Music should be something that makes you gotta move, inside or out." The tendency to move to music sometimes results in athletes' synchronizing their movements with the tempo of the music. When movement is performed consciously in time with music, the music is said to be used synchronously. Synchronous music is most obvious in sports such as figure skating, rhythmic gymnastics, and dance aerobics.

Scientific studies that have examined the effects of synchronizing training activities with music tempo consistently report that synchronous music significantly enhances work rate. In other words, when athletes work in time to music, they often work harder for longer. A recent study led by the first author revealed that synchronizing stride rate during 400-meter time trials to upbeat music led to an average improvement of half a second when compared to a no-music control condition.

A follow-up study examined the effects of upbeat music on treadmill endurance. The subjects started at 75 percent of their maximal aerobic capacity ($\dot{V}O_2$max) and were requested to synchronize their stride rate to a music tempo and then continue exercising until exhaustion. When a motivational music condition was compared to a no-music control, there was a 15 percent improvement in endurance. When motivational music was compared to *oudeterous* (neutral) music, a 6 percent improvement in endurance resulted. (Back in 1999 we coined the term *oudeterous* to mean music that is neither motivational nor demotivational.)

In contrast to synchronous music, asynchronous music is played in the background without any expectation that athletes will synchronize their movements with it. That is not to say that unintentional synchronous movement does not occur. For example, the Brazilian football team is accompanied by a section of percussion players among their supporters. Many journalists and commentators have noted that the Brazilian style of play emulates the lilting swing of the samba, a rhythm embedded in Brazilian culture—the team has even been nicknamed the Samba Boys. Hence, it is plausible that background samba rhythms may give the Brazilian players a slight advantage over their European rivals.

Our assertion that, as humans, we have an innate response to the rhythmic qualities of music has been detailed in many texts written by philosophers and musicologists. A century ago, philosopher R. MacDougall proposed that people find rhythm pleasurable because its structure replicates natural forms of physical activity such as walking and running. To experience this, think about performing a physical task such as step-ups that involves a strict four-stage movement pattern. This is comparable to a marching rhythm in 4/4 time. Alternatively, join your arms by putting the palms of your hands together and swing them from side to side in a pendulum-like motion (as if you were striking an imaginary golf ball). This will have a "*one*-two-three" feel that

Jona Nyachae and the Musical Running Method

Jona Nyachae is a middle-distance runner who has just completed her first season on the European grand prix circuit. She was World Junior Champion over 1500 meters but took a few years to make her mark in the senior ranks. In the past, her training was fairly sporadic, and she relied heavily on her considerable natural talent. The demands of the grand prix and major championships have necessitated a more structured approach to both training and preparation.

When Jona was growing up in Kenya, she found that when music was piped through the public address system of her local stadium, it put a real spring in her step. Pace judgment was always a problem for Jona in both training and competition. Frequently, she would start too fast, but musical accompaniment helped her regulate her stride. A performance specialist in Europe suggested that Jona apply synchronous music to her interval training—music preselected to coincide in tempo with her cadence at various running speeds.

Jona worked out that she took 200 strides on average when performing 400-meter intervals in 60 seconds. This coincided with musical selections that had a tempo of 100 beats per minute (Jona took two strides to each beat). Appropriate musical selections included "Single Ladies" by Beyoncé and Jordin Sparks' "One Step At A Time (Ultimix)." Jona made similar calculations for other common interval distances that she completed in training—600 meters, 800 meters, and so on. She used an ergonomically designed Sony W series MP3 player that attached snugly to the back of her head along with in-ear headphones to ensure that the audio equipment did not offset her smooth running stride. For longer distances, Jona was able to take one stride for each beat of the music as her stride rate per minute decreased to coincide with up-tempo selections such as "Beat It" by Michael Jackson.

In competition, the use of music was not permitted (other than for an occasional exhibition race), so Jona ran the musical selection that corresponded with her intended time in her mind, which helped her to pace the race evenly. This had two added benefits. First, she could resist allowing her rivals to dictate the pace because the musical method allowed her to run consistently fast times using an even pace. This meant that she could even hang around the back of a field in a "suicidally paced" opening lap, safe in the knowledge that she would come back strongly in the closing stages of the race. Second, in the opening stages of the race at least, hearing the music in her mind distracted her from the physical sensations of hard running and almost seemed to buffer the effects of the onset of lactic acid. Her thought process made the experience of racing more pleasurable. The inspirational lyrics also gave her a hard competitive edge: "Beat it, no one wants to be defeated."

is like a waltz in 3/4 time (three beats to the bar). Athletes routinely apply the force of rhythm for their specialized purposes. Our own research has demonstrated that the response to the rhythmic components of music is the most important factor in determining its motivational qualities. This is because people lock into the rhythmic components of music immediately; the melodic and harmonic aspects of music have a secondary effect on mental and physical functioning.

Dissociation and Mood Effects

Another way music may influence physical performance is by narrowing your attention, which may divert it from feelings of fatigue during training or competition. The amount of information your mind can process at any given moment is quite limited; hence, focusing on an external stimulus such as music may alter your perception of effort. In short, music can make training and endurance activities seem less hard. Music can therefore increase work output and enhance the emotional experience of physical activity by blocking out the negative sensations associated with physical exertion and fatigue.

Scientists commonly refer to focusing on music for its reputed distraction effect as a dissociation technique. Other well-known dissociation techniques that athletes use include imagery, focusing on their surroundings, and mental arithmetic. Some athletes hum, whistle, or sing their preferred music to dissociate from a tough workout.

Our research has shown that music inhibits muscular discomfort only at low to moderate levels of physical exertion. During high-intensity activity, when you feel the accumulation of lactic acid in your muscles, your attention switches involuntarily from external stimuli, such as music, to the internal sensations of fatigue. Hence, although music can divert attention, it is best used in training for repetitive activities at a submaximal level such as running, rowing, and cycling.

We have quantified the effect of music on perceived exertion, as have other researchers. A fairly consistent finding is that music reduces perceived exertion by around 10 percent up to exercise intensities of 75 percent of maximal aerobic capacity ($\dot{V}O_2$max). Our most recent research has shown that although music does not reduce the perception of effort during high-intensity workouts (>75 percent of $\dot{V}O_2$max), it does improve the *experience* of the workout; in other words, it makes hard training seem more fun and shapes how you interpret the symptoms of fatigue.

Louise the Triathlete

Louise is an excellent cyclist and runner but a relatively weak swimmer, which has prevented her from reaching the highest echelons of her sport. She makes a concerted effort to improve by swimming at least 50 miles (80 km) in training each month. This is often a lonely and arduous task with little variation. Her coach aims to make Louise a more efficient swimmer. To do this, she needs to relax and not waste energy through unwanted muscular tension. With this aim, Louise uses a specially designed waterproof MP3 player in her swimming cap. She listens to soulful ballads and soft, relaxing music. The vocal harmony group Ladysmith Black Mambazo performs her favorite music. She associates this African music with the fine tradition of endurance athletes from East Africa, and this inspires her. The harmonies within the music create a positive mood while the flowing rhythms and slower tempos of the music help her to relax and maintain an efficient and regular stroke rhythm. The music also provides a focus on long-duration swims and distracts her from the negative bodily sensations associated with fatigue. In fact, the effects of the music can be quite hypnotic, and after a while she feels as though she is gliding through the water.

Accordingly if you are running on a treadmill at 85 percent of your $\dot{V}O_2$max, listening to music will not make the task seem any easier in terms of the information that your muscles and vital organs send to your brain, although you are likely to interpret the experience as more enjoyable. The bottom line is that during a hard workout, music has limited power in influencing *what* you feel but has considerable power in influencing *how* you feel it.

The first author uses loud asynchronous music in a circuit training session that he runs every Monday evening at his university. The session is for track and field athletes, and they enjoy the blare of upbeat, inspirational music to dull the pain and alleviate the monotony of the repetitive conditioning exercises. Softer and slower music is used to accompany recovery periods. The change in music indicates to the athletes when they should stop working on a particular station and refreshes them prior to the next burst of energy.

Hence, the music not only provides cues by which to regulate the entire session but also unifies the group. An appropriate musical program raises their spirits and gives them the impetus to push that little bit harder. To increase the effectiveness of the music even further and prevent athletes from becoming desensitized to it, the author uses no music at all every fourth session. Also, he changes the music program every week and updates it each semester to incorporate current hits that the students might be familiar with in their everyday music listening environments.

Arousal Control

Arousal refers to a person's physiological state and ranges on a continuum from deep sleep at one end to panic at the other. Music can influence performance by altering arousal levels; it can be used as a legal stimulant or sedative prior to and during competition. When employed prior to competition, it is known as pretask music. It seems unlikely that music will ever be on the list of banned substances published by the International Olympic Committee, and of course, music does not carry the same risks as some other ergogenic aids.

Music affects arousal levels for at least two reasons. First, physiological processes tend to react to the rhythmic components of music; fast, upbeat music increases respiration rate, heart rate, sweat secretion, and other indicators of physical activation. Second, arousal is increased through extramusical associations; in other words, the music promotes thoughts that inspire either physical activity or heroic deeds. Just as the association between your first love and "your song" can be very strong, so is the relationship between music and sporting endeavor.

For example, when many people involved in soccer (but not classical music!) hear the operatic aria "Nessun Dorma," which was performed by the late great Luciano Pavarotti to celebrate the 1990 Soccer World Cup in Italy, they immediately think of that competition and are reminded of the buzz and excitement generated by the World Cup. Similarly, many boxers who hear any of the musical motifs from the five Rocky movies think of Sylvester Stallone's Herculean efforts in and out of the ring, which may inspire them. Such associations are built up by repetition and the powerful images provided by cinema, television, radio, and the Internet. These agents of popular culture have a powerful influence on music preferences.

Iwan Thomas, 400-Meter Runner

Iwan Thomas was a 400-meter international track runner. He won gold at the 1997 World Championships in the 4 × 400-meter relay and, in the following year, took individual gold at the European Championships and Commonwealth Games. His event requires an explosive and concerted burst of energy lasting around 44 seconds. Iwan is a very easygoing person, and he found that music used in a stimulative role helped him to increase his levels of arousal to an optimal state, both physically (release of adrenaline) and mentally (feelings of excitement and urgency). For this purpose, he used a piece of up-tempo dance music with an insistent and driving rhythm: "Firestarter" by The Prodigy.

Iwan found that the combination of the strong rhythmic features and the lyrics, which incite aggressive action, created a hostile energy that empowered him and gave him the killer instinct he believed he needed to surpass his opposition. He used the minutes before he was called to the blocks to listen to the music and stare down his lane. While he was doing this, he imagined himself running in a dominant and ultimately victorious way; the music promoted that kind of imagery in his mind. Also, while he was listening to the music, he assumed confident and assertive postures, clenching his fists and nodding his head in time with the beat. He sensed that his rivals noticed his positive body language, and believed they would be disconcerted by it. Meanwhile, he ignored them in the knowledge that most of them were unable to ignore him.

Photo courtesy of Job King

British 100-meter record holder Montell Douglas in full flight.

When the media promote an association between specific pieces of music and sporting activities, this often creates a conditioned response that can trigger a particular mindset. In a similar way, music can just as easily trigger tranquillity and relaxation. Its therapeutic, anxiety-relieving properties have been used for centuries. For example, think of Bach's "Air On The G-String," the piece that accompanied the long-running series of Hamlet cigar television commercials in the UK. The piece is so slow, so simple, and so beautifully structured that you immediately begin to feel more at ease, even by just imagining listening to it.

Many writers have acknowledged the anxiety-relieving properties of music. Montell Douglas, the athlete who recently broke Kathy Cook's 27-year-old British record for 100 meters, put it like this: "When I switch on my iPod, I am ready. I am unstoppable. I fear nothing. I am totally at one with myself—focused entirely on the task at hand in my own listening bubble."

Skill Learning

An established benefit of music lies in its capacity to improve skill learning. Think back to your days in elementary school when your first physical education classes were probably set to music. Music gave you the opportunity to explore various planes of motion and to improve coordination skills through dance and play. Scientific studies have consistently shown that the application of purposefully selected music can have a positive effect on the style characteristics of movement in sport.

Researchers in Belgium investigated the influence of music on the development of gymnastics skills among female physical education students over a three-month period. One group of students learned the skills with a musical accompaniment; and the other, without. Although the technical aspects of the skills were not affected by music, the stylistic aspects were. Interestingly, the subjects' musical perception abilities were found to contribute significantly to the effectiveness of the music.

Musical perception refers to the extent to which subjects can process a musical stimulus without any deterioration in performance. Hence, higher musical perception abilities equate with better task performance. A New Zealand–based study also looking at gymnastics found that music made learning skills more enjoyable while also promoting "greater freedom of bodily expression" and a "superior quality of movement presentation."

Paul Jernberg Jr., a former swimming coach at Arizona State University, conducted applied research into the use of music during swimming training. He initiated a "musical method" of motor development in which the swimmers were taught to develop an awareness of music and internalize the ability to swim at different tempos. To help the swimmers progress, the tempo of the music was gradually increased to push them to new levels. Jernberg also used specific tracks for each of his swimmers to assist in real-time visualization of their races. He found that swimming performed with a rhythmic stimulus was more efficient, and key skills were picked up more rapidly. Accordingly, the swimmers were able to perform with greater economy of effort.

Three explanations have been given to account for the learning effects reported in the preceding studies and others like them. First, in its structure, music replicates forms of bodily rhythm. Hence, music guides the body in adopting effective movement patterns, almost as if the body visually expresses the sound. Second, the lyrics in music can reinforce important aspects of sporting technique. For example, the "Old Skool" classic "Push It" by Salt-N-Pepa can reinforce to young track and field athletes that they should attempt to putt the shot rather than throw it—the most common technical error. Third, music makes the learning environment more fun, which, in turn, increases the intrinsic motivation to master skills (see also chapter 1).

We have reviewed five ways music can have a positive influence on physical performance, and you may by now be wondering, How can I best harness such benefits? The answer lies in how you select and apply music. Before we get to music applications, however, it is important to outline when music is likely to be ineffectual or even have a negative effect in sport.

Musical Approach to Training

A musical approach to training has been used with great success by U.S. football team the Dallas Cowboys. Their coaches teach defensive skills and conduct tackle bag drills to driving and aggressive music. The sound of the music induces the type of mindset required to complete the skills successfully. We have noted a similar trend in the UK among Premiership soccer teams such as Manchester United and Arsenal, both of which use music as an accompaniment for teaching ball control skills. In soccer, music is employed for its rhythmic qualities to encourage slicker, more efficient execution of the skills.

Wade Jackson/YCJ/Icon SMI

Premiership soccer teams like Manchester United use music to assist ball control skills.

WHEN NOT TO USE MUSIC

Despite all the potential benefits of music, at times its use can lead to a detriment in performance or a less-than-optimal mood state. This is particularly the case when new skills need to be learned and music is likely to be a distraction. The human brain has limited capacity, and research has consistently shown that when music is combined with learning a skill that has high technical demands, such as a triple salchow in figure skating or throwing a hammer in field athletics, it can inhibit learning.

Learning new skills requires maximum concentration, and listening to music can detract considerably from athletes' ability to concentrate on what they should be learning. Similarly, when a coach or teacher is giving instructions, music can be an unwanted distraction. Thus, session leaders should turn music off or down before giving detailed instructions. The International Amateur Athletic Federation has banned in-competition use of personal listening devices to ensure that athletes can hear instructions from officials and receive instructions from their coaches.

Research has shown that music is relatively ineffective in reducing athletes' perception of effort when they are working at a very high intensity (>80 percent of $\dot{V}O_2$max). Fatigue-related symptoms dominate attention at very high levels of effort, and so external cues such as music become far less relevant. In many instances, internally focused attention is needed to maintain high-intensity activity such as sprinting, and background music can be an unnecessary distraction. Stimulative pretask music is often more effective in the case of short-duration, high-intensity tasks.

Another consideration is how athletes typically attend to sensory information. Some have what is termed an associative attentional style. This means that they prefer to focus on the regulation of their bodies. For such athletes, music can be an unwanted distraction. We interviewed double Olympic decathlon gold medalist Daley Thompson toward the end of his athletic career. He told us: "I get so immersed in my training that music is a real turn-off. I just don't need it." Thompson was an extraordinary athlete with his own unique approach. In our experience though, most athletes report a preference for background music during physical conditioning work.

To identify whether you are an "associator" or a "dissociator" in training, you can apply a simple attentional style test that we have devised (exercise 8.1 on page 208). Simply check either Yes or No in response to each question, giving the answer that best represents you.

TUNED IN TO TRAINING

Anyone who has ever worked in a gymnasium, club, bar, or restaurant knows that it is impossible to satisfy the musical tastes of every customer. This is because we differ greatly in our musical preferences. However, a group of athletes of similar cultural background who are willing to adhere to some simple guidelines can derive some real benefit from music. A culturally similar group is one whose members have been exposed to similar cultural experiences during their upbringing, such as watching shows on MTV each week or listening to an ethnic radio station such as BBC Asian Network.

As a starting point, it is important to consider the context in which you are operating. What type of activity are you undertaking? How does the activity affect other people? What are the instrumental objectives of the session? What music-playing facilities are available?

Some activities lend themselves very well to musical accompaniment, particularly those that are repetitive and laborious. Such activities include warm-ups, weight and circuit training, and stretching. In each case, you should select music whose rhythm and tempo match the activity. For example, if your goal during your warm-up is to elevate your heart rate to 120 bpm, limit your music to songs with a tempo in the range of 115 to 125 bpm; or even better, choose songs that gradually increase in tempo up to 120 bpm. If others operating in the vicinity are likely to be disturbed by the music, use a personal listening device. This is the approach that many athletes use while mentally preparing for competition.

Contrastingly, if the intent is to increase team unity and promote a positive prematch group mindset, a hi-fi or public address system might be a more appropriate means of

Exercise 8.1
Attentional Style Test

		Yes	No
1	Do you often find that your mind drifts during training without a detriment in your performance?		
2	When you are out walking, do you like to look at everything going on around you?		
3	Do you like to focus on your breathing during a tough workout?		
4	When your muscles really hurt, do you try to think about something else?		
5	Do you enjoy the company of a training partner when you work out?		
6	Are you often so focused on your performance that you sometimes don't hear what your coach or instructor is saying?		
7	Do you enjoy chatting during training?		
8	When a session is really painful, do you block out the physical sensations by thinking about something else?		
9	When you train, do you often find yourself humming a tune in your head?		
10	Do you find that physical exercise helps you to work out problems that you are experiencing in your life?		

Scoring the Attentional Style Test

Add up the scores from the 10 questions using the following scoring scheme:

Item 1: Yes = 1, No = 2   Item 6: Yes = 2, No = 1

Item 2: Yes = 1, No = 2   Item 7: Yes = 1, No = 2

Item 3: Yes = 2, No = 1   Item 8: Yes = 1, No = 2

Item 4: Yes = 1, No = 2   Item 9: Yes = 1, No = 2

Item 5: Yes = 1, No = 2   Item 10: Yes = 1, No = 2

You will obtain a score between 10 and 20. If your score is in the range of 17 to 20, you are an "associator," which means that you like to focus on the regulation of your body by thinking about your breathing, your form, and your working muscles. You are unlikely to benefit significantly from background music, although it might well enhance your mood. If your score is in the range of 14 to 16, you do not have a dominant attentional style in terms of association or dissociation; rather, you may well use the style that is most appropriate at any given time. You are likely to derive benefit from music, particularly during workouts that you find really monotonous. If your score is in the range of 10 to 13, you are a "dissociator," which means that you actively seek distractions to alleviate any discomfort that accompanies a tough session. You are likely to derive a great deal of benefit from music playing in the background. In fact, you will be the one asking for the volume to be cranked up!

From C.I. Karageorghis and P.C. Terry, 2011, *Inside sport psychology* (Champaign, IL: Human Kinetics).

music delivery. If a public address system is available, the fans can also be drawn into the prematch ritual by playing songs that relate to their sporting identity. Just a brief word of warning, though: music can sometimes cause offense. We stumbled across the case of the Pittsburgh Pirates announcer Brian Kirsch playing the Carl Douglas song "Kung Fu Fighting" as a South Korean opposition player was walking out to bat. Kirsch was sacked for his choice of music, which was deemed to be offensive to the batter because it reinforced racial stereotypes. Earlier in the season he had been warned following a similar incident involving David Bowie's "China Girl."

Listeners' Backgrounds

As we mentioned earlier, cultural background shapes music preference. The kind of music experienced during the formative years, in particular, has a very strong influence. Playing Britpop music for basketball players in Harlem, New York, is as poor a match as, say, playing Brazilian samba for a German soccer team.

Our research has shown that gender also influences music selection. Females rate the importance of rhythmic qualities and the "danceability" of music more highly than males do. However, males rate extramusical associations higher than females do. One of our recent studies showed that female participants derived greater benefit from synchronizing their movements to music tempo during an exhaustive circuit-type task than males did. Despite these findings, we have found no gender differences in response to pretask music for sport-related tasks such as strength tests.

Among teams with varied nationalities and cultural backgrounds, such as Chelsea FC in the English Premiership, music selection can be quite difficult to get right. The unity of the team can be increased by having shared ownership of the musical selections. One way to do so is to have the players establish a pool of appropriate music. Many teams have their own team song that is used to build cohesion. Manchester United FC, for example, uses "Glory Glory Man United" as its team chant, whereas Liverpool FC uses the anthemic "You'll Never Walk Alone," which was popularized by Gerry and the Pacemakers in the 1960s.

Music Preferences

Preferences for music are influenced by many factors. One of the most prevalent is peer influence: we tend to listen to the same types of music as our close friends. In fact, music often defines groups or cliques that subscribe to specific subcultures such

---

Glen's Going for Gold

Glen Rate is a trampolinist aspiring to represent Great Britain at the 2012 Olympic Games in London. He often feels agitated before big events, particularly when he knows that his closest rivals will also be competing. To help himself focus better for the impending competition, he listens to the 1980s pop classic "Gold" by Spandau Ballet. Glen associates the song with success, and he finds that after listening to it on a loop for 10 or 15 minutes, he is focused solely on the task at hand. Indeed, as the song suggests, he feels "indestructible."

as hip-hop, grime, and goth. The media also play a critical role in shaping preferences by repeatedly playing and promoting certain tracks and genres.

Personality can also influence music preference. A well-known British psychologist, Professor Hans Eysenck, who passed away at the end of the last century, devoted his life to investigating personality and the kinds of sensory experiences sought by people with different types of personality. He argued that extroverted and outgoing people constantly seek stimulation and thus are more likely to enjoy loud, upbeat, frenetic, and lively music. Conversely, introverted and insular people demonstrate a preference for soft, slow, structured, and sedate music. Eysenck's theory has received only limited support. Most team sport players tend to be quite extroverted and may

Katherine and the Tour de France Féminin

Katherine LeBlanc is a cyclist who competes in a tough season of European tour events, including the grueling Tour de France Féminin. During the last three years, she has suffered an unlikely string of injury setbacks and two notable tragedies in her personal life that have blighted her attempt to reach her athletic potential and left her clinging onto her cycling career by her fingertips.

As part of her effort to save her athletic career, Katherine consulted a sport psychologist. He suggested that she use a signature tune as a motivational trigger to inspire her. She selected the heartfelt ballad "Something Inside So Strong" by Labi Siffre. The song expresses the feelings of a whole nation if not a whole race of people who have been oppressed and victimized but who fight back to assert their natural rights and free themselves from suffrage. Katherine could readily relate this powerful motif to her own struggles in life and sport.

Hence, although she did not typically use the song during her training sessions, she listened to it on a regular basis and it reminded her how important her struggle to compete is, and that she must not give up. The music gave her the determination to adhere to her tough training schedule and to face injury and other setbacks with renewed determination.

Her long struggle culminated in a strong performance in one of the mountain stages in the Tour de France Féminin. She led the field at the last checkpoint and looked certain to win the stage when disaster struck; one of her tires was punctured. Her coach and support team were following in a car and arrived at the scene to replace the wheel. It was clear as Katherine set off again that she was severely distressed and would possibly not even complete the stage. But her coach had an idea. With the car shadowing Katherine's descent of the mountain, he opened up all the windows and the sunroof and played Katherine's song on the car audio system.

At first, Katherine slowed because hearing the music slightly disoriented her, but then she knew just what to do. She found a new burst of energy, and with each bar of the song, total despair turned into total determination. By the end of the song the transformation was complete: she found she had more gears than her bike and used enormous reserves of strength to get up and win by the narrowest of margins. Her victory was covered by national television crews and made sporting headlines all over France. Even though Labi Siffre's ballad is neither fast nor particularly rhythmic, it exerted an ergogenic effect on Katherine's performance because of the personal meaning it held for her.

therefore derive benefits from stimulating music prior to competition. This tendency does not hold true in all cases, though, and it is prudent to establish a pool of preferred selections for each athlete.

Having a pool of preferred tracks presents two distinct advantages. First, common preferences among a group of athletes can be identified and used. Second, the pool can be rated to identify the pieces of music with the highest motivational qualities. We have developed a questionnaire called the Brunel Music Rating Inventory (BMRI) to serve this purpose (see exercise 8.2). We originally developed the questionnaire in the late 1990s to help researchers and practitioners select music in a more structured manner.

Exercise 8.2
The Brunel Music Rating Inventory-3

This questionnaire is designed to assess the extent to which the piece of music you are about to hear would motivate you during [*insert activity here*]. For our purposes, the word *motivate* means that you would want to pursue [*insert activity here*] with greater intensity, stay with it for longer, or both. As you listen to the piece of music, indicate the extent of your agreement with the six statements listed by circling *one* of the numbers to the right of each statement. Provide an honest response to each statement. Give the response that best represents your opinion, and avoid dwelling too long on any single statement.

		Strongly disagree						Strongly agree
1	The rhythm of this music would motivate me during [*insert activity here*].	1	2	3	4	5	6	7
2	The style of this music (i.e., rock, dance, jazz, hip-hop) would motivate me during [*insert activity here*].	1	2	3	4	5	6	7
3	The melody (tune) of this music would motivate me during [*insert activity here*].	1	2	3	4	5	6	7
4	The tempo (speed) of this music would motivate me during [*insert activity here*].	1	2	3	4	5	6	7
5	The sound of the instruments used (i.e., guitar, synthesizer, saxophone) would motivate me during [*insert activity here*].	1	2	3	4	5	6	7
6	The beat of this music would motivate me during [*insert activity here*].	1	2	3	4	5	6	7

BMRI-3 Scoring Instructions

Add the items for a score between 6 and 42. A score in the range of 36 to 42 indicates high motivational qualities in the piece of music, a score in the range of 24 to 35 indicates moderate motivational qualities, and a score below 24 indicates that the track lacks motivational qualities.

From C.I. Karageorghis, 2008, The scientific application of music in sport and exercise. In *Sport and exercise psychology: Topics in applied psychology*, edited by A.M. Lane (London: Hodder Education), 115. Reproduced with permission of Hodder Education.

Coordinating Music With the Task

As we indicated earlier, effective music selection is just one half of the task of harnessing the power of music. The other half entails coordinating the music with specific activities, which will provide the maximum benefit. As we are about to explain, music can be used in many ways in training and competition.

Music can be coordinated with a task to facilitate the specific goals of a training session. Such music should match both the sociocultural upbringing of the athletes and the nature of the activity. Also, the music can parallel the arousal level required. Recently, we tested the relationship between working heart rate and preference for music tempo during a static cycling task. As shown in figure 8.2, the ideal range of music tempo for exercise is 125 to 140 bpm, but at high work intensities (>70 percent of $\dot{V}O_2$max), there is a ceiling effect. Playing very fast music during high-intensity exercise is not likely to result in a heightened aesthetic response to the music.

To find the tempo of any given piece of music, try searching on the Internet. More and more Web sites are dedicated to presenting various characteristics of music, including tempo. Examples include www.bpm4djs.com, www.thebpmbook.com, and www.ez-tracks.com. Software such as Tangerine (www.potionfactory.com) can assess the tempo of each track on your PC and automatically add this information to an iTunes library. The sidebar Useful Web Sites for Planning Music Programs (page 215) lists state-of-the-art Web-based technology that can aid music selection in the domain of sport. Table 8.1 contains popular tracks used in sport and exercise along with their associated tempos.

Another approach is simply to ask a DJ or a dance aerobics instructor about the tempo of specific tracks. These professionals routinely review pieces of music that they mix into coherent musical programs for a club environment or a class. They are likely to be local experts in selecting, mixing, and applying music for maximum effect. The authors often have lengthy discussions with professional DJs before formulating

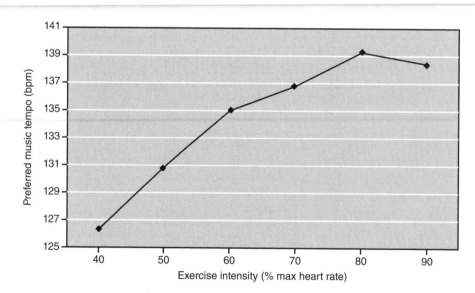

Figure 8.2 Relationship between exercise intensity and preferred music tempo.

Table 8.1 Popular Tracks for Sport and Exercise

Track title	Artist(s)	Tempo (bpm)	Style	Length (mins.)
We Are The Champions	Queen	64	Rock	2:59
Rockstar	Nickelback	73	Pop/rock	4:14
Hard Knock Life	Jay-Z	76	Hip-hop	3:58
Live Your Life	T.I. feat. Rihanna	80	R'n'B/hip-hop	5:39
No Air	Jordin Sparks feat. Chris Brown	81	R'n'B	4:24
Empire State Of Mind	Jay-Z feat. Alicia Keys	87	Hip-hop	4:37
Faith	George Michael	95	Pop	3:16
Swing Low, Sweet Chariot	China Black feat. Ladysmith Black Mambazo	96	Pop	3:51
Hips Don't Lie	Shakira	100	Latin pop	3:41
The Best	Tina Turner	104	Pop	4:11
Valerie	Mark Ronson feat. Amy Winehouse	107	Pop	3:39
Jump Around	House of Pain	108	Hip-hop	3:37
Gettin' Jiggy With It	Will Smith	108	Hip-hop	3:48
The Power	Snap!	109	Dance/hip-hop	5:42
Dance Wiv Me	Dizzee Rascal feat. Calvin Harris	113	Grime/pop	3:25
Number 1	Tinchy Stryder feat. N-Dubz	115	R'n'B/hip-hop	3:34
The Way I Are	Timbaland feat. Keri Hilson	115	Hip-hop	2:59
Holiday	Dizzee Rascal feat. Calvin Harris	118	Dance/grime	3:39
Just Dance	Lady Gaga	119	Pop	4:02
American Boy	Estelle feat. Kanye West	119	R'n'B	4:44
Fight For This Love	Cheryl Cole	123	Pop	3:52
Livin' On A Prayer	Bon Jovi	123	Rock	4:12
Don't Stop The Music	Rihanna	123	R'n'B	4:27
Run To You	Bryan Adams	126	Rock	3:54
Miami 2 Ibiza	Swedish House Mafia vs. Tinie Tempah	126	Hip-hop	4:22

(continued)

Table 8.1 *(continued)*

Track title	Artist(s)	Tempo (bpm)	Style	Length (mins.)
Raider's March (theme music from Indiana Jones movies)	Composer: John Williams	126	Classical / soundtrack	5:05
In The Air	TV Rock	128	Dance	3:35
I Like The Way (You Move)	BodyRockers	128	Rock	3:44
I See You Baby	Groove Armada (Fatboy Slim Remix)	128	House	4:40
Put Your Hands Up For Detroit	Fedde Le Grande	129	Dance	2:30
Mercy	Duffy	130	Pop	3:41
Meet Me Halfway	Black Eyed Peas	130	Pop/hip-hop	4:44
Ace Of Spades	Motörhead	141	Rock/metal	2:49
Firestarter	The Prodigy	142	Dance	4:42
I Got You (I Feel Good)	James Brown	146	Funk	2:47
Now You're Gone	Basshunter	149	Dance	2:34
I Need A Hero	Bonnie Tyler	150	Pop/rock	4:29
Rockafeller Skank	Fatboy Slim	152	Dance	6:53
Don't Stop Me Now	Queen	155	Pop	3:29
Underdog	You Me at Six	156	Rock	2:27
Danger Zone (from *Top Gun* movie soundtrack)	Kenny Loggins	158	Rock/pop	3:36
Freestyler	Bomfunk MCs	163	Dance	5:44
Reach	S Club 7	167	Pop	4:07
I'm A Believer	The Monkees	167	Rock	2:41

playlists for athletes or the general public. Some athletes simply prefer to use trial and error to find appropriately paced tracks. Use the method that best suits your needs.

Synchronizing Music With Activity

Exercise participants often report that they like exercising to music because they can synchronize their movements to the beat or tempo. This enables them to regulate their work output, which makes the exercise seem less laborious (see Jona Nyachae and the Musical Running Method on page 201). It also enhances the stylistic aspects of their movements. You can derive similar benefits by using music in training or to regulate a precompetitive warm-up.

Useful Web Sites for Planning Music Programs

www.jogtunes.com

This is a multipurpose site for runners to select music that is aligned in tempo with their stride rates.

http://nikerunning.nike.com/nikeos/p/nikeplus/en_GB

This page describes a wireless accelerometer (made by Nike and concealed in the sole of a training shoe) that is used to feed back information regarding stride rate to an iPod. The music player can then manage its output in terms of tempo to best accompany the runner's performance.

www.run2r.com

This site sells music from a variety of composers that is specially compiled by the site's founder, pianist-composer Gary F. Blake. He believes the rhythms he has produced are particularly conducive to efficient running.

www.djsteveboy.com/podrunner.html

This site features Podrunner, a free weekly series of fixed-bpm dance music mixes produced by Los Angeles DJ Steve Boyett for running, jogging, power walking, aerobics, spinning, or any fixed-tempo physical activity.

www.fitmix.co.uk

This site features various links, MP3 playlists, and mixed (segued) music selections that can be purchased.

www.wetronome.com

This site describes an underwater metronome that can be used for pacing swimming strokes.

www.ministryofsound.com

This site is for dance music aficionados and contains a number of mixes compiled specifically for fitness activities that include the *Run to the Beat 2010* album, which was developed by the first author in collaboration with Ministry of Sound.

The primary consideration when synchronizing music with training activities is to carefully assess movement patterns, intensity, and movement duration. Movement patterns determine the rhythmic qualities of the music. For example, a 4/4 rhythm suits running, cycling, and cross-country skiing, whereas a 3/4 rhythm suits rowing, triple jumping, and numerous running drills (in a 3/4 rhythm there are three beats to the bar and the main emphasis rests on the first beat, as in the most played song in history, "Happy Birthday To You"). There are many other types of rhythm, but these are the main ones. In Western popular music, the 4/4 rhythm is by far the most common and is often referred to as "common time".

The intensity of the exercise, or how hard you are working, determines the tempo of the music. Very gentle exercise requires slow tempo music, whereas high-intensity exercise requires music of a faster tempo. For example, a gentle jog can be performed at a tempo of 90 to 110 bpm. This corresponds with the typical tempo of gentle soul, slow rock, or hip-hop tracks. Push-ups or bench dips can be performed at a tempo of 120 to 140 bpm, with each half of the movements (flexion and extension) corresponding to one beat. This matches the tempo used in most commercial dance music including house, grime, and garage.

Using Background Music

Background music is best used when you want to either enhance your mood or distract your attention from a monotonous or repetitive drill (without synchronizing your movements to the beat). If distraction is an important consideration, the volume of the music needs to be set quite high (70 to 80 decibels) but not so high that it is uncomfortable. Also, bear in mind that a musician's greatness is absolutely no guarantee of his or her suitability to the context of sport. However much you may love Chris de Burgh, you will have to accept that "Lady In Red" only works at the end of a romantic night out; the same holds for Barry White, the reformed Take That, Julio Iglesias, and most of Ronan Keating. As we said earlier, appropriate selection and coordination with the type of activity you are engaged in are critical.

Good examples of situations in which to use background music include conditioning work, all gym sessions, and during the practice of rhythmic skills. In each case, the volume needs to be set so as not to block out the instructor's voice. A prematch routine can be punctuated by the blast of a classic song with inspirational lyrics such as "Search For The Hero" by M People or "Don't Stop Me Now" by Queen. Sometimes teams make their own music. In contact sports such as American football and rugby union, for example, this is commonplace. Further, military units use rhythmic chants to alleviate the pain of long stomps and to keep their spirits high.

The duration of an activity determines the duration of the musical selection(s). When performing training that involves intervals or circuits, prerecord a music program so that the music changes for each activity. This not only regulates the training session and makes it feel professional but also makes it more fun.

Music for Workouts

Most athletes use music for at least one of their weekly workouts—usually a gym-based workout. Pulsating background music is almost omnipresent in gyms nowadays. This section is for those who have a say in which music is played. Some gyms hold a license to play only music from a certain music supplier or are contracted to use a particular radio station.

One of the key considerations is the mindset you want to achieve for a particular type of workout. If the actions required are explosive or motoric (using large muscle groups), then driving, aggressive music is probably the best accompaniment. For example, double Olympic gold medal–winning rower James Cracknell used the persistent rhythms of the Red Hot Chili Peppers in his preevent routine. If the movements are steady and rhythmic, the music should not have fluctuations in tempo; rather, it should parallel the speed of the movements.

So, if you are warming up on a cycle ergometer at a pace of around 65 rpm, commercial dance music, which is typically in the tempo range of 120 to 130 bpm, is ideal;

you can take half a pedal revolution to each beat of the music. For a stretching routine that is conducted as part of a warm-up, inspirational slow music is the perfect adjunct, whereas for a warm-down routine, relaxing, slow music is good. Inspirational slow music is typified by ballads with powerful lyrics such as those performed by Alicia Keys and Leona Lewis; relaxing, slow music can be classical or gentle instrumental music mixed with the sounds of nature.

Another important consideration is how to program the music to punctuate a workout. As we described earlier, essentially you have three choices. You can either perform movements in time with the music (synchronous music) or have music playing in the background (asynchronous music). Some athletes like to use a combination of both, whereas others like to listen to music just before they start (pretask music) to get into an appropriate mood state (see chapter 5).

Research conducted in industry has shown that music can be most effective when played at a point when workers reach a plateau in work output. If we apply this principle to sport, music will likely have the most potent effect if you switch it on when your work level begins to decline as fatigue sets in.

Table 8.2 shows a list of workout segments and the music chosen to accompany them. Look these over, and then fill out the blank table with your own workout segments and musical selections. Establish how you will use the music (synchronously or asynchronously), and estimate either the work rate for synchronous use or the

Table 8.2 Musical Selections for the Components of a Typical Training Session

Workout component	Track title	Artist	Tempo (bpm)
Mental preparation	Gonna Fly Now	Rocky Orchestra	94
Warm-up activity	Let's Get It Started	Black Eyed Peas	105
Stretching	Start Without You	Alexandra Burke feat. Laza Morgan	92
Strength component	Boom Boom Pow	Black Eyed Peas	130
Endurance component	It Feels So Good	Sonique	135
Cool-down activity	Strong Again	N-Dubz	105

Workout component	Track title	Artist	Tempo (bpm)
Mental preparation			
Warm-up activity			
Stretching			
Cool-down activity			

From C.I. Karageorghis and P.C. Terry, 2011, *Inside sport psychology* (Champaign, IL: Human Kinetics).

predicted heart rate for asynchronous use. Once you have established the tempo for a range of suitable tracks, prepare the music program. The latest generation of wireless MP3 players and headphones, such as the Sony W series, facilitate the use of music during vigorous activities. One note of caution: If you use headphones, be aware of your immediate environment so you do not compromise your safety.

Now prepare your own version of table 8.2, and use the music program to give your training sessions a boost:

To take music use to a more advanced level, you can program components of training to coincide with segments of music. Work time and recovery time can be punctuated by music so that soft and slow music follows loud and fast music. This approach is especially suited to highly structured workouts such as circuit and interval training. Sydney Olympics rowing gold medalist Tim Foster, now a respected coach, uses music to regulate all of the indoor workouts he leads. He finds that this increases the motivation of the rowers as well as making sessions far more enjoyable.

MUSIC IN COMPETITION

To use music effectively on the day of competition, you need to prepare carefully. First, you must be aware of your optimal level of arousal (see chapter 4) so you know whether to use music to psych up or psych down. Gentle music with powerful lyrics is ideal for keeping from bubbling over, whereas driving rhythms and movement-related lyrics are good for increasing physiological arousal levels. You can coordinate a visualization routine with your music program if that suits (see chapter 7). In a team situation, a coach or team manager might create an entire music-related routine to prepare for the impending contest.

Your music program should build toward competition gently so that by the time you switch off the last track, you are in an optimal psychological state to compete. The last piece of music is likely to stay in your head, so leave the most inspirational piece until last. You should be prepared to switch your music on and off because your preevent routine may not go exactly as planned. Develop strategies for delays, poor

Swing Low, Sweet Chariot

The use of anthemic chanting that reverberates around a rugby or soccer crowd can be a great source of inspiration to the players. Most great teams have a signature chant or song. For example, England rugby fans sing the stirring spiritual "Swing Low, Sweet Chariot." This recital, whether in the stands or the players' dressing room, promotes feelings of patriotism, unity, and competitive zeal. Although long associated with club rugby, the anthem was spontaneously adopted for the England team in March 1988 during a Five Nations match against Ireland at Twickenham. Following quite a barren patch for the England team, a black player named Chris Oti scored a sensational hat-trick of tries. A group of pupils from a Benedictine school initiated the vocal salute, and they were very soon joined by the remainder of the crowd.

The Great Britain Olympic Bobsled Team

The second author worked as team psychologist for the Great Britain bobsled team at the 1998 Olympic Winter Games in Nagano, Japan. The GB team had chipped away at the advantage of the world's most successful nations over the previous decade, finishing sixth in the 1992 Albertville Games and fifth in Lillehammer in 1994. Nagano was planned as their moment to finally clinch the Olympic medal that had remained elusive to Britain since 1964. As they approached the bob run each day for training and on the two competition days, the team would listen to Whitney Houston's "One Moment In Time" while visualizing themselves calmly and decisively seizing the moment. On the final race day, that's exactly what they did in a storming last run that won them the bronze by the narrowest of margins.

weather, and even starting ahead of schedule. It is also advisable to have a strategy for when an MP3 player breaks down or runs out of batteries. Hearing a song in your head is a particularly effective strategy in this instance.

You will want to arrange your music program around your preevent routine. Thus, you may wish to raise the tempo for a warm-up jog and slow it down for stretching and mental rehearsal. If you feel lethargic after a long journey, you may need a little extra stimulation for the initial part of your warm-up. In a team situation, this might involve playing some dance music in the changing room prior to the formal team preparation. We suggest that you change your music program every four to six weeks to avoid getting bored with it or to alternate two or three music programs. Variety is always important when selecting music, because excessive exposure to certain pieces can sometimes lead to irritation rather than inspiration.

A final consideration is the nature of your sport. If you need to be listening to instructions from match officials or team management, then clearly it is not advantageous to listen to music the entire time before your event. Plan your listening to ensure that you receive all of the information relevant to your event. If you are a sprinter about to compete in the first round of a championship that has a large entry, as well as checking in, you should find out which heat you are competing in so that you can plan your preparation to perfection. This links in to the point we made earlier about the need for flexibility in your preevent routine. At some championships, there can be a 45-minute difference between the first and last heats of an opening round. This is often announced only *after* athletes have warmed up and officials know how many athletes have checked in.

MUSIC FOR RELAXATION
AND RECUPERATION

We have devoted a great deal of coverage to how music can raise spirits and increase arousal levels for training and competition. Given the many forms music can take, it is equally effective in relieving tension, psyching down, and aiding relaxation. In many respects, it is far easier to select music for this purpose than selecting it as an "upper" because literally thousands of suitable compilations and downloads are available.

Further, relaxing music tends to be more universally applicable than motivational music because familiarity, lyrical content, and extramusical associations are of lesser importance in producing a relaxation response. Relaxing music tends to work at a more subliminal level than motivating music, and your body will often have an immediate physiological response typified by a lowering of heart rate and blood pressure. You will also notice your breathing rate slowing down.

We have encouraged athletes to use relaxing music on the eve of competition to relieve anxiety and aid a restful night's sleep. On numerous occasions, we have produced personalized MP3 files with imagery or relaxation scripts set to calming music of the athlete's choice (see chapters 4 and 7). Some athletes are so highly motivated that most of the interventions we apply are designed to keep them from boiling over. The combination of music and imagery is a particularly potent intervention. In many sports such as golf and shooting, there are long gaps between the action, and participants need to learn to switch their energy channels on and off to ensure that they do not expend too much psychological energy early on.

Listening to relaxing music between rounds of an event or during the evenings at multiday championships is a great way to switch off and unwind. Begin by determining exactly how relaxed you want to feel. If a particular selection sends you into a deep sleep, do not use it when you have limited time between rounds; it would be far more appropriate to use it as the last selection you listen to in bed.

Conversely, selections that would be suitable between rounds of an event might have a slow beat but inspirational lyrics to keep you in touch with the fact that more effort will soon be required while keeping your body from expending energy unnecessarily. Tracks that contain sounds such as birdsong and crashing waves may not be the most appropriate in this instance because the sounds of nature produce an innate and profound relaxation response. Ambient sounds are best used late at night or when a particularly deep relaxation response is sought.

In terms of using music to recuperate from competition, injury, or a tough workout, we suggest a tempo in the range of 60 to 70 bpm, which is close to resting heart rate. The music should be played on soothing, "warm" instruments such as strings, clarinet, or piano, and its emotional qualities should be neutral or relaxing. The length of recuperative tracks is generally longer than that of regular music tracks (more than 10 minutes), and the rhythmic patterns tend to be very simple. The key is to become absorbed in the music, so jarring or irritating selections do not work well. Good examples of recuperative music include the slow-tempo classical works of Vivaldi, Handel, and Bach, or for a more contemporary sound, tracks by Enya or Enigma.

SUMMARY

Music can be applied in many ways to training and competition. It goes without saying that music should be purchased on original recordings or downloaded legally. You may already use music in your training or competition, but until now, there have been no comprehensive guidelines available to guide its effective use. In some situations the use of music may be disadvantageous, such as in the early stages of learning a complex motor skill. At other times, such as when you cycle on the roads, avoid music altogether for safety. We hope that by using the principles outlined in this chapter, you will be able to harness the stimulative, sedative, and work-enhancing effects of music with greater precision.

A particular advantage of MP3 technology is that you can construct playlists very easily to suit your needs. For example, you can group tracks with a similar tempo or arrange the order of tracks in such a way that they match the physiological demands of an event or a workout. Preparing playlists also complements the process of mental rehearsal (see chapter 7) because it helps you think carefully about the demands of your discipline.

The latest International Amateur Athletic Federation rules dictate that personal listening devices cannot be taken into the competitive arena or be used during long-duration events such as road and cross-country running. In response to this, mass participation running events have been organized with live musical accompaniment that is scientifically selected to enhance the experience for athletes and their performance levels (e.g., www.runtothebeat.co.uk). This is one of the latest developments in a long-established relationship between music and physical activity.

We believe that it would be inappropriate for us to be prescriptive when it comes to the selection of specific pieces of music; we have just provided a few examples of how we have applied music in our own work with athletes. Different pieces of music are suitable for different athletes for different reasons; there is no "vitamin model" associated with music use whereby a piece of music has a predictable benefit for everyone who listens to it. As the great Roman philosopher Lucretius put it, "One man's meat is another man's poison".

You should now have a better idea of how to make effective music selections and integrate them into a performance routine. Music has the power to motivate the individual athlete, lift a team to superior levels of performance, and drive sports fans into a frenzy. Happy listening!

SUGGESTED RESOURCES

Books

Abrams, M. (2010). *Anger management in sport.* Champaign, IL: Human Kinetics.

Andersen, M.B. (Ed.). (2000). *Doing sport psychology.* Champaign, IL: Human Kinetics.

Anderson, M.B. (Ed.). (2005). *Sport psychology in practice.* Champaign, IL:Human Kinetics.

Anshel, M. (2002). *Sport psychology: From theory to practice* (4th ed.). San Francisco: Benjamin Cummings.

Bateman, A.J., & Bale, J.R. (Eds.). (2009). *Sporting sounds: Relationships between sport and music.* London: Routledge.

Beauchamp, M.R. (2008). *Group dynamics in sport psychology: Contemporary themes.* New York: Routledge.

Beauchamp, M.R., & Eys, M.A. (2007). *Group dynamics in sport psychology.* New York: Routledge.

Blumenstein, B., Bar-Eli, M., & Tenenbaum, G. (Eds.). (2002). *Brain and body in sport and exercise.* Chichester, UK: Wiley.

Brewer, B. (Ed.). (2009). *Sport psychology.* Chichester, UK: Wiley-Blackwell.

Burton, D., & Raedeke, T. (2008). *Sport psychology for coaches.* Champaign, IL: Human Kinetics.

Carlstedt, R. (2004). *Critical moments during competition: A mind-body model of sport performance when it counts the most.* New York: Psychology Press.

Carron, A.V., Hausenblas, H.A., & Eys, M.A. (2005). *Group dynamics in sport* (3rd ed.). Morgantown, WV: Fitness Information Technology.

Cashmore, E. (2008). *Sport psychology: The key concepts* (2nd ed.). London: Taylor and Francis.

Clifford, C., & Feezell, R.M. (2010). *Sport and character: Reclaiming the principles of sportsmanship.* Champaign, IL: Human Kinetics.

Cockerill, I. (2002). *Solutions in sport psychology.* London: Thomson.

Coe, S. (2009). *The winning mind: My inside track on great leadership—developing inspirational leadership and delivering winning results.* New York: Business Plus.

Cox, R.H. (2006). *Sport psychology: Concepts and applications* (6th ed.). New York: McGraw-Hill.

Csikszentmihalyi, M. (2008). *Flow: The psychology of optimal experience.* New York: Harper & Row.

Dosil, J. (Ed.). (2006). *The sport psychologist's handbook: A guide for sport-specific enhancement.* Chichester, UK: Wiley.

Farrow, D., Baker, J., & MacMahon, C. (Eds.). (2007). *Developing sport expertise: Researchers and coaches put theory into practice.* New York: Routledge.

Feltz, D.L., Short, S., & Sullivan, P. (2008). *Self-efficacy in sport: Research and strategies for working with athletes, teams, and coaches.* Champaign, IL: Human Kinetics.

Galluci, N.T. (2007). *Sport psychology: Performance enhancement, performance inhibition, individuals, and teams.* Hove, UK: Psychology Press.

Gardner, F., & Moore, Z. (2005). *Clinical sport psychology.* Champaign, IL: Human Kinetics.

Gavin, J. (2005). *Exercise and sport psychology.* Champaign, IL: Human Kinetics.

Gill, D.L. (2008). *Psychological dynamics of sport and exercise* (3rd ed.). Champaign, IL: Human Kinetics.

Hackfort, D., Duda, J.L., & Lidor, R. (Eds.). (2005). *Handbook of research in applied sport and exercise psychology: International perspectives.* Morgantown, WV: Fitness Information Technology.

Hagger, M.S. (2007). *Intrinsic motivation and self-determination in exercise and sport.* Champaign, IL: Human Kinetics.

Hagger, M.S., & Chatzisarantis, N.L.D. (2005). *The social psychology of exercise and sport.* New York: McGraw-Hill.

Hanin, Y.L. (2000). *Emotions in sport.* Champaign, IL: Human Kinetics.

Hanrahan, S.J., & Andersen, M.B. (Eds.). (2010). *The Routledge handbook of applied sport psychology: A comprehensive guide for students and practitioners.* London: Routledge.

Hemmings, B., & Holder, T. (Eds.). (2009). *Applied sport psychology—A case-based approach.* London: Wiley-Blackwell.

Hill, K.L. (2001). *Frameworks for sport psychologists: Enhancing sport performance.* Champaign, IL: Human Kinetics.

Honeybourne, J. (2006). *Acquiring skill in sport: An introduction.* New York: Routledge.

Horn, T. (Ed.). (2008). *Advances in sport psychology* (3rd ed.). Champaign, IL: Human Kinetics.

Jarvis, M. (2006). *Sport psychology: A student's handbook.* New York: Routledge.

Jowett, S., & Lavallee, D. (Eds.). (2007). *Social psychology in sport.* Champaign, IL: Human Kinetics.

Kauss, D.R. (2001). *Mastering your inner game.* Champaign, IL: Human Kinetics.

Kellmann, M. (2002). *Enhancing recovery: Preventing underperformance in athletes.* Champaign, IL: Human Kinetics.

Kerr, J.H. (2001). *Counselling athletes: Applying reversal theory.* New York: Routledge.

Kerr, J.H. (2008). *Rethinking aggression and violence in sport.* New York: Routledge.

Kornspan, A.S. (2009). *Fundamentals of sport and exercise psychology.* Champaign, IL: Human Kinetics.

Kremer, J., & Moran, A.P. (2007). *Pure sport: Practical sport psychology.* Hove, UK: Psychology Press.

Lane, A.M. (Ed.). (2007). *Mood and human performance: Conceptual, measurement, and applied issues.* New York: Nova Science.

Lane, A.M. (Ed.). (2008). *Sport and exercise psychology.* London: Hodder Education.

Lavallee, D., Kremer, J., Moran, A.P., & Williams, M. (2004). *Sport psychology: Contemporary themes.* London: Palgrave Macmillan.

Lavallee, D., Williams, J., & Jones, M. (2008). *Key studies in sport and exercise psychology.* New York: McGraw-Hill.

Leith, L.M. (2002). *The psychology of coaching team sports: A self-help guide.* Toronto: Sports Book Publishers.

Leith, L.M. (2008). *The psychology of achieving sports excellence: A self-help guide for all athletes.* Toronto: Sports Book Publishers.

LeUnes, A., & Nation, J.R. (2008). *Sport psychology* (4th ed.). Pacific Grove, CA: Wadsworth.

Lidor, R., & Bar-Eli, M. (Eds.). (2001). *Sport psychology: Linking theory and practice.* Morgantown, WV: Fitness Information Technology.

Lidor, R., Morris, T., Bardaxoglou, N., & Becker Jr., B. (Eds.). (2001) *The world sport psychology sourcebook.* Morgantown, WV: Fitness Information Technology.

Liggett, D. (2000). *Sport hypnosis.* Champaign, IL: Human Kinetics.

Mellalieu, S., & Hanton, S. (2008). *Advances in sport psychology.* New York: Routledge.

Moran, A.P. (2004). *Sport and exercise psychology: A critical introduction.* New York: Routledge.

Moran, A.P. (2006). *The psychology of concentration in sport performers: A cognitive analysis.* Hove, UK: Psychology Press.

Morris, T., Spittle, M., & Watt, A.P. (Eds.). (2005). *Imagery in sport.* Champaign, IL: Human Kinetics.

Morris, T., & Summers, J. (2004). *Sport psychology: Theory applications and issues.* Chichester, UK: Wiley.

Morris, T., & Terry, P.C. (Eds.). (2011). *The new sport and exercise psychology companion.* Morgantown, WV: Fitness Information Technology.

Morris, T., Terry, P.C., & Gordon, S. (Eds.). (2007). *Sport and exercise psychology: International perspectives.* Morgantown, WV: Fitness Information Technology.

Murphy, S.M. (2005). *The sport psych handbook.* Champaign, IL: Human Kinetics.

Nesti, M. (2006). *Existential sport psychology.* London: Routledge.

Nesti, M. (2009). *Sport and spirituality: An introduction.* London: Routledge.

Nideffer, R.M., & Sagal, M. (2001). *Assessment in sport psychology.* Morgantown, WV: Fitness Information Technology.

Orlick, T. (2008). *In pursuit of excellence: How to win in sport and life through mental training* (4th ed.). Champaign, IL: Human Kinetics.

Porter, K. (2003). *The mental athlete.* Champaign, IL: Human Kinetics.

Raedeke, T.D., & Smith, A.L. (2009). *The Athlete Burnout Questionnaire manual.* Morgantown, WV: Fitness Information Technology.

Richardson, S.O., Andersen, M., & Morris, T. (2008). *Overtraining athletes: Personal journeys in sport.* Champaign, IL: Human Kinetics.

Roberts, G.C. (2001). *Advances in motivation in sport and exercise.* Champaign, IL: Human Kinetics.

Rushall, B.S. (2003). *Mental skills training for sports* (3rd ed.). Spring Valley, CA: Sports Science Associates.

Ryba, T., Schinke, R.J., & Tenenbaum, G. (2010). *The cultural turn in sport psychology.* Morgantown, WV: Fitness Information Technology.

Schinke, R.J., & Hanrahan, S.J. (Eds.). (2009). *Cultural sport psychology.* Champaign, IL: Human Kinetics.

Shaw, D., Gorely, T., & Corban, R. (2004). *Instant notes in sport and exercise psychology.* London: Taylor and Francis.

Sheard, M. (2009). *Mental toughness: The mindset behind sporting achievement*. New York: Routledge.

Shields, D.L., & Bredemeier, B.L. (2009). *True competition: A guide to pursuing excellence in sport and society*. Champaign, IL: Human Kinetics.

Silva, J.M., & Stevens, D.E. (Eds.). (2002). *Psychological foundations of sport*. Boston: Allyn & Bacon.

Singer, R., Hausenblas, H., & Janelle, C. (2001). *Handbook of sport psychology* (2nd ed.). New York: Wiley.

Smith, D., & Bar-Eli, M. (2007). *Essential readings in sport and exercise psychology*. Champaign, IL: Human Kinetics.

Taylor, J., & Wilson, G. (Eds.). (2005). *Applying sport psychology: Four perspectives*. Champaign, IL: Human Kinetics.

Tenenbaum, G. (Ed.). (2001). *Reflections and experiences in sport and exercise psychology*. Morgantown, WV: Fitness Information Technology.

Tenenbaum, G. (Ed.). (2001). *The practice of sport and exercise psychology: International perspectives*. Morgantown, WV: Fitness Information Technology.

Tenenbaum, G., & Eklund, R.C. (Eds.). (2007). *Handbook of sport psychology* (3rd ed.). Hoboken, NJ: Wiley.

Thompson, R., & Sherman, R. (2010). *Eating disorders in sport*. New York: Routledge.

Vernon, D. (2009). *Human potential: Exploring techniques used to enhance human performance*. New York: Routledge.

Weinberg, R.S., & Gould, D. (2007). *Foundations of sport and exercise psychology* (4th ed.). Champaign, IL: Human Kinetics.

Weiss, M. (Ed.). (2003). *Developmental sport and exercise psychology: A lifespan perspective*. Morgantown, WV: Fitness Information Technology.

Williams, A.M., & Hodges, N.J. (2004). *Skill acquisition in sport: Research, theory and practice*. New York: Routledge.

Williams, J.M. (Ed.). (2009). *Applied sport psychology: Personal growth to peak performance* (6th ed.). New York: McGraw-Hill.

DVDs

Cohn, P.J. (2010). *The focused team: A coach's guide* [DVD]. Orlando, FL: Peak Performance Sports.

Cohn, P.J. (2010). *Golfer's mental edge program* [DVD]. Orlando, FL: Peak Performance Sports.

Dale, G. (2003). *Coach's guide to team building* [DVD]. Ames, IA: Championship Productions.

Dale, G. (2004). *Becoming a champion athlete: Goal setting for success* [DVD]. Ames, IA: Championship Productions.

Dale, G. (2004). *Becoming a champion athlete: Making every practice count* [DVD]. Ames, IA: Championship Productions.

Dale, G. (2004). *Becoming a champion athlete: Mastering pressure situations* [DVD]. Ames, IA: Championship Productions.

Dale, G. (2004). *Goal setting for success: A coach's guide* [DVD]. Ames, IA: Championship Productions.

Dale, G. (2005). *Becoming a champion: An athlete's guide to self confidence* [DVD]. Ames, IA: Championship Productions.

Dale, G. (2005). *Coaching the perfectionist athlete* [DVD]. Ames, IA: Championship Productions.

Dale, G. (2005). *Developing confident athletes: A coach's guide* [DVD]. Ames, IA: Championship Productions.

Dale, G. (2005). *Promoting a positive athletic experience: The parent's guide* [DVD]. Ames, IA: Championship Productions.

Dale, G. (2005). *The coach's guide to dealing effectively with parents* [DVD]. Ames, IA: Championship Productions.

Dale, G. (2005). *The coach's guide to team building: Volume II* [DVD]. Ames, IA: Championship Productions.

Gould, D. (2001). *Teaching mental skills for sport* [DVD]. Wilbraham, MA: Virtual Brands.

Gould, D. (2004). *Mental skills for young athletes* [DVD]. Wilbraham, MA: Virtual Brands.

Gould, D. (2005). *Five essential mental skills for sport* [DVD]. Wilbraham, MA: Virtual Brands.

Jaure, P. (2008). *Golf psychology: The pre-shot routine* [DVD]. Fairfield, OH: Cooper Sports.

Lynch, J. (2007). *The way of the champion: Developing self-awareness* [DVD]. Ames, IA: Champion Productions.

Lynch, J. (2007). *The way of the champion: Developing strategic positioning* [DVD]. Ames, IA: Champion Productions.

Lynch, J. (2007). *The way of the champion: Developing team unity* [DVD]. Ames, IA: Champion Productions.

Lynch, J. (2007). *The way of the champion: Having the right stuff* [DVD]. Ames, IA: Champion Productions.

Lynch, J. (2008). *Mental strategies for physical injury: A coach's & trainer's guide to managing wounded athletes* [DVD]. Ames, IA: Champion Productions.

Moore, M. (2007). *Coaching psychology for health, fitness, and mental health professionals* [DVD]. Monterey, CA: Healthy Learning.

Moore, M. (2007). *Peak performance and well-being: Positive psychology in action* [DVD]. Monterey, CA: Healthy Learning.

Petitpas, A., & Balague, G. (2005). *An inside look at sport psychology consulting* [DVD]. Wilbraham, MA: Virtual Brands.

Petitpas, A., & Gould, D. (2004). *Teaching mental skills for sport* [DVD]. Wilbraham, MA: Virtual Brands.

Petitpas, A., Ravizza, K., & Murphy, S. (2004). *Three approaches to sport psychology consulting* [DVD]. Wilbraham, MA: Virtual Brands.

Petitpas, A., Nilsson, P., & Marriott, L. (2004). *COACH54: Golf fundamentals for the future* [DVD]. Wilbraham, MA: Virtual Brands.

Ravizza, K. (2007). *Mental skills for competitive athletes* [DVD]. Wilbraham, MA: Virtual Brands.

Ravizza, K. (2008). *Keys to effective sport psychology consulting* [DVD]. Wilbraham, MA: Virtual Brands.

Ravizza, K., Van Raalte, J., Zaichovsky, L., & Giges, B. (2008). *Brief contact interventions in sport psychology* [DVD]. Wilbraham, MA: Virtual Brands.

Schuijers, R. (2008). *Mental skills for equestrian athletes* [DVD]. Wilbraham, MA: Virtual Brands.

Solivan, E. (2007). *Mind mastery for basketball* [DVD]. Champaign, IL: Human Kinetics.

Solivan, E. (2007). *Mind mastery for golf* [DVD]. Champaign, IL: Human Kinetics.

Solivan, E. (2007). *Mind mastery for pitching* [DVD]. Champaign, IL: Human Kinetics.

Solivan, E. (2007). *Mind mastery for soccer* [DVD]. Champaign, IL: Human Kinetics.

Solivan, E. (2007). *Mind mastery for tennis* [DVD]. Champaign, IL: Human Kinetics.

Solivan, E. (2007). *Mind mastery for winning* [DVD]. Champaign, IL: Human Kinetics.

Zaichowsky, L.D., Van Raalte, J.L., Giges, B., & Ravizza, K. (2002). *Brief contact interventions in sport psychology* [DVD]. Wilbraham, MA: Virtual Brands.

INDEX

PLEASE NOTE: Page numbers followed by an italicized *f, t, or e* show figures, tables, or exercises will be found on those pages, respectively.

ABOUT THE AUTHORS

Costas Karageorghis is internationally recognized for his research on the psychophysical and ergogenic effects of music. He is the author of 50 peer-reviewed and 90 professional articles in sport and exercise psychology. Karageorghis has also made 60 conference presentations nationally and internationally for which he has won several awards. His work has been featured in newspapers around the world, including the *Times* (London), *Independent*, *New York Times*, *Wall Street Journal*, *Washington Post*, and *Sydney Morning Herald*.

Karageorghis is a chartered member of the British Psychological Society and a double-accredited member and Fellow of the British Association of Sport and Exercise Sciences. He is best known for leading the *Run to the Beat* series of half-marathons in the UK and across mainland Europe (see www.runtothebeat.co.uk). Since May 2007 he has been head coach of the Great Britain student athletics team.

Karageorghis is currently a reader in sport psychology and deputy head (research) of the School of Sport and Education at Brunel University, United Kingdom.

Peter Terry is a registered psychologist who has held professorial positions in the United Kingdom and Australia. As an internationally recognized sport psychologist, he has been a consultant at almost 100 major international events, including 8 Olympic Games, 18 World Championships, 30 World Cup competitions, and 9 Wimbledon Championships.

Terry has authored three books on sport psychology and more than 150 scholarly articles. He has served two terms as president of the Australian Psychological Society's College of Sport Psychologists and sits on the managing council of the Asian-South Pacific Association of Sport Psychology. He has also been a member of the British Olympic Association's psychology advisory board, a long-time advisor to the Women's Tennis Association, and psychology coordinator for the Queensland Academy of Sport. He is a Fellow of both the British Association of Sport and Exercise Sciences and the Australian Psychological Society.

Terry is currently a professor of psychology in the Department of Psychology at the University of Southern Queensland, Australia.

You'll find other outstanding mental training resources at

www.HumanKinetics.com/mentaltrainingforathletes

In the U.S. call 1-800-747-4457

Australia 08 8372 0999 • Canada 1-800-465-7301
Europe +44 (0) 113 255 5665 • New Zealand 0800 222 062

HUMAN KINETICS
The Premier Publisher for Sports & Fitness
P.O. Box 5076 • Champaign, IL 61825-5076 USA